Teaching in the Digital Age:
A Guide to Modernizing Higher Education

(From Chalkboard to Keyboard: An Introduction to Digital Tools for Teachers)

Teaching in the Digital Age:
A Guide to Modernizing Higher Education

(From Chalkboard to Keyboard: An Introduction to Digital Tools for Teachers)

Dr. Shanmuga Sundaram Anandan
B.E.,M.E.,Ph.D.
Director and Principal
Sree Sastha Institute of Engineering and Technology, Chennai

Dr. Kanchana Venkatesan
B.Sc., M.Sc.,Ph.D.
Professor, Department of Chemistry
Sree Sastha Institute of Engineering and Technology, Chennai

Jagannathan Sundarababu
B.E., M S
Assistant Professor
Department of Mechanical and Automation Engineering
Sree Sastha Institute of Engineering and Technology, Chennai

BSP BS Publications
An Imprint of **BSP Books Pvt. Ltd.**
4-4-309/316, Giriraj Lane,
Sultan Bazar, Hyderabad - 500 095

Teaching in the Digital Age: A Guide to Modernizing Higher Education
(From Chalkboard to Keyboard: An Introduction to Digital Tools for Teachers)
***by* Dr. Shanmuga Sundaram Anandan, Dr. Kanchana Venkatesan and Jagannathan Sundarababu**

Disclaimer: The author and publishers have taken due care to provide authentic, reliable and up-to-date information related to the subject. However, neither the author nor the publisher shall be responsible for any liability for any damage caused because of the use of this book. The respective users must check the accuracy from other sources too.

Published by:

BS Publications
An Imprint of **BSP Books Pvt. Ltd.**
4-4-309/316, Giriraj Lane,
Sultan Bazar, Hyderabad - 500 095
Phone: 040 - 23445688
e-mail: info@bspbooks.net
www.bspbooks.net

ISBN: 978-93-48734-63-1 (Hardback)

Preface

Welcome to "Teaching in the Digital Age: A Guide to Modernizing Higher Education"! As educators, we face a decisive era where in technology has radically altered our approaches toward teaching and learning. From traditional chalkboards to today's advanced digital tools, education has undergone an exceptional metamorphosis.

"From Chalkboard to Keyboard: An Introduction to Digital Tools for Teachers," is a guidebook crafted specifically as an aide for educators who are navigating the uncharted waters of digital teaching. This handbook aims to equip both experienced professors and novice instructors with valuable knowledge, skills, and resources that will enable them not just to survive but excel in today's modern classroom.

Throughout the upcoming pages, we will investigate numerous methods by which technology can enrich higher education's teaching and learning. We'll thoroughly examine recent digital resources and tactics such as interactive whiteboards, multimedia presentations, online educational platforms, and virtual reality simulations that encourage student involvement while promoting collaboration among learners.

This book has a purpose beyond being a simple inventory of electronic devices and accessories. Its mission is to guide educators toward embracing an education model that puts the learner at its center, challenging traditional teaching practices. As we embark on this journey together, our quest will focus specifically on how technology can assist teachers in creating stimulating and inclusive environments filled with meaningful interactions tailored to meet current student's diverse needs.

In this book, practical pointers, actual case studies, and examples from forward-thinking educators who are spearheading digital progress abound. Whether you're inclined towards the idea of switching your classroom approach with innovative tactics like gamification or blended learning models, there's an abundance of inspiration and direction to aid in unleashing technology's efficacy within your teaching practice.

Let's begin this thrilling journey into the digital era of education with a willingness to explore and an open attitude toward each chapter. Whether you've grown up in the age of technology or are acclimating yourself as an adult learner, there is always something fresh waiting for us all to learn, uncover, and generate within the constantly progressing world of teaching and learning.

As we embark on this journey together, let us leave the chalkboard behind and embrace the keyboard. The time has come to take advantage of technology's opportunities for a more dynamic, inclusive, and captivating learning adventure that will make education brighter than ever before.

Have a joyful teaching experience!

- Authors

Acknowledgement

The rewarding journey of writing "Teaching in the Digital Age: A Guide to Modernizing Higher Education" was made possible by the invaluable support, guidance and inspiration received from numerous individuals and organizations.

We would like to express our deepest appreciation to our education colleagues and peers. Their pioneering methods and steadfast dedication to teaching excellence have always been a source of inspiration for us. The knowledge they shared with us has played a pivotal role in shaping the material of this book.

Our sincere appreciation goes to the educators and administrators, who took part in our research study, shared their experiences as well as challenges. The diverse viewpoints provided by your insightful contributions have significantly enhanced this guide's richness and depth.

Our families deserve a heartfelt appreciation for their constant encouragement and understanding during the writing process. Their unwavering support and patience have been our source of strength throughout.

We would like to express our gratitude towards the technical experts and digital education innovators who have expanded the limits of contemporary education. Your ground breaking efforts have established a strong base for this book's creation.

Our heartfelt gratitude to Prof. Kartheekeyan J., Chairman of Sree Sastha Institute of Engineering and Technology, Chennai. Your exceptional guidance and foresight in advancing education have been a tremendous source of motivation for us. We deeply value your backing, which has played an indispensable part in bringing this book to fruition.

We extend our heartfelt gratitude to the publisher for their unwavering faith in this endeavour and adeptness in publishing that has played a pivotal role in materializing this book. Your proficient mentorship and backing have been immensely valued.

To all the readers of this book, we extend our heartfelt gratitude for your unwavering commitment to enhancing education in today's digital world. Our earnest desire is that this manual would be a valuable asset in your quest to revolutionize tertiary learning and trigger fresh ideas as well as novel innovations when it comes to teaching techniques.

Expressing gratitude,

- Authors

Contents

Chapter 2

Essential Digital Tools for Teachers

Chapter 3

Interactive Learning with Multimedia

Chapter 4

Online Coding Courses and Tutorials

Chapter 8

Data-Driven Teaching with Digital Tools

Chapter 11

Digital Marketing and Analytics Training Programs

Chapter 12

Chapter 13

Online Project Management and Collaboration Tools for Technical Education

Chapter 14

Web Development and Programming Bootcamps

Chapter 15

Virtual Laboratories and Simulations for Science and Engineering Education

Chapter 16

Professional Development for Tech-Savvy Teachers

Chapter 17

Overcoming Challenges and Ensuring Equity

Chapter 18

A Roadmap for Implementing and Operating Digital Tools

Chapter 19

Conclusion and Future of Digital Tools in Technical Education

CHAPTER 1

Introduction to Digital Tools for the Modern Teacher

The book entitled "Teaching in the Digital Age: A Guide to Modernizing Higher Education" is intended to provide teachers with comprehensive training on incorporating technology into their teaching methodologies. Throughout this program, instructors will gain insight and proficiency in an assortment of digital tools such as learning management systems, interactive whiteboards, educational apps, and online collaboration platforms. Moreover, educators will be equipped with strategies that promote student engagement while simultaneously facilitating personalized learning experiences whilst streamlining administrative duties serving as a unified resource center directly aimed towards academic growth requirements about virtual classrooms facilitated by modern education standards embodied across various contemporary institutions globally.

1.1 The Importance of Digital Tools in Technical Education

In today's rapidly evolving digital age, educators must embrace the use of digital tools in education. These tools have changed the way we teach and learn, offering countless benefits and opportunities for students and teachers. The objective of this subchapter is to emphasize the value of integrating digital tools into the contemporary classroom. It also serves as an introduction for teachers to the world of digital tools for education.

First and foremost, digital tools provide a wide range of engaging and interactive learning experiences. Gone are the days when traditional blackboards and textbooks were the only source of knowledge. Digital tools enable teachers to deliver information in new formats, including video, interactive presentations, and multimedia content. This not only engages students' attention but also increases their understanding and retention of critical concepts.

Additionally, the advantage of digital tools is the ability to tailor and customize learning experiences according to individual needs and preferences. Each student has unique learning needs and preferences, and digital tools enable teachers to address these individual differences. For example, online options can provide personalized learning pathways with content and pace tailored to each learner's ability. This ensures that no student is left behind and allows each student to reach their full potential.

Digital tools play an important role in creating digital content and teaching graphic design. With access to powerful software like Adobe Photoshop and Illustrator, students can express their creativity and learn the principles of design. They can create stunning images, manipulate images, and have a keen eye for aesthetics. These skills are valuable not only in graphic design but also in tasks that require a strong visual presence.

Moreover, virtual reality, an augmented reality teaching tool, has changed the way engineering courses are taught. Through immersive experiences, students can explore and visualize complex concepts in previously unimaginable ways. Whether exploring the human body in a biology class or conducting research like that in medicine, these tools make learning engaging and interactive.

E-learning platforms have also emerged as powerful tools for technology acquisition. Platforms like Coursera, Udemy, and Khan Academy allow students to access a wide range of courses and learn from industry experts. From digital marketing analytics training programs to data science analytics courses, these workshops offer a wealth of knowledge that can be traditional classroom learning.

Collaboration is an important part of technology education, and online project management collaboration tools have changed the way students collaborate. Platforms like Trello, Asana, and Slack allow students to communicate in real time, share resources, and collaborate on projects. This fosters teamwork, enhances problem-solving skills, and prepares students for the collaborative nature of the professional world.

Finally, virtual labs and simulations have made science and engineering education more accessible and engaging. Students can conduct experiments and simulations in a safe and controlled environment, allowing them to learn from their mistakes and gain practical experience. These virtual tools bridge the gap between theory and practice and equip students with the skills they need to excel in their chosen fields.

In conclusion, digital tools have become indispensable in the field of technical education. By embracing these tools, teachers and scholars can enhance the learning experience, provide students with valuable skills, and prepare them for success in the digital age. Whether it's online coding courses, digital design tools, or virtual reality simulations, digital tools have the power to revolutionize technical education and equip students with the skills they need to thrive in the modern world. As we move from chalkboard to keyboard, teachers must embrace these tools and adapt their teaching practices to meet the needs of the modern learner. The further subchapters serve as an introduction to the world of digital tools for teachers, equipping them with the knowledge and understanding to harness the power of technology in the classroom and create meaningful learning experiences for their students.

1.2 The Benefits of Incorporating Technology in the Classroom

In today's digital age, technology has played an important role in education. As educators, it's important to adapt and embrace digital tools to create dynamic and engaging learning environments. This subchapter explores the many benefits of integrating technology into the classroom, focusing on how it enhances the teaching and learning experience for students and teachers.

One of the main benefits of using technology in the classroom is the ability to personalize instruction. Digital tools provide a wide range of resources and platforms that cater to different learning styles and allow teachers to tailor their lessons to meet students' individual needs. Whether through interactive presentations, educational apps, or online assessments, technology enables teachers to differentiate instruction and provide targeted support to students.

Furthermore, technology allows us to create a collaborative learning environment. Digital tools enable students to collaborate on projects, share ideas, and work together in real-time, regardless of physical location. It develops teamwork, critical thinking, and problem-solving skills, preparing students for the demands of the modern workplace.

Integrating technology into the classroom keeps students engaged and motivated. By integrating multimedia elements such as videos, audio clips, and interactive simulations, teachers can make their lessons interactive and motivating. This helps keep students' attention and encourages active participation, leading to deeper understanding and retention of information.

1.3 Enhancing Personalized Learning with Digital Tools

One of the key advantages of the usage of technology within the classroom is the ability to personalize guidance. Digital equipment offers a huge variety of resources and systems that cater to numerous mastering styles, allowing instructors to tailor their classes to fulfill the character needs of college students. Whether it's through interactive presentations, instructional apps, or online checks, era lets teachers distinguish training and offer targeted help to college students.

1.4 Encouraging Collaboration and Critical Thinking in Education with Technology

Furthermore, generations permit us to create a collaborative studying environment. With the help of digital tools, college students can collaborate on initiatives, percentage thoughts, and work collectively in actual time, irrespective of their bodily area. This fosters teamwork, vital thinking, and hassle-fixing abilities, making ready college students for the needs of the modern-day place of job.

How Technology Can Boost Classroom Engagement and Motivation

Incorporating technology in the classroom additionally enhances scholar engagement and motivation. By integrating multimedia elements consisting of films, audio clips, and interactive simulations, teachers can make their instructions more interactive and stimulating. This enables college students' interest and encourages active participation, resulting in deeper expertise and retention of the cloth.

1.5 The Digital Age: A Gateway to Knowledge and Resources

Additionally, the era offers entry to a substantial amount of information and assets. With only a few clicks, college students can explore numerous online databases, studies articles, and academic websites to expand their knowledge past the textbook. This is not the most effective promote independent mastering, however, additionally cultivates virtual literacy skills which can be crucial in a state-of-the-art statistics-pushed society.

1.6 The Importance of Integrating Technology in Study Rooms for College Students

Lastly, integrating technology within the study room equips college students with important digital abilities that can be vital for their destiny fulfillment. By using digital equipment, college students broaden their proficiency in the use of software programs, navigating online platforms, and using critical questioning to evaluate records. These competencies are transferable and put together for the demands of better training and the task market.

1.7 Enhancing Instructional Strategies with Digital Tools for Educators

First and foremost, digital tools provide teachers with a wide range of materials and resources to improve their teaching strategies. By having online coding courses and tutorials, teachers can add interactive exercises, real-world examples, and hands-on coding activities to their lessons. Not only does this engage students in the learning process but helps them develop skills, a useful, technical skill that is in high demand in the job market.

1.8 Maximizing Digital Production and Design Education with Digital Tools

Furthermore, the use of digital tools can greatly enhance digital production and design education. Students can learn and apply graphic design techniques using specialized software, create visually appealing projects, and hone their creativity. Virtual reality and augmented reality teaching tools take this one step further, allowing students to engage in realistic simulations and experiences, allowing them to understand complex concepts in a fun and intuitive way.

1.9 The Advantages of Digital Tools in Education: E-Learning Platforms

Another important benefit of digital tools in the classroom is e-learning platforms. These platforms provide a flexible and flexible learning environment, allowing students to access learning materials and activities anytime and anywhere. This is particularly beneficial for developing technology skills, as students can learn at their own pace and revise concepts whenever necessary.

1.10 The Power of Digital Marketing Analytics and Data Science Education

In today's digital economy, digital marketing analytics training programs and data science analytics courses and tools provide students with the essential skills needed to excel in their careers. Equipping students with digital tools in the classroom is crucial, as there is a growing demand for professionals in these industries. By doing so, students are better poised for future career opportunities.

1.11 Preparing Students for the Workforce with Web Development and Operations Bootcamp

In addition, online management systems and collaboration tools facilitate teamwork and communication among students, preparing them for the collaborative nature of the staff. The Web Development and Operations Bootcamp offers in-depth training in coding and web development, giving students the skills they need to succeed in the digital age.

1.12 The Benefits of Virtual Labs and Simulations in Science and Technology Education

Finally, virtual labs and simulations provide students with hands-on experience in learning science and technology. These tools allow students to conduct experiments, analyze data, and solve problems in a virtual environment, bridging the gap between theory and practice.

In conclusion, the benefits of integrating digital tools into the classroom are vast and varied. From providing teachers with more diversity to developing students' technology skills and preparing them for the digital economy, these tools have the potential to transform technology education. Embracing digital tools enables educators to create dynamic and engaging learning environments that prepare students for the challenges and opportunities of the modern world. Personalized education, collaboration, student engagement, get right of entry to data, and the development of virtual skills are just a few advantages that technology brings to the contemporary trainer. As educators, it's miles vital that we embody this digital equipment to create a dynamic and innovative knowledge of surroundings that prepares our students for the demanding situations of the digital era.

1.13 Challenges and Limitations of Using Digital Tools in Education

In recent years, the introduction of digital tools in education has changed the way teachers deliver information and engage students in the classroom. However, despite many benefits, educators, and scholars in digital tools and technology education need to be aware of the challenges and limitations that come with their use.

One of the key challenges to implementing digital tools in education is the digital divide. Not all students have the necessary technology or internet connectivity at home, which can make a difference in learning opportunities. This issue is most pronounced in low-income communities, where students do not have reliable access to computers or the internet outside of school hours and as a result, teachers must manage these limitations and find ways another way to provide information to students who do not have access to digital tools.

Another challenge is the need for technical support and training. While digital tools offer great potential, they also require specific technical skills from teachers. Not all teachers have the necessary skills to effectively integrate digital tools into their teaching practices, which may hinder their effectiveness. It is important to provide teachers with ongoing training and support to feel confident and competent in using these tools.

Furthermore, the effectiveness of digital gear in education may be restricted by way of the dearth of personalized mastering experiences. While these tools can offer individualized feedback and adaptive getting-to-know pathways, they frequently depend upon algorithms and pre-set content material that may not meet the precise needs of every scholar. Teachers must strike a balance between making use of virtual gear and offering customized practice to ensure that each student's knowledge of needs are met.

Lastly, the fast pace of technological advancements affords an undertaking for instructors and scholars to keep up with state-of-the-art tools and tendencies. As new virtual tools emerge, it can be overwhelming for educators to constantly adapt their coaching practices to comprise this gear efficiently. Continuous professional improvement and staying updated with modern research and great practices are essential to conquer this task.

In conclusion, even as digital gear offers severe benefits in training, teachers, and scholars in the field of digital gear and technical schooling need to be aware of the demanding situations and barriers associated with their use. By addressing troubles together with the digital divide, presenting technical aid and training, making sure personalized studying experiences, and staying abreast of technological improvements, educators can successfully navigate those challenges and leverage virtual gear to enhance technical schooling.

1.14 Overcoming Resistance to Digital Tools

In the rapidly evolving digital age, teachers need to embrace and effectively use digital tools in the classroom. However, many teachers face resistance to incorporating these tools into their teaching practices. This subchapter aims to address the most common challenges faced by teachers and to provide strategies for overcoming resistance to digital tools.

One of the main reasons for resistance to digital tools is fear of the unknown. Teachers feel overwhelmed by so many options and may not know how to navigate them and incorporate them into their curriculum. To overcome this fear, teachers need to spend time learning about and using different digital tools. Attend conferences, webinars, or professional development workshops that focus on providing digital tools for teachers. By gaining hands-on experience, teachers can gain confidence and realize the value of integrating digital tools into their teaching.

Another common barrier is the perception that digital tools are time-consuming and complex. Teachers are often concerned that the introduction of technology will disrupt their established classroom routines and therefore require extensive training. However, with proper planning and preparation, digital tools can save time and enhance the learning experience. Start by selecting a few easy-to-use tools that align with your learning goals and gradually incorporate them into your lessons. Seek help from tech-savvy colleagues or instructional technology specialists who can help troubleshoot and provide guidance. By taking small steps, teachers can gradually integrate digital tools without feeling overwhelmed.

Resistance to change is an inherent human trait, so it is not uncommon for teachers to stick to traditional teaching methods. However, it is important to recognize that today's students are growing up in a digital world. By integrating digital tools into the classroom, teachers can engage students in new and engaging ways, making learning more interactive and relevant. Emphasize the value of digital tools for student's future success, such as developing digital literacy and critical thinking skills.

In conclusion, overcoming resistance to digital tools requires a shift in mindset and a willingness to embrace change. By taking the time to teach, plan, and seek support, teachers can effectively integrate digital tools into their teaching practices. Embracing digital tools will not only enrich students' learning experiences but also provide them with the skills they need to succeed in today's world.

1.15 Understanding the Digital Divide in Education

In today's technologically advanced world, it is important to equip teachers with digital tools to better engage and educate their students. However, not all teachers have the same access to these tools, creating a phenomenon known as the "digital divide." This sub-chapter aims to provide a deeper understanding of the digital divide in education and its implications for teachers.

The digital divide distinguishes between individuals or groups who access, use, and benefit from digital technologies and those who do not. In education, the digital divide manifests itself as differences in student access to technology, internet connectivity, and digital literacy skills. Such differences can have a significant impact on students' academic performance and prospects.

Teachers need to be aware of the digital divide and its impact on their students. By understanding the different ways their students access digital tools, teachers can tailor their instructional strategies to provide equal opportunity for all. This subchapter will examine the causes of the digital divide, as well as economic, geographic, social, and cultural aspects.

Additionally, it will include measures to bridge the digital divide in education. Teachers will be exposed to other approaches such as blended learning, which combines traditional face-to-face classes with online resources for students with limited access to technology. In addition, the mini-chapter will examine more closely the importance of digital literacy skills for teachers and students, emphasizing the need for professional development opportunities to enhance teachers' digital competencies.

In addition, this subchapter will discuss the role of planners, school administrators, and the broader community in narrowing the digital divide. It will focus on the importance of investing in infrastructure, providing equal access to technology and fostering partnerships with community organizations to ensure every student has the same opportunity to continue to succeed in the digital age.

By understanding the digital divide in education, educators can be proactive agents of change, advocate for educational equity, and use digital tools to meet student needs. In doing so, they will be better equipped to navigate the evolution of digital tools and provide a quality education for all students, regardless of background or technology.

As teachers begin their journey to embrace digital tools for today's classroom, understanding the digital divide becomes an important part of their professional development. This sub-chapter aims to create an inclusive and equitable learning environment for all students by equipping educators with the necessary knowledge and tools to bridge the digital divide.

1.16 Navigating the Ethical Use of Technology in Teaching

In an era of rapid technological advancement, educators face the challenge of integrating digital tools into their classrooms to ensure ethical use. As educators, it is important to consider the implications and consequences of bringing technology into our teaching practices. The purpose of this subchapter is to provide teachers with a comprehensive understanding of the ethical considerations involved in the use of digital tools, and how to navigate them responsibly.

First and foremost, educators need to recognize the importance of protecting privacy and data when using digital tools. With the increasing collection and storage of student data, protecting personal information has become paramount. Teachers should be aware of the data privacy policy of any digital tools they plan to use, to ensure compliance with legal and ethical standards. In addition, they should educate their students on the importance of digital citizenship, teach them to be responsible digital users, and promote a culture that respects privacy.

Another area of ethical concern is the digital divide, which refers to differences in students' access to technology. As educators, we must strive to bridge this divide by providing equal opportunities for all students to engage with digital devices This may require funding for technology resources, advocating for Internet access to underserved areas, or providing students without personal devices with alternatives by addressing the digital divide, teachers can ensure that technology is used ethically and inclusively in the classroom.

Additionally, teachers need to be aware of potential bias and discrimination that can be perpetuated with digital tools. Algorithms used in educational technology can reinforce existing biases, leading to gaps in student achievement. It is therefore important for teachers to scrutinize the tools they use, considering their potential impact on different student populations. By actively seeking inclusive and equitable digital tools, educators can create fair and equitable learning environments.

In conclusion, the ethical use of technology for educational purposes requires careful consideration of privacy, the digital divide, and the possibility of bias. By prioritizing data security, bridging the digital divide, and carefully evaluating digital tools, educators can address the ethical challenges associated with integrating technology into their classrooms. By doing so, we can empower our students to be responsible digital citizens and ensure that technology enhances their educational experience rather than disrupting it.

1.17 Overview of the Roadmap for Implementing and Operating Digital Tools

In today's digital age, it's important to equip teachers with the tools and techniques they need to successfully integrate technology into their classrooms. The rapidly evolving nature of digital tools offers countless opportunities to improve teaching and learning experiences. But many teachers feel overwhelmed and don't know where to start. That's why this subchapter is "Learn, Click, Use: A Guide to Using and Leveraging Digital Tools" – to provide a comprehensive guide and roadmap for teachers who want to start their digital journey.

This subchapter, "An Overview of the Roadmap for Implementing and Operating Digital Tools," serves as the foundation for the rest of the book. It outlines key steps and strategies teachers should consider when introducing and implementing digital tools in their classrooms.

The roadmap begins with a self-assessment, enabling teachers to assess their current technology skills and identify areas for improvement. This step is important because it sets the stage for personal and professional growth, ensuring teachers have the support they need to succeed.

The road map then guides teachers in the process of selecting digital tools that align with their instructional goals and meet the needs of their students. It emphasizes the importance of thorough research and getting recommendations from reliable sources to make informed decisions.

Once the digital tools are selected, the roadmap provides a comprehensive implementation plan. This includes ways to introduce tools to students, provide clear instruction, and foster positive digital learning environments. It highlights the importance of ongoing support and problem solving to address any potential challenges.

The proper use of digital tools is another area covered in this subchapter. Emphasize the importance of regular research and reflection on the impact of equipment on student learning. Teachers are encouraged to collect data, analyze it, and adjust their teaching practices accordingly.

Throughout the orientation, there is an emphasis on collaboration and professional learning units. Teachers are encouraged to network with colleagues, attend meetings, and participate in online forums to share ideas and experiences. This collaborative approach ensures that teachers can learn from each other and stay abreast of the latest trends and best practices in educational technology.

In conclusion, this subchapter provides an outline of the roadmap for imposing and running virtual gear. It serves as a treasured aid for teachers seeking to navigate the digital panorama and decorate their teaching practices. By following this roadmap, instructors can expectantly integrate virtual gear into their school rooms and provide their students with engaging and meaningful knowledge of studies.

Digital learning, also known as e-learning, is a rapidly growing trend in education. It uses digital technology to deliver educational content to students. Implementing digital learning in your school or organization can have many benefits, including increased engagement, improved learning outcomes, and greater flexibility.

Here are some steps to implement your digital learning:

1. Determine your needs and objectives: Before you start using digital learning, it's important to consider your needs and objectives. What is your reason for wanting to use digital learning? What kind of information do you want to provide? What materials do you need? The answers to these questions will help you create a clear implementation plan.
2. Choose the right tools: There are many digital tools available to deliver educational content, such as learning management systems (LMS), virtual classrooms, and instructional services. Choose the equipment that best meets your needs and purposes.
3. Train your students: Digital learning requires different skills and knowledge than traditional learning. Make sure your teachers receive proper training in how to use the tools and deliver digital content effectively.
4. Develop content: Creating digital content can be time-consuming, but it is an important step in implementing digital learning. Work with your students to develop engaging and interactive content that aligns with your learning objectives.
5. Pilot tests the program: Before sending the system to all students, conduct a pilot test with a small group of students. This will help you identify any issues or challenges that need to be addressed before maximizing the use of the system.
6. Monitor and adjust: After implementing digital learning, evaluate its effectiveness and adjust as needed. Use the data to measure student engagement and learning outcomes, and adjust your program as needed.

By following these steps, you will be able to successfully implement digital learning in your school or institution and offer your students an engaging and effective modern learning experience.

CHAPTER 2

Essential Digital Tools for Teachers

Essential digital tools for teachers include learning management systems (LMS) like Google Classroom or Schoology, which allow teachers to easily organize and distribute assignments online. Communication tools such as email, messaging apps, or video conferencing platforms facilitate effective communication with students and parents. Productivity tools like word processors, spreadsheets, and presentation software enable teachers to create engaging lesson materials and assessments. Additionally, interactive whiteboards or smart boards can enhance classroom instruction by allowing teachers to display multimedia content and interact with the material in real-time.

2.1 Overview of Digital Tools for Technical Education

In today's digital age, integrating technology into education has become imperative, especially in technology. The use of digital tools has revolutionized teaching and learning processes, allowing teachers to enhance technology learning and provide students with interactive and engaging learning experiences. This subchapter will look at the different types of digital tools available for the teaching-learning process in modern education.

Digital tools are needed for course content development, course planning and execution, promotion and visibility enhancement, and evaluation and certification.

Digital tools and technology education are ongoing, providing teachers and students with a wealth of resources and platforms to explore. Online coding courses and tutorials have become increasingly popular, offering step-by-step instructions for students of all levels. These resources not only teach programming language but also develop critical thinking and problem-solving skills.

Digital design and graphic arts instruction has also grown tremendously, equipped with tools that allow students to create stunning images and graphics. These tools allow students to showcase their creativity and enhance their understanding of graphic design concepts.

Virtual reality (VR) and augmented reality (AR) educational tools have revolutionized technology education by providing immersive experiences that mimic real-world contexts. Students can explore complex concepts and environments through virtual labs and simulations, to increase their understanding and knowledge retention.

E-learning platforms have become essential to access technology, with a wide range of courses and programs. These platforms offer learning flexibility, allowing individuals to access technology at their own pace and convenience.

Digital advertising and analytics training applications have gained recognition in recent years, helping individuals develop abilities in the ever-developing field of virtual advertising and marketing. These programs offer insights into advertising and marketing strategies, information analysis, and using analytics equipment to optimize marketing campaigns.

Data technology and analytics courses and tools have also become critical in technical education. With the increasing emphasis on fact-driven decision-making, those tools enable students to develop skills in statistics analysis, visualization, and interpretation.

Online undertaking control and collaboration tools have transformed how technical training is conducted. These gears permit college students to work on projects remotely, collaborate with friends, and manage tasks successfully.

Web development and programming boot camps offer intensive education in internet development and programming languages. These boot camps offer hands-on revel and equip college students with the capabilities had to excel in the era industry.

In the end, the mixing of digital gear in technical schooling has opened new avenues for coaching and getting to know. Whether it's miles coding courses, digital fact simulations, or statistics analytics tools, these resources cater to the wishes of instructors, pupils, and numerous niches in the field. The use of digital tools no longer complements technical education but also equips students with the abilities required for success within the contemporary world.

2.2 Digital Resources for Today's Educators

In today’s dynamic educational environment, integrating digital tools has become imperative for educators seeking to improve classroom experiences, encourage collaboration, and facilitate administrative tasks. These tools not only provide effective teaching-learning but also empower students to engage with content in new ways. From learning management systems to interactive whiteboard software, the educational technology ecosystem offers a variety of features to help educators create dynamic and interactive learning environments.

As a teacher, having the right digital tools to support your learning is important. These tools have become a necessity in modern classrooms. Technology has become an integral part of modern education, providing educators with many benefits, including enhanced communication, collaboration, and collaboration. Here are some of the most important digital tools teachers can use to make their teaching-learning experience more productive and enjoyable (see Table 2.1).

2.3 Exploring the Essential Tools for Course Content Development and Delivery

Creating, organizing, and presenting instructional materials in various educational contexts requires the use of course content development and delivery tools. To assist you in this effort, we have compiled a list of tools categorized by their functions in course content development and delivery (See Table 2.2).

2.4 Enhancing Teaching Strategies with Digital Tresentation Tools

The digital age has changed how we teach and learn. Traditional blackboards and textbooks have been replaced by powerful digital tools that allow teachers to create engaging and interactive lessons. In this subchapter, we will explore the best instructional tools available to teachers looking to improve their teaching strategies and engage students in the learning process.

Microsoft PowerPoint is one of the most popular presentation tools for teachers. Its versatility allows teachers to create engaging visuals with text, images, video, and audio. PowerPoint provides templates and themes that make it easy for teachers to create professional-looking presentations. Integration with other Microsoft tools, such as Word and Excel, also provides interactive assessment tools that teachers can use to further engage students.

Prezi is another powerful presentation tool that offers a unique zooming interface. With Prezi, teachers can create non-linear content that encourages active use and exploration through its dynamic and visually appealing layout. For topics such as geography or history, students can "zoom in" to explore specific locations or events in depth.

Nearpod is an excellent resource for teachers looking to incorporate multimedia content into their presentations. This allows teachers to create interactive lessons that can be delivered to students' devices in real-time. Nearpod allows teachers to incorporate quizzes, polls, and interactive activities into their presentations, ensuring active student engagement. Teachers can also track student progress and identify areas for improvement through the tool's data and analytics.

For teachers who prefer a more collaborative approach, Google Slides is an excellent choice. It allows multiple users to work on a presentation simultaneously, making it ideal for group projects or brainstorming sessions. Google Slides also offers seamless integration with other Google tools such as Google Drive and Google Classroom, enabling teachers to easily share and collaborate on presentations with their students.

In conclusion, digital presentation tools have revolutionized how teachers deliver lessons and engage students in the learning process. Using PowerPoint, Prezi, Nearpod, or Google Slides, teachers can create visually appealing, interactive, and engaging presentations that enhance student learning, foster creativity, and make lessons more enjoyable and memorable.

2.5 Exploring the Best Digital Presentation Tools for Educators

In today's digital age, educators have a plethora of options to create engaging and interactive content for their students. Here are some of the most popular digital presentation tools: When selecting a digital presentation tool, consider factors such as ease of use, collaboration features, integration capabilities, and the specific needs of your teaching style and content. Many of these tools offer free versions with basic features and premium versions with additional functionalities.

2.6 Exploring Collaboration Platforms for Enhanced Student Interaction

In today's digital age, technology is increasingly used by teachers to promote student engagement and create a collaborative learning environment. Collaboration platforms are one of the most effective ways to encourage student interaction. These platforms provide students with virtual spaces to work together, share ideas, and collaborate on projects, regardless of their physical location. This subchapter reviews various collaboration platforms that are specifically designed to facilitate student interaction, ensuring that teachers have the necessary digital tools to create an engaging and inclusive learning experience.

Google Classroom is a popular collaboration platform built on the powerful G Suite for Education. It allows teachers to create virtual classrooms where they can distribute assignments, provide feedback, and facilitate discussions. Students can collaborate on documents, presentations, and spreadsheets in real-time, fostering teamwork and peer-to-peer learning. Google Classroom integrates seamlessly with other Google tools, such as Google Drive and Google Meet, making it a comprehensive platform for student interaction.

Microsoft Teams is another noteworthy collaboration platform designed specifically for educational settings. It offers a wide range of features that promote student engagement and collaboration. Teachers can create virtual classrooms, share resources, and facilitate discussions through video conferencing and chat functionalities. Students can work together on documents, presentations, and projects, leveraging the power of Microsoft Office 365. With its user-friendly interface and robust set of tools, Microsoft Teams is an excellent choice for enhancing student interaction in classrooms.

Besides mainstream collaboration platforms, there are also specialized tools designed specifically for student interaction and collaboration. For example, Padlet allows students to create virtual bulletin boards to post and share ideas, images, videos, and documents. This visual and interactive platform encourages creativity and collaboration among students, enabling them to engage in meaningful discussions and brainstorming sessions.

2.7 Enhancing Student Interaction with Collaboration Platforms: A Comprehensive Guide

Collaboration platforms are vital in promoting communication, and interaction and facilitating collaborative learning environments. Below are some excellent collaboration platforms that educators can explore to foster student interaction:

In conclusion, collaboration platforms offer teachers a powerful means to foster student interaction and create dynamic learning environments. Teachers have a wide array of options to choose from, whether it's through the comprehensive features of Google Classroom and Microsoft Teams or the specialized functionalities of tools like Padlet. By embracing these digital tools, teachers can unlock the full potential of their students, promoting active participation, collaboration, and creativity in the classroom. When choosing a collaboration platform, consider factors such as the specific needs of your students, ease of use, integration capabilities, and security features. Exploring different platforms can help educators find the best fit for their teaching style and the unique requirements of their courses.

Table 2.1 Tools for Digital Education.

Teaching / Learning activities	Digital Tools	Usage
Tools or Content Creation Tools	Canvas, Articulate Storyline, Adobe Captivate, and Lectora.	Educators and instructional designers create interactive and engaging e-learning content.
Learning Management System (LMS)	Moodle, Canvas, Google Classroom	Organize course content, distribute assignments, and facilitate communication between teachers, students, and parents.
Online Collaboration Tools	Google Workspace (Docs, Sheets, Slides), Microsoft 365	Facilitate collaborative document creation, editing, and sharing among students and teachers.
Video Conferencing	Zoom, Microsoft Teams, Google Meet	Conduct virtual classes, host meetings, and enable real-time communication with students and parents.
Educational Websites and Resources	Khan Academy, TED-Ed, National Geographic Kids	Supplement classroom instruction with interactive and engaging online resources.
Interactive Whiteboard Software	SMART Notebook, Promethean ActivInspire	Create interactive lessons and presentations to engage students in a digital environment.
Formative Assessment Tools	Kahoot, Quizizz, Socrative	Gauge student understanding in real-time through quizzes, polls, and interactive assessments.
Digital Note-Taking	OneNote, Evernote	Encourage students to take digital notes, organize information, and collaborate on shared documents.
Screen Recording and Screen casting	Screencast-O-Matic, Loom	Create instructional videos, provide feedback, and demonstrate concepts through screen recordings
Digital Classroom Management	ClassDojo, Classcraft	Manage and monitor student behavior, track achievements, and communicate with parents.
Document and File Management	Google Drive, Dropbox	Store, organize, and share documents, presentations, and other files with students and colleagues.
Parent-Teacher Communication Platforms	Remind, ClassTag	Facilitate communication between teachers and parents through announcements, messages, and event scheduling.
Adaptive Learning Platforms	Khan Academy, DreamBox, IXL	Provide personalized learning experiences based on individual student needs and progress.

Table 2.1 ***Contd…***

Teaching / Learning activities	Digital Tools	Usage
Virtual Reality Tools	Google Expeditions, Merge Cube	Enhance learning with immersive experiences and virtual field trips.
Teacher Professional Development Platforms	Edmodo, LinkedIn Learning	Access online courses, webinars, and resources to support ongoing professional development.
Data Analytics and Assessment Tools Authoring	Edpuzzle, MasteryConnect	Analyze student performance data, track progress, and inform instructional decisions.

Table 2.2 Course Content Development Tools.

Activities	Tools/ Platform	Functionality
Learning Management Systems (LMS)	Moodle, Canvas, Blackboard	Centralized platforms for organizing course materials, delivering content, managing assessments, and facilitating communication.
Authoring Tools	Articulate Storyline, Adobe Captivate, Camtasia	Create interactive and multimedia-rich e-learning content, including simulations, videos, and quizzes.
Content Management Systems (CMS)	WordPress, Drupal	Platforms for creating and managing digital content, including websites, blogs, and online resources.
Interactive Whiteboard Software	SMART Notebook, Promethean ActivInspire	Create interactive lessons, presentations, and activities using digital whiteboard technology.
Video Editing Software	Adobe Premiere Pro, iMovie, Camtasia	Edit and enhance instructional videos for effective content delivery.
Graphic Design Tools	Canva, Adobe Spark, Piktochart	Create visually appealing graphics, infographics, and presentations for course materials.
Document Collaboration	Google Workspace, Microsoft 365	Facilitate real-time collaboration on documents, spreadsheets, and presentations among students and educators.
Mind Mapping Tools	MindMeister, XMind	Create visual mind maps to organize and represent complex information.
Screen Recording and Screen casting	Screencast-O-Matic, Loom, OBS Studio	Record and share instructional videos, tutorials, and software demonstrations.

Table 2.3 Course Content Delivery Tools.

Activity	Tools	Functionality
Video Hosting Platforms	YouTube, Vimeo, Wistia	Upload, share, and manage instructional videos for students to access.
Web Conferencing	Zoom, Microsoft Teams, Google Meet	Conduct live virtual classes, webinars, and meetings with students.
Podcasting Platforms	Anchor, Podbean, Libsyn	Share audio content, such as lectures, discussions, or interviews, in podcast format.
Interactive Quizzing	Kahoot!, Quizizz, Google Forms	Create interactive quizzes and assessments to gauge student understanding.
Learning Analytics Platforms	Edpuzzle, H5P, Learning Locker	Collect and analyze data on student engagement and performance to inform instructional decisions.
Virtual Classroom Platforms	ClassDojo, Edmodo, Flipgrid	Facilitate communication, collaboration, and engagement within a virtual classroom environment.
Augmented Reality (AR) and Virtual Reality (VR) Tools	Google Expeditions, Merge Cube, Oculus	Enhance learning experiences with immersive AR and VR content.
Adaptive Learning Platforms	Khan Academy, DreamBox, Smart Sparrow	Provide personalized learning experiences based on individual student progress.

Table 2.4 Popular Digital Presentation Tools.

Tools	Specific Functionality
Microsoft PowerPoint	• A classic presentation tool with a wide range of features for creating slideshows. • Integrates with Microsoft 365 for collaboration and cloud storage.
Google Slides	• A cloud-based presentation tool that allows real-time collaboration. • Integrates seamlessly with Google Workspace.
Prezi	• Offers a unique zooming interface for dynamic and non-linear presentations. • Useful for creating visually engaging and interactive presentations.
Canva	• Beyond presentations, Canva allows the creation of visually appealing graphics, posters, and infographics. • Offers a user-friendly drag-and-drop interface
Adobe Spark	• A suite of creative tools for designing web pages, graphics, and videos. • Great for creating multimedia-rich presentations.

Table 2.4 ***Contd…***

Tools	Specific Functionality
Powtoon	• An animated video creation tool that can be used for educational content. • Engages students with animated characters and dynamic presentations.
Haiku Deck	• Focuses on simplicity and visual appeal, providing access to a library of high-quality images. • Ideal for creating aesthetically pleasing presentations.
Emaze	• Offers a variety of presentation templates with 3D effects and animations. • Enables the creation of visually stunning presentations.
Nearpod	• Combines interactive presentations with activities, quizzes, and virtual reality. • Facilitates student engagement and participation.
Pear Deck	• Integrates with Google Slides to create interactive and formative assessments. • Engages students with real-time questions and discussions.
Sway	• A Microsoft tool for creating interactive reports, presentations, and newsletters. • Focuses on a smooth and dynamic design.
Slides Carnival	• Provides a collection of free, professionally designed presentation templates for Google Slides. • Useful for adding a polished look to presentations.
Venngage	• Primarily a tool for creating infographics but also supports presentation creation. • Ideal for visual storytelling and data visualization.
Visme	• A versatile platform for creating presentations, infographics, and other visual content. • Offers a wide range of templates and customization options.
Beautiful.ai	• Focuses on creating aesthetically pleasing and professionally designed presentations. • Uses artificial intelligence to assist with slide design.

Table 2.5 Platforms for Enhanced Student Interaction.

Platform	Features	Benefits
Google Workspace (formerly G Suite for Education)	• Google Docs, Sheets, and Slides for real-time collaborative document editing. • Google Classroom for assignment distribution and communication.	Seamless integration, accessibility, and a suite of collaborative tools.
Microsoft 365 Education	• Microsoft Teams for communication, collaboration, and virtual meetings. • OneNote for collaborative note-taking and sharing.	Integration with Microsoft Office applications, and robust collaboration features.

Table 2.5 ***Contd...***

Platform	Features	Benefits
Slack for Education	• Channels for organized communication. • File sharing and integrations with various apps.	Real-time communication, and efficient team collaboration.
Canvas	• Learning Management System (LMS) for course organization. • Integrated tools for assignments and assessments.	Centralized platform for course content and collaboration.
Edmodo	• Secure a social media-like platform for class discussions. • Assignment distribution and grading features.	User-friendly interface, social learning environment.
Padlet	• Virtual boards for collaborative brainstorming. • Real-time updates and commenting.	A versatile, creative collaboration tool.
Flipgrid	• Video discussion platform for asynchronous communication. • Short video responses for engaging interactions.	Enhances student voice and expression.
Zoom	• Video conferencing for virtual classes and meetings. • Screen sharing and collaborative annotation.	Reliable video communication, easy to use.
Trello	• Boards, lists, and cards for project organization. • Collaboration through task assignments and comments.	Visual and flexible project management.
Remind	• Messaging platform for secure communication with students and parents. • Announcement broadcasting and file sharing.	Simplifies communication enhances parent-teacher interaction.
Cisco Webex Teams	• Messaging, file sharing, and virtual meetings. • Spaces for team collaboration and communication.	Enterprise-grade collaboration and communication.
Discord	• Chat channels for text and voice communication. • Server organization for different topics or subjects.	Informal and gamer-friendly, suitable for certain educational contexts.

2.8 Assessment and Feedback Tools for Effective Evaluation

In today's modern era of education, teachers are increasingly relying on digital tools to enhance their teaching methods and engage students in new and exciting ways. The integration of technology in the classroom not only improves student learning outcomes but also streamlines the assessment and feedback process. This subchapter provides a comprehensive overview of various assessment and feedback tools that can revolutionize the way teachers evaluate their students' progress.

2.8.1 Online Quizzes and Tests

One of the most popular assessment tools is online quizzes and tests. Platforms like Google Forms or Quizizz allow teachers to create interactive quizzes with immediate feedback and automatic grading. These tools save valuable time and provide students with instant insights into their performance, enabling them to identify areas for improvement.

2.8.2 Digital Portfolios

Digital portfolios are another powerful assessment tool. By leveraging platforms like Seesaw or Google Sites, teachers can encourage students to compile their best work in a digital format. This allows for a comprehensive evaluation of student's progress over time, as well as the opportunity for self-reflection and goal setting. Digital portfolios enable teachers to provide personalized feedback and engage in meaningful conversations with students about their growth and achievements.

2.8.3 Peer Assessment Tools

Peer assessment tools facilitate peer-to-peer feedback, allowing students to evaluate and provide constructive criticism of their peers' work. Applications like Peergrade or Flipgrid foster a collaborative learning environment and enhance students' critical thinking and communication skills.

2.8.4 Formative Assessment Tools

Formative assessment tools such as Kahoot or Socrative encourage active student participation and provide real-time feedback. These tools allow teachers to gauge students' understanding during a lesson or gather valuable data to inform their instructional strategies. By using formative assessment tools, teachers can address misconceptions immediately and adapt their teaching accordingly.

In conclusion, the integration of digital tools in the assessment and feedback process revolutionizes the way teachers evaluate student progress. Online quizzes, digital portfolios, peer assessment tools, and formative assessment applications all contribute to effective evaluation. By utilizing these tools, teachers can save time, provide personalized feedback, foster collaboration, and enhance student engagement. Embracing digital tools for assessment and feedback ensures that teachers are equipped with the necessary resources to meet the needs of the modern classroom and facilitate student success.

2.9 Digital Tools to Enhance Your Assessment and Feedback Process

Are you looking for ways to streamline and enhance your evaluation process? Here are some assessment and feedback tools that you can use to make your work easier.

The tools listed in Table 2.6 offer a wide range of assessment options, from traditional quizzes to innovative forms of evaluation. When choosing the right tools for your needs, consider the type of feedback you want to provide and the preferences of both educators and students.

Table 2.6 Assessment Tools.

Platform	Key features
Google Forms	• Create quizzes and surveys. • Autograding and instant feedback.
Quizizz	• Gamified quizzes with leaderboards. • Self-paced and live quiz options.
Kahoot	• Interactive quizzes with a competitive element. • Real-time feedback and discussion.
Formative	• Real-time assessment with instant feedback. • Ability to upload images and use diverse question types.
Edpuzzle	• Create interactive video lessons. • Track student engagement and understanding.
Socrative	• Real-time quizzes and polls. • Reports on individual and overall performance
Turnitin	• Originality checking for written assignments. • Facilitates peer review.
Grade Craft	• Gamified platform for grading and feedback. • Analytics to track student progress.
Speed Grader (Canvas)	• Integrated with the Canvas LMS. • Instant access to student submissions.
Voice Thread	• Allows multimedia presentations with voice comments. • Supports asynchronous communication.

Table 2.6 ***Contd…***

Platform	Key features
Peer grade	• Facilitates peer assessment. • Rubric-based evaluations.
Feedback Fruits	• Supports various feedback activities. • General Assessment and Feedback Platforms
Blackboard Learn	• Comprehensive LMS with assessment tools. • Discussion boards for collaborative learning.
Moodle	• Open-source LMS with assessment modules. • Grade book for tracking student progress.
Canvas	• LMS with robust assessment features. • Speed Grader for efficient grading.
Brightspace (D2L)	• LMS with assessment and feedback tools. • Intelligent Agents for personalized feedback.

2.10 Exploring the World of Learning Management Systems (LMS)

Learning Management Systems (LMS) is a type of software platform that facilitates the administration, documentation, tracking, reporting, and delivery of educational courses or training programs. They are widely used in educational institutions, corporations, and organizations to manage and enhance the learning experience (See Table 2.7).

Table 2.7 Some of the popular LMS systems.

Tool	Description
Moodle	• Open-source platform. • Customizable and flexible.
Canva	• Cloud-based platform. • User-friendly interface.
Blackboard Learn	• Comprehensive LMS. • Grade Center for efficient grading.
Schoology	• User-friendly interface. • Collaboration and communication tools.
D2L Brightspace	• Cloud-based and mobile-friendly. • Intelligent Agents for personalized learning.
Google Classroom	• Part of Google Workspace for Education. • Integrates with other Google apps.
Edmodo	• Social learning platform. • Collaboration and communication tools.
Sakai	• Open-source LMS. • Collaboration and project tools.

Table 2.7 ***Contd…***

Tool	Description
Adobe Captivate Prime	• Focuses on corporate training. • User-friendly interface.
Totara Learn	• Open-source platform based on Moodle.
EduBrite	• Cloud-based LMS. • Social learning features.
Docebo	• Cloud-based LMS with AI capabilities. • Focuses on scalability and user engagement.
LearnDash	• WordPress-based LMS. • Intuitive course builder.
TalentLMS	• Cloud-based platform. • Supports blended learning. • Gamification features.

When choosing an LMS, it's essential to consider factors such as the specific needs of your organization or institution, scalability, user-friendliness, integration capabilities, and support services. Additionally, some LMS platforms are more suitable for specific sectors, such as education, corporate training, or professional development.

2.11 Organization and Productivity Apps for Teachers

In today's fast-paced digital age, teachers are constantly seeking efficient ways to stay organized and maximize their productivity. With the advent of smartphones and tablets, a plethora of apps have been developed specifically to cater to the needs of educators. This subchapter aims to introduce teachers to a range of organization and productivity apps that can revolutionize their teaching experience.

- **Evernote**

One such app is Evernote, a versatile tool that allows teachers to create digital notebooks to store and organize lesson plans, resources, and even student work. Not only can teachers access their notes from any device, but they can also collaborate with colleagues and share resources effortlessly.

- **Trello**

Trello is a fantastic app for managing tasks and projects. With its intuitive interface, teachers can create boards, lists, and cards to keep track of various teaching responsibilities. Whether it's planning lessons, setting deadlines, or monitoring student progress, Trello helps teachers stay on top of their workload.

- **Google Drive**

Google Drive is a cloud-based storage solution that offers not only ample space for storing files but also seamless collaboration features. Teachers can create and edit documents, spreadsheets, and presentations, all while easily sharing them with students and colleagues.

- **Todoist**

Todoist provides a simple yet powerful way to manage to-do lists and stay organized. Teachers can create tasks, set due dates, and even assign priorities to ensure nothing falls through the cracks. With its reminders and notifications, Todoist helps teachers maintain focus and meet deadlines effortlessly.

- **Communication Apps**

Lastly, teachers can enhance their productivity with the use of communication apps like Slack or Microsoft Teams. These platforms allow for instant messaging, file sharing, and video conferencing, making collaboration with colleagues and students more efficient than ever.

In conclusion, the digital tools mentioned in this subchapter are just a starting point for teachers looking to embrace technology and boost their organization and productivity. By utilizing apps such as Evernote, Trello, Google Drive, Todoist, Slack, or Microsoft Teams, teachers can streamline their teaching experience, save time, and ultimately enhance student learning. Embracing digital tools is essential for the modern teacher, and these organization and productivity apps are the perfect stepping stones towards a more efficient and effective teaching practice.

2.12 Communication Tools for Seamless Operations

In today's digital age, effective communication between teachers and parents is more crucial than ever. As teachers, we understand the importance of keeping parents informed about their children's progress and ensuring a collaborative approach towards their education. With the advent of various digital tools, communication has become easier and more efficient. In this subchapter, we will explore the communication tools that can help foster seamless teacher-parent communication.

Email

One of the most used tools for communication is email. Email provides a convenient and efficient way for teachers to share updates, homework assignments, and important announcements with parents. It allows for quick and direct communication, ensuring that parents are always in the loop about their child's academic journey. Additionally, email provides a written record of the communication, which can be helpful for future reference.

- **Online Platforms and Apps**
    - Another powerful tool for teacher-parent communication is the use of online platforms and apps. These platforms, such as Google Classroom or Edmodo, provide a centralized space where teachers can share resources, assignments, and grades with parents. They also allow for parent-teacher discussions and feedback, creating a collaborative environment for supporting the student's learning.
- **Video Conferencing Tools**
    - Some digital tools go beyond simple messaging and provide a more interactive experience for teacher-parent communication. Video conferencing tools like Zoom or Microsoft Teams enable face-to-face meetings between teachers and parents, regardless of geographical limitations. This allows for more personalized discussions and a deeper understanding of the child's needs.
- **Parent Portals**
    - Additionally, many schools now utilize parent portals, which provide parents with access to their child's grades, attendance records, and other important information. This transparency fosters a sense of involvement and encourages parents to actively participate in their child's education.

It is worth mentioning that while these digital tools offer numerous benefits, it is essential to strike a balance between digital and face-to-face communication. Some parents may prefer traditional methods such as phone calls or in-person meetings. As educators, we should be mindful of this and adapt our communication strategies accordingly.

In conclusion, digital tools have revolutionized teacher-parent communication in the modern era. Whether through email, online platforms, video conferencing, or parent portals, these tools provide opportunities for seamless and effective communication. By leveraging these tools, teachers can enhance parent involvement, strengthen educational partnerships, and ultimately contribute to their students' success.

2.13 Organization and Productivity Apps for Teachers

In today's fast-paced digital age, teachers are constantly seeking efficient ways to stay organized and maximize their productivity. With the advent of smartphones and tablets, a plethora of apps have been developed specifically to cater to the needs of educators. This subchapter aims to introduce teachers to a range of organization and productivity apps that can revolutionize their teaching experience.

2.13.1 Organization Apps

- **Evernote:** A versatile tool that allows teachers to create digital notebooks to store and organize lesson plans, resources, and even student work. Teachers can access their notes from any device and collaborate with colleagues easily.
- **Trello:** A fantastic app for managing tasks and projects. Teachers can create boards, lists, and cards to keep track of various teaching responsibilities.

2.13.2 Productivity Apps

- **Google Drive:** A cloud-based storage solution that offers ample space for storing files and seamless collaboration features. Teachers can create and edit documents, spreadsheets, and presentations and easily share them with students and colleagues.
- **Todoist:** A simple yet powerful way to manage to-do lists and stay organized. Teachers can create tasks, set due dates, and assign priorities to ensure nothing falls through the cracks. With reminders and notifications, Todoist helps teachers maintain focus and meet deadlines effortlessly.
- **Communication Apps:** Platforms like Slack or Microsoft Teams allow for instant messaging, file sharing, and video conferencing, making collaboration with colleagues and students more efficient than ever.

In conclusion, these digital tools are just a starting point for teachers looking to embrace technology and boost their organization and productivity. By utilizing apps such as **Evernote, Trello, Google Drive, Todoist, Slack, or Microsoft Teams,** teachers can streamline their teaching experience, save time, and ultimately enhance student learning. Embracing digital tools is essential for the modern teacher, and these organization and productivity apps are the perfect stepping stones towards a more efficient and effective teaching practice.

In today's fast-paced world, teachers need all the help they can get to streamline their daily tasks, manage resources, and enhance overall efficiency. Thankfully, there are a plethora of organization and productivity apps that can help. Here are some of the most useful apps that span different categories like Task and Time Management (See Table 2.8), Making and Organization (See Table 2.9), Communication and Collaboration (See Table 2.10), Grade Book and Assessment (See Table 2.11), File Management (See Table 2.12), Virtual Classroom and Online Teaching (See Table 2.13), and Professional Development and Learning (See Table 2.14).

Table 2.8 Task and Time Management.

Tool	Description
Todoist	• Task management app with features like due dates, priority levels, and project organization. • Supports collaboration for group projects. • Available on various platforms.
Trello	• Visual project management app using boards, lists, and cards. • Ideal for organizing lesson plans, tasks, and collaborative projects. • Allows attachments, checklists, and due dates.
Any.do	• Task and time management app with a simple interface. • Supports tasks, reminders, and to-do lists. • Integrates with calendars for seamless planning.

Table 2.9 Notetaking and Organization.

Tool	Description
Evernote	• Digital note-taking app for organizing lesson plans, resources, and ideas. • Supports multimedia notes, checklists, and document scanning. • Syncs across devices.
Microsoft OneNote	• Digital notebook for organizing lesson plans, research, and notes. • Supports multimedia notes, drawing, and collaboration. • Integrates with other Microsoft Office applications
Notability	• Note-taking app for iPads with features like handwriting, sketching, and annotating PDFs. • Ideal for creating interactive and visual lesson materials.

Table 2.10 Communication and Collaboration.

Tool	Description
Slack	• Team communication app for real-time messaging and collaboration. • Organizes conversations into channels for different subjects or projects. • Supports file sharing and integrations with other apps.
Remind	• Communication app designed for teacher-student and teacher-parent communication. • Allows for broadcast announcements, messaging, and document sharing.
ClassDojo	• Classroom communication app that allows teachers to share updates, photos, and videos with parents. • Supports behavior tracking and positive reinforcement.

Table 2.11 Gradebook and Assessment.

Tool	*Description*
Gradekeeper	• Gradebook app for tracking student grades and attendance. • Supports various grading systems and customizable reports. • Available for Windows, macOS, and iOS.
ZipGrade	• Grading app that uses the device's camera to scan and grade multiple-choice assignments. • Provides detailed reports and analysis. • Ideal for quick and efficient grading.

Table 2.12 File Management.

Tool	Description
Google Drive	• Cloud storage and file-sharing app. • Collaborative document editing and sharing. • Integrates with other Google Workspace apps.
Dropbox	• Cloud-based file storage and collaboration app. • Easily share files and collaborate on documents. • Syncs files across devices.

Table 2.13 Virtual Classroom and Online Teaching.

Tool	Description
Zoom	• Video conferencing app for virtual classrooms and meetings. • Supports screen sharing, breakout rooms, and recording. • Ideal for online teaching and virtual collaboration.
Google Classroom	• Platform for creating and managing classes, assignments, and communication. • Integrates seamlessly with other Google Workspace apps. • Facilitates virtual collaboration and submission of assignments.

Table 2.14 Professional Development and Learning.

Tool	Description
LinkedIn Learning	• Online learning app offering courses on a wide range of topics. • Ideal for professional development and acquiring new skills. • Provides certificates upon course completion.
Edmodo	• Social learning platform that supports communication, collaboration, and assignment distribution. • Allows for the creation of a virtual learning community. • Supports quizzes, polls, and discussions.

These apps can significantly enhance teachers' organization and productivity by providing tools for efficient communication, lesson planning, grading, and collaboration. The choice of apps may depend on personal preferences, device compatibility, and specific teaching needs.

2.14 Communication Tools for Seamless Teacher-Parent Communication

In today's digital age, it's more crucial than ever for teachers to communicate effectively with parents. Collaborative relationships between teachers and parents are essential for ensuring a student's academic success, and various digital tools have made communication more efficient than ever before. In this subchapter, we will explore how these tools can be utilized to foster seamless communication.

Email is one of the most used tools for teacher-parent communication. It provides an easy way for teachers to share updates, homework assignments, and important announcements with parents. It also allows for direct communication and offers a written record that can be useful for future reference.

Online platforms and apps such as Google Classroom or Edmodo provide a centralized space where teachers can share resources, assignments, and grades with parents. They also facilitate parent-teacher discussions and feedback, creating a collaborative environment for supporting the student's learning.

Video conferencing tools like Zoom or Microsoft Teams enable face-to-face meetings between teachers and parents, regardless of geographical limitations. This allows for more personalized discussions and a deeper understanding of the child's needs.

Many schools now utilize parent portals, which provide parents with access to their child's grades, attendance records, and other important information. This transparency fosters a sense of involvement and encourages parents to actively participate in their child's education.

While digital tools offer numerous benefits, it's important to strike a balance between digital and face-to-face communication. Some parents may prefer traditional methods such as phone calls or in-person meetings. As educators, we should be mindful of this and adapt our communication strategies accordingly.

In conclusion, digital tools have revolutionized teacher-parent communication. Whether through email, online platforms, video conferencing, or parent portals, these tools provide opportunities for seamless and effective communication. By leveraging these tools, teachers can enhance parent involvement, strengthen educational partnership, and ultimately contribute to their students' success.

Effective communication between teachers and parents is essential for a student's academic success and positive learning experience. Here are some communication tools that can help facilitate seamless and efficient communication between teachers and parents:

Table 2.15 Communication Tools for Seamless Teacher-Parent Communication.

Tool	Description
Remind	• A messaging app created to connect teachers, parents, and students.
Class Dojo	• A classroom communication app that enables teachers to share updates, photos, and videos with parents. • Supports behavior tracking and positive reinforcement.
Seesaw	• A digital portfolio tool that promotes communication and collaboration between teachers and parents. • Teachers can share students' work, announcements, and updates.
Google Classroom	• Part of Google Workspace for Education, Google Classroom streamlines communication and assignment distribution.
Class Tag	• A comprehensive communication platform that includes messaging, event scheduling, and volunteer coordination.
Parent Square	• A unified communication platform for schools that combines messaging, event scheduling, and parent-teacher conferences.
Bloomz	• A communication and coordination app for teachers and parents.
TalkingPoints	• A multilingual messaging platform designed to bridge language gaps between teachers and parents.
Class Messenger	• A communication app that allows teachers to send messages, photos, and files to parents. • Includes features like announcements and event scheduling.
Edmodo	• A social learning platform that facilitates communication between teachers, students, and parents. • Teachers can share resources, assignments, and announcements. • Parents can monitor their child's progress and receive updates.

When choosing a communication tool, consider factors such as ease of use, accessibility, security, and specific features that align with the communication needs of both teachers and parents. It's also vital to ensure that the chosen tool complies with privacy regulations and school policies.

CHAPTER 3

Interactive Learning with Multimedia

In today's digital age, multimedia has become an integral part of our daily lives. It has transformed the way we learn and assimilate information. Interactive learning with multimedia combines various forms of media, such as text, images, audio, and video, to create engaging and immersive learning experiences. This approach has proven to be highly effective in enhancing understanding, promoting retention, and increasing overall student engagement. In this article, we will explore the benefits of interactive learning with multimedia and discuss how it can be effectively implemented in educational settings.

3.1 Benefits of Interactive Learning with Multimedia

Enhanced Engagement: Multimedia elements, such as videos, animations, and interactive graphics, capture students' attention and make the learning process more enjoyable. This increased engagement leads to better focus, improved information retention, and a deeper understanding of the subject matter.

1. Improved Retention: Studies have shown that multimedia-based learning improves long-term retention of information. By presenting information through various media formats, learners can process and encode the information in multiple ways, making it easier to remember and recall later.
2. Personalized Learning: Interactive multimedia allows for personalized learning experiences tailored to individual needs and preferences. Learners can navigate through the content at their own pace, review materials as needed, and choose the media format that best suits their learning style.
3. Active Learning: Interactive multimedia encourages active participation and hands-on exploration. Learners can interact with the content, solve problems, and engage in real-life simulations. This active learning approach promotes critical thinking, problem-solving skills, and a deeper understanding of the subject matter.

4. Multisensory Learning: By combining text, images, audio, and video, multimedia appeals to multiple senses, enhancing the learning experience. This multisensory approach stimulates different parts of the brain, leading to better comprehension and knowledge retention.
5. Real-World Applications: Interactive multimedia can simulate real-world scenarios, allowing learners to apply their knowledge in practical contexts. This helps bridge the gap between theory and practice, preparing students for real-life situations and improving their problem-solving abilities.

3.2 Implementation of Interactive Learning with Multimedia

To effectively implement interactive learning with multimedia, educators can consider the following strategies:

1. Curriculum Integration: Incorporate multimedia elements into the curriculum to supplement traditional teaching methods. Use videos, animations, and interactive simulations to reinforce key concepts and engage students in active learning.
2. Online Learning Platforms: Utilize online learning platforms that offer interactive multimedia content. These platforms provide a wide range of resources, including videos, quizzes, and interactive exercises, to facilitate self-paced learning and student engagement.
3. Collaborative Projects: Encourage collaborative learning by assigning group projects that require students to create multimedia presentations or videos. This fosters teamwork, communication skills, and creativity while incorporating multimedia into the learning process.
4. Virtual Reality (VR) and Augmented Reality (AR): Explore the use of virtual reality and augmented reality technologies to create immersive learning experiences. These technologies can transport students to virtual environments, allowing them to explore complex concepts in a hands-on and interactive manner.
5. Gamification: Gamify the learning experience by incorporating game elements, such as leaderboards, badges, and rewards, into educational multimedia content. This approach increases motivation, engagement, and active participation among learners.

Interactive learning with multimedia offers numerous advantages in today's educational landscape. By leveraging various media formats, educators can create engaging and immersive learning experiences that enhance student engagement, retention, and understanding. Implementing interactive multimedia strategies in classrooms and online learning environments can transform traditional teaching methods and provide students with personalized, active, and multisensory learning experiences. As technology continues to advance, interactive learning with multimedia will undoubtedly play a crucial role in shaping the future of education.

3. 3 Incorporating Videos and Animations in Lessons

Incorporating videos and animations into lessons has become an essential tool for the modern teacher. This subchapter aims to introduce teachers to the benefits and strategies of using videos and animations in their lessons, equipping them with the necessary digital tools to enhance their teaching methods.

3.3.1 The Advantages of Using Videos and Animations in Teaching

- Visual content stimulates students' interest and helps them better understand complex concepts.
- Videos and animations can be used to demonstrate real-life scenarios or historical events, making the learning experience more immersive and memorable.
- Multimedia content caters to diverse learning styles since different students have different learning preferences.

3.3.2 Effective Use of Videos and Animations in Lessons

- Teachers need to be familiar with the various digital tools available to effectively incorporate videos and animations in their lessons.
- It is crucial to consider the appropriate use of videos and animations within lessons, selecting content that aligns with learning objectives and curriculum, age-appropriate and of high quality.
- Integrating interactive elements, such as quizzes or discussions, can further enhance students' engagement and comprehension.

Incorporating videos and animations in lessons is a valuable strategy for modern teachers. By leveraging these multimedia tools, teachers can make their lessons more engaging, accessible, and effective in reaching diverse learners. Teachers must explore the available digital tools and integrate videos and animations thoughtfully to maximize their educational impact.

3.4 Enhancing Learning with Video and Animation: Tools and Platforms for Educators

Teachers can improve learning outcomes and inspire curiosity by incorporating videos and animations into their lessons. Here are some useful tools and platforms that educators can use for creating or finding educational videos and animations (See Table 3.1), and (See Table 3.2).

Table 3.1 Tools for Creating Videos and Animations.

Tool	Description
Camtasia	• Screen recording and video editing tools. • Voiceover and webcam integration.
Powtoon	• Animated video creation platform. • Templates for various educational topics. • Drag-and-drop interface for creating animated presentations
Adobe Spark Video	• Easy-to-use animated video creation tool. • Storytelling tools with text, images, and icons.
Vyond	• Animation software for creating animated videos. • Customizable characters and scenes.
Moovl	• Create animated videos and presentations. • Library of templates, objects, and transitions.
Explain Everything	• Interactive whiteboard platform. • Screen recording and annotation.
YouTube	• Vast library of educational channels and videos. • Many educational content creators cover various subjects.
Khan Academy	• Extensive collection of instructional videos. • Covers a wide range of subjects and grade levels.
TED-Ed	• Educational platform with animated lessons. • Lesson creation tools for educators.
National Geographic Education	• Educational videos and resources on science, geography, and culture. • Stunning visuals and storytelling.
PBS Learning Media	• Educational videos, lesson plans, and interactive activities. • Aligned with curriculum standards.
Discovery Education	• Digital content library with videos and resources. • Curriculum-aligned materials. • Virtual field trips and interactive content.

Table 3.2 Interactive Learning Platforms.

Platforms	Description
Edpuzzle	• Embed questions and quizzes into videos. • Track student progress and engagement. • Support for flipped classroom models.
PlayPosit	• Create interactive video lessons. • Embed assessments and discussions. • Analyze student performance.
Nearpod	• Interactive lessons with multimedia content. • Collaboration and formative assessments. • Virtual reality and 3D lessons.

These tools and platforms offer educators a range of options for incorporating videos and animations into lessons. Whether creating original content or leveraging existing resources, adding multimedia elements can make lessons more engaging and effective.

3.5 Creating Interactive Presentations with Multimedia Tools

In today's rapidly evolving digital age, teachers must utilize multimedia tools to engage and captivate their students. The days of traditional chalkboard lectures are long gone, and modern educators must embrace technology in the classroom. This subchapter will delve into the various multimedia tools available to teachers, introducing digital tools for the modern teacher.

Multimedia tools offer an array of possibilities for creating dynamic and interactive presentations. By incorporating multimedia elements into their lectures, teachers can cater to different learning styles and capture their students' attention. These tools include videos, animations, audio clips, and interactive quizzes, among others.

PowerPoint is one of the most popular multimedia tools for creating interactive presentations. Its user-friendly interface and vast array of features allow teachers to incorporate multimedia elements into their slides easily. Teachers can add animations, transitions, and interactive features to make their presentations more engaging. Additionally, PowerPoint offers the option to save presentations as interactive videos or create online versions that can be accessed remotely.

Another powerful multimedia tool is Prezi, which offers a unique and visually stunning way to present information. Prezi allows teachers to create zooming and panning presentations, offering a more dynamic and interactive experience for students. With its ability to incorporate multimedia elements and seamless integration with other platforms, Prezi is an excellent choice for teachers looking to create captivating presentations.

Teachers can also consider other multimedia tools, such as Google Slides, Haiku Deck, and Adobe Spark, each offering its unique features and benefits. By exploring these tools and experimenting with different multimedia elements, teachers can create engaging presentations that resonate with their students.

In conclusion, creating interactive presentations with multimedia tools is an essential skill for the modern teacher. These tools offer endless possibilities for engaging students and enhancing the learning experience. By embracing technology and incorporating multimedia elements into their presentations, teachers can captivate their students' attention, cater to different learning styles, and create a truly immersive and interactive classroom environment.

Creating interactive presentations with multimedia tools can significantly enhance engagement and comprehension. Here are several tools that allow you to integrate various multimedia elements into your presentations.

Table 3.3 Creating Interactive Presentations with Multimedia Tools.

Platform	Features
Microsoft PowerPoint	• Embedded images, videos, and audio clips. • Add hyperlinks for interactive navigation. • Incorporate animations and transitions. • Use features like PowerPoint Designer for design suggestions.
Features	• Collaborative editing and real-time sharing. • Embedded videos from YouTube. • Insert images, shapes, and text boxes. • Add links for navigation.
Prezi	• Non-linear presentation structure. • Zooming and panning effects for visual engagement. • Embed images, videos, and links. • Collaborative editing in real-time.
Haiku Deck	• Simplified and visually appealing presentations. • Access to a library of high-quality images. • Integration with Creative Commons for image search.
Adobe Spark	• Create web pages, videos, and graphics. • Incorporate images, icons, and text. • Add narration to video presentations. • Easy-to-use interface.

Table 3.3 ***Contd...***

Platform	Features
Canva	• Design visually appealing presentations. • Access to a vast library of templates and elements. • Embed videos, images, and links. • Collaborative design with team members.
Mentimeter	• Interactive presentations with live polls and quizzes. • Engage audiences through Q&A sessions. • Real-time data visualization. • Supports remote and in-person presentations.
Sway (Microsoft)	• Create interactive and responsive presentations. • Embed multimedia elements seamlessly. • Dynamic design that adjusts to different screens. • Real-time collaboration.
Emaze	• 3D templates for visually stunning presentations. • Animated and interactive elements. • Embed videos, 3D objects, and charts.

3.6 Gamification and Educational Games for Active Learning

In today's constantly evolving digital landscape, teachers are exploring new ways of engaging and motivating their students. One approach that has gained significant traction in recent years is the use of gamification and educational games for active learning. This subchapter delves into the concept of gamification, its benefits in the classroom, and how teachers can effectively incorporate educational games into their instruction.

3.6.1 What is Gamification?

Gamification refers to the integration of game elements, such as competition, rewards, and challenges, into non-game contexts, such as education. By incorporating game-like elements into the learning process, teachers can tap into students' natural inclination towards competition and play, making education more enjoyable and stimulating. This approach can significantly enhance student engagement and motivation, leading to improved learning outcomes.

3.6.2 What are Educational Games?

Educational games are specifically designed to facilitate learning while providing an interactive and entertaining experience. These games often simulate real-world scenarios, allowing students to apply their knowledge and skills in practical contexts. From math puzzles and language quizzes to virtual science experiments and historical simulations, the possibilities for educational games are vast and cater to a wide range of subjects and grade levels.

3.6.3 The Benefits of Gamification and Educational Games

The benefits of gamification and educational games in the classroom are numerous. Firstly, they foster active learning, as students are actively involved in solving problems, making decisions, and exploring concepts. This hands-on approach promotes critical thinking, problem-solving skills, and creativity. Additionally, gamification enhances student motivation by providing immediate feedback, rewards, and the opportunity for students to track their progress and compete with peers. These elements create a sense of achievement and encourage students to persist and excel.

3.7 Incorporating Gamification and Educational Games into Instruction

To effectively incorporate gamification and educational games into their instruction, teachers must first identify the learning objectives and select appropriate games that align with the curriculum. They should also consider the level of challenge, age appropriateness, and accessibility of the games. Technology plays a crucial role in this process, as many educational games are digital and require devices such as computers, tablets, or smartphones. Teachers should familiarize themselves with the available digital tools and platforms that host educational games, ensuring they are user-friendly and secure.

Furthermore, teachers should actively participate in the game-based learning experience, providing guidance, support, and feedback to students. They can also design their games or modify existing ones to suit their specific teaching goals and student needs. Collaboration and reflection should be encouraged, allowing students to discuss their experiences and insights gained from the game.

In conclusion, gamification and educational games offer a powerful tool for educators to create a dynamic and engaging learning environment. By leveraging the natural affinity students have for games, teachers can enhance student motivation, active learning, and critical thinking skills. As teachers embrace digital tools for the modern classroom, gamification, and educational games should be considered essential components of their instructional toolbox.

Gamification and educational games are effective tools to encourage active learning and engagement in the classroom. Consider using the following tools to create educational games and implement gamification (See Table 3.4).

Table 3.4 Tools to Create Educational Games.

Platform	Features
Kahoot	• Create and play interactive quizzes. • Supports multiple-choice questions, surveys, and discussions. • Real-time feedback and leaderboard for added excitement.
Quizizz	• Gamified quizzes with a competitive element. • Self-paced learning options. • Memes and avatars for a fun and engaging experience.
Classcraft	• Gamify the entire classroom experience. • Students create characters and go on quests. • Points and rewards system for positive behavior.
Breakout EDU	• Digital and physical escape room challenges. • Encourages critical thinking and collaboration. • Offers various educational themes.
Minecraft	• Educational version of the popular game. • Build, explore, and learn in a virtual world. • Teacher controls for a safe and structured environment.
Prodigy	• Math-focused game with adaptive learning. • Aligns with curriculum standards. • Tracks student progress and provides personalized challenges.
GooseChase	• Create and participate in scavenger hunt games. • Supports both indoor and outdoor activities.
Socrative	• Real-time quizzes and assessments. • Gamified Space Race mode. • Immediate feedback and data analysis.
Gimkit	• Quiz-based game with an emphasis on strategy. • Incentivizes students to collaborate and compete. • Teachers can create and customize games.

3.8 Augmented Reality and Virtual Reality in the Classroom

In today's digital age, technology has transformed the way we approach education. Teachers are now exploring innovative methods to engage and educate their students using digital tools. One such technology that holds immense potential for transforming the classroom experience is Augmented Reality (AR) and Virtual Reality (VR). These emerging technologies offer exciting opportunities to create immersive and interactive learning environments that can greatly enhance students' understanding and retention of complex concepts.

3.8.1 AR and VR Integration in Education

AR involves the integration of digital information, such as images, videos, or 3D models, into the real-world environment. By using AR apps or devices, teachers can create a more tangible and relatable experience for students when exploring abstract ideas. For example, instead of simply explaining the solar system, students can use AR to explore and interact with virtual planets in real time, fostering a deeper understanding of celestial bodies and their movements. AR can also be utilized to create interactive historical or geographical tours, allowing students to virtually visit famous landmarks or ancient civilizations.

On the other hand, VR offers a fully immersive experience by completely replacing the real-world environment with a simulated one. With VR headsets, students can be transported to different times, places, or even fictional worlds. This technology not only captivates students' attention but also enables them to actively participate in their learning. For instance, biology lessons can be transformed into virtual dissections, allowing students to explore the human body in a safe and controlled environment. Similarly, VR can be used to recreate historical events, enabling students to witness and understand significant moments firsthand.

3.8.2 Benefits of AR and VR in Education

AR and VR promote active learning, as students become active participants rather than passive recipients of information. By engaging multiple senses, these technologies stimulate students' curiosity and help them retain knowledge more effectively. Furthermore, these tools cater to different learning styles, accommodating visual, auditory, and kinesthetic learners alike.

3.8.3 Potential Challenges

Teachers need to ensure that the use of AR and VR aligns with the learning objectives and curriculum. While these technologies offer exciting possibilities, they should be seen as complementary tools rather than replacements for traditional teaching methods. Teachers must also consider the accessibility and affordability of AR and VR devices, as well as the potential challenges associated with their implementation. In conclusion, AR and VR have the potential to revolutionize education by creating immersive and interactive learning experiences. By embracing these digital tools, teachers can engage and inspire students in ways that were previously unimaginable. As modern educators, it is essential to explore and harness the power of digital tools like AR and VR to prepare students for the ever-evolving digital landscape they will encounter in the future.

3.9 Innovative Tools for Educators to Integrate AR and VR into their Lesson

Augmented and virtual reality technologies offer immersive experiences that can transform traditional classroom settings. These are some of the best tools and platforms that educators can use to integrate AR and VR into their teaching (See Table 3.4), and (See Table 3.5).

Table 3.5 Tools and Platforms for Augmented Reality (AR).

Tools/Platforms	Description
AR Flashcards	• Enhances traditional flashcards with AR technology. • Supports a variety of subjects
Google Expeditions	• Virtual field trips with 360-degree panoramas. • Allows teachers to guide and narrate the journey.
Aurasma	• Create and share augmented reality experiences. • Ideal for interactive presentations and projects.
Metaverse	• Create AR experiences without coding. • Supports collaboration and sharing.
Quiver	• Coloring pages come to life with AR. • Supports various subjects.

Table 3.6 Tools and Platforms for Virtual Reality (VR).

Tools/Platforms	Description
Google Cardboard	• Affordable VR solution using cardboard headsets. • Compatible with many VR apps and experiences.
Nearpod VR	• Integrates VR experiences into lessons. • Virtual field trips and 3D models for enhanced learning.
ClassVR	• VR content designed for educational settings. • Teacher controls for managing VR sessions.
Alchemy VR	• Educational VR content for science and history. • Designed for classroom use.
CoSpacesEdu	• Create, explore, and share virtual worlds. • Supports coding within the VR environment.
Expeditions	• Google's VR platform for virtual field trips. • Teacher controls and guided tours.
ZSpace	• Combines AR and VR for interactive learning. • 3D models and simulations for STEM education.
ThingLink VR	• Create interactive 360-degree images. • Embed information, links, and multimedia.
Minecraft	• Virtual building and exploration.

These tools provide educators with the means to integrate AR and VR into their lessons, creating more immersive and engaging learning experiences for students. When using these technologies, it's essential to consider the age group, curriculum alignment, and specific learning objectives for the most effective implementation.

3.10 Using Podcasts and Audio Tools to Enhance Learning

In today's fast-paced digital world, traditional teaching methods are evolving at a rapid pace to keep up with the changing needs and interests of modern students. As educators, it's critical to stay up-to-date with the latest digital tools that can enhance the learning experience and engage students in new and exciting ways. One such tool that has gained immense popularity is podcasts and audio tools.

Offering a unique way to deliver educational content, podcasts provide an auditory experience that can be easily accessed and consumed by students at their convenience. They are accessible on smartphones and other portable devices, allowing students to listen while commuting, exercising, or during any downtime. This accessibility makes podcasts an efficient tool for extending learning beyond the walls of a traditional classroom.

Teachers can use podcasts to supplement their lessons by creating their own or curating existing ones. By incorporating audio content into the curriculum, teachers can reinforce key concepts, provide additional examples, or even introduce new perspectives. This approach helps students develop a deeper understanding of the subject matter and enhances their critical thinking skills.

Audio tools, on the other hand, provide teachers with a range of options for creating interactive and engaging learning experiences. Audio recording software enables teachers to create their audio lessons, explaining complex ideas clearly and concisely. Students can revisit the recordings as many times as required, allowing them to grasp the content better.

Audio tools can also be used to create interactive quizzes or assessments. Teachers can record questions or prompts, and students can respond by recording their answers. This method provides immediate feedback and helps students improve their speaking and listening skills.

Podcasts and audio tools also offer opportunities for collaborative learning. Teachers can assign group projects where students create their podcasts, discussing a particular topic or presenting their research findings.

This approach encourages students to work together and develop their communication and presentation skills.

In conclusion, podcasts and audio tools are valuable additions to the digital toolkit of any modern teacher. By incorporating these tools into their teaching strategies, educators can create engaging and interactive learning experiences that cater to the diverse needs and preferences of their students. So, embrace the power of podcasts and audio tools and unlock a world of endless possibilities in the classroom.

3.11 Enhancing Education with Podcasts and Audio Tools

Incorporating podcasts and audio tools into education can be a game-changer, providing a fresh and interesting alternative way for students to learn. Here are several tools that educators can use to integrate podcasts and audio into their teaching (See Table 3.6) and See (Table 3.7). By using podcasts and audio tools, educators can cater to different learning styles, provide flexible learning opportunities, and enhance engagement. Whether creating podcasts, leveraging existing educational content, or using audio for assignments, these tools offer a range of possibilities for audio-based learning experiences.

Table 3.7 Podcast Creation and Hosting Tools.

Tools	Description
Anchor	• This free platform is perfect for creating and hosting podcasts. • It has an easy-to-use interface with built-in recording and editing tools.
Audacity	• This free, open-source audio editing software lets you record, edit, and mix audio files.
Podbean	• This podcast hosting and monetization platform boasts a user-friendly interface for creating and managing podcasts.
Spreaker	• This live streaming and podcast hosting platform has integrated recording and editing tools.
Libsyn	• This podcast hosting service is perfect for those who want robust analytics.
TED Talks Education	• This podcast features inspiring talks from educators, researchers, and thought leaders.
The EdSurge Podcast	• This podcast focuses on the intersection of technology, education, and the future.
Teaching in Higher Ed	• This podcast addresses topics relevant to higher education and includes interviews with educators, authors, and experts. • It focuses on teaching, learning, and technology.

Table 3.7 ***Contd...***

Tools	Description
The Cult of Pedagogy Podcast	• Hosted by Jennifer Gonzalez, this podcast focuses on effective teaching strategies.
GarageBand	• This music creation and audio editing software is ideal for creating podcasts, music, and soundtracks.
Adobe Audition	• This professional audio editing software has multitrack editing and mixing capabilities.
Hindenburg Journalist	• This audio editing software is specifically designed for journalists and podcasters. • It has an intuitive interface for recording and editing and automatic sound leveling for consistent audio quality.

Table 3.8 Audio Collaboration and Sharing Tools.

Tools	Description
Soundtrap by Spotify	• This online collaborative music and podcast studio allows for real-time collaboration with other users. • It also has cloud-based storage for easy access.
Vocaroo	• This simple online voice recording tool does not require an account. • Easily share recordings through links.
SpeakPipe	• This voice recording tool is ideal for feedback, questions, or reflections, and integrates with websites and blogs.

CHAPTER 4

Online Coding Courses and Tutorials

In today's world, coding has become a vital skill for both individuals and businesses. With the demand for software developers on the rise, online coding courses and tutorials have made coding accessible from the comfort of one's own home.

There are numerous online coding courses and tutorials to choose from, catering to various skill levels and programming languages. From novice to advanced learners, there is a course suitable for everyone. Interactive learning experiences offered by many online coding courses enable learners to practice coding in real time and receive instant feedback.

Apart from coding courses, several online coding communities and forums are available to connect with other coders and share knowledge. These communities can be a valuable resource for individuals looking to expand their coding skills and stay up to date with the latest industry trends.

Overall, online coding courses and tutorials are an excellent way to enhance coding skills, advance careers, and remain competitive in the ever-evolving tech industry.

4.1 The Significance of Learning Coding in the Digital Age: Top Online Platforms

In today's digital era, coding has become a critical skill for students to master. It opens a world of opportunities for those who aspire to become software developers, data scientists, or entrepreneurs. Luckily, there are various online platforms available that cater to different types of learners and skill levels. This subchapter highlights some of the most famous online platforms for learning coding, providing teachers and students with valuable resources to enhance technical education.

1. Codecademy: Codecademy is a widely known online learning platform that offers interactive coding courses in various programming languages. With its hands-on exercises and user-friendly interface, Codecademy allows students to learn coding concepts through practical application.

2. Udacity: Udacity offers nano degree programs in collaboration with industry leaders such as Google and IBM. These programs provide comprehensive training in various technical fields, including coding. Students can learn at their own pace and receive personalized feedback from mentors.
3. Coursera: Coursera is a leading online learning platform that partners with leading universities and organizations to offer coding courses. With a wide range of courses, students can learn coding fundamentals or specialize in specific areas such as web development or data science.
4. Khan Academy: Khan Academy provides free coding courses for students of all ages. Its interactive coding environment enables students to learn coding concepts while creating projects such as animations and games.
5. edX: edX offers coding courses from renowned institutions such as Harvard and MIT. Students can choose from a variety of programming languages and learn through video lectures, quizzes, and hands-on assignments.
6. FreeCodeCamp: FreeCodeCamp is a nonprofit organization that offers free coding courses and projects. It provides a supportive community where students can collaborate and learn from each other.
7. Pluralsight: Pluralsight offers a vast library of coding courses and tutorials. Its learning paths guide students through a structured curriculum, ensuring they acquire the necessary skills to succeed in their chosen field.
8. GitHub: GitHub is a web-based platform that allows students to collaborate on coding projects and showcase their work. It also provides a rich resource of open-source projects for students to learn from.

These online platforms offer a wealth of resources that educators can incorporate into their teaching strategies to empower students to develop essential coding skills. Whether students are interested in web development, data science, or virtual reality, these platforms offer a diverse range of courses and tools to cater to their individual needs and interests, preparing them for the digital future.

Learning to code on these platforms allows individuals to acquire practical skills, work on real projects, and build a strong foundation in programming languages, making them well-prepared for the demands of the digital age.

4.2 Why Coding is Important in the Digital Age and Top Online Platforms to Learn

Nowadays, learning how to code is of great significance as coding skills are becoming more essential in various fields. Here are some reasons why acquiring coding skills is important in the digital age.

4.2.1 Significance of Learning Coding

In the context of today's digital era, acquiring coding skills has become increasingly crucial. Not only does it allow individuals to cultivate several highly sought-after abilities in the job market, such as problem-solving and logical thinking, but also creativity enhancement is attainable through coding education. Furthermore, mastering programming languages equips learners with a comprehensive understanding of technology manipulation; enabling them to craft websites or develop mobile applications while automating complex tasks effectively – all valuable proficiencies given automation advancements within various industries. Moreover, collaborative work strategies are often involved in coding projects and provide opportunities for teamwork fostering growth among coworkers by sharing perspectives from other professionals' backgrounds positively. As technological innovation continues shaping our society at a rapid pace globally, contributively learning how code functions will undoubtedly lead to personal development alongside professional success prospects significantly increasing. The significance of obtaining this skillset cannot be underestimated due to its paramount capacity opening an extensive range of possibilities and expanding horizons indefinitely in today's progressively driven technological world. Learning coding holds immense significance mentioned in Figure 3.1.

Table 4.1 Significance of Coding.

Parameters	Highlights
Problem-Solving	• Coding teaches logical thinking and problem-solving skills. • It enables individuals to break down complex problems into smaller, more manageable parts.
Digital Literacy	• In a digitally driven world, coding is a fundamental aspect of digital literacy. • Understanding code allows individuals to navigate and comprehend technology more effectively.
Career Opportunities	• Many high-demand and well-paying jobs require coding skills. • Coding is essential in fields such as software development, data science, artificial intelligence, and web development.

Table 4.1 ***Contd....***

Parameters	Highlights
Creativity and Innovation	• Coding empowers individuals to bring their creative ideas to life. • It is a tool for innovation and enables the development of new solutions and products.
Critical Thinking	• Coding requires attention to detail and precision, fostering critical thinking. • Debugging and troubleshooting are integral parts of the coding process.

Table 4.2 Top Online Platforms for Learning Coding.

Tools	Usage
Codecademy	• Interactive coding lessons with hands-on projects. • Courses cover various programming languages. • Free and paid subscription options.
Coursera	• Offers coding courses from universities and institutions. • Specializations and degree programs available. • range of programming languages and topics.
edX	• Online courses from universities and organizations. • Verified certificates and degree programs. • Diverse coding courses and specializations.
Udacity	• Nanodegree programs with a focus on practical skills. • Mentorship and real-world projects. • Courses in programming, data science, and more.
Khan Academy	• Free coding courses suitable for beginners. • Interactive challenges and projects. • Focus on JavaScript and SQL.
FreeCodeCamp	• Free coding curriculum with hands-on projects. • Full-stack web development certification. • Coding challenges and community support.
GitHub Learning Lab	• Interactive coding tutorials hosted on GitHub. • Hands-on projects with real-world applications. • Covers various programming languages.
Hackerrank	• Platform for practicing coding challenges. • Compete in coding contests. • Interview preparation kits for coding interviews.
SoloLearn	• Mobile app for learning coding on the go. • Courses in various programming languages. • Code playground for practice.

Table 4.2 *Contd....*

Tools	Usage
MIT Open Courseware	• Free online courses from MIT. • Computer Science and Electrical Engineering courses available. • In-depth coverage of coding principles.
LinkedIn Learning	• Coding courses and tutorials. • Access to a broad range of professional development content. • Certificates of completion for courses.

Learning to code is easy through these platforms, as they provide practical skills, real projects, and a solid foundation in programming languages, making individuals well-prepared for the demands of the digital age.

4.3 Advantages of Online Coding Courses for Education

Online coding courses have become increasingly popular in technical education over the past few years. These courses have revolutionized the way we acquire and master technical skills and offer great benefits to both teachers and students. This section explores the advantages of online coding courses and sheds light on their significance in enhancing education.

One of the key advantages of online coding courses is their accessibility. These courses can be accessed from anywhere with an internet connection, allowing teachers and scholars to learn at their own pace and convenience. This flexibility eliminates geographical barriers and time constraints, enabling individuals to fit learning into their busy schedules. Moreover, online courses often offer lifetime access to course materials, allowing learners to revisit and reinforce their understanding whenever needed.

Online coding courses are also known for their interactive and engaging nature. Many platforms use innovative teaching methods such as gamification, quizzes, and interactive coding exercises to make the learning experience enjoyable and effective. This not only helps in retaining information but also fosters a sense of motivation and curiosity among learners.

In addition, online coding courses provide a vast range of resources and support. Learners can access forums, communities, and chat groups where they can discuss problems, seek guidance, and engage with fellow enthusiasts and experts. This collaborative learning environment enhances the overall learning experience and encourages the exchange of ideas and best practices.

Furthermore, online coding courses often offer certifications upon successful completion. These certifications hold value in the job market and can boost career prospects for scholars. Employers recognize the significance of continuous learning and appreciate candidates who have taken the initiative to upgrade their technical skills through online courses.

Finally, online coding courses provide access to cutting-edge tools and technologies. Many platforms offer virtual laboratories, simulations, and programming environments that allow learners to practice and experiment without the need for expensive physical equipment. This hands-on experience with the latest tools and technologies ensures that scholars are well-prepared for the demands of the industry.

To sum up, online coding courses offer numerous advantages for technical education. Their accessibility, interactive nature, vast resources, and certifications make them a valuable tool for both teachers and scholars. By embracing online coding courses, educators can enhance technical education and equip learners with the skills needed to thrive in the digital age.

CHAPTER 5

Digital Design and Graphic Arts Education

Digital art and design education have become increasingly important in today's world. With the rise of technology and the internet, there is a growing need for talented individuals who can create informative and visually appealing digital content.

Digital design and graphic arts education programs teach students basic design principles such as typography, color theory, composition, and layout. They also gain technical skills to create various digital products such as logos, brochures, websites, and social media posts using software such as Adobe Photoshop, Illustrator, and InDesign.

The pursuit of digital art and graphic design benefits from versatility. Graduates can work in a variety of industries, including advertising, marketing, web design, and print media. They can also choose to work as freelancers, offering their services to clients in need of digital content.

In conclusion, digital design and illustration courses are a valuable investment for anyone interested in pursuing a creative career. It also equips individuals with the skills and knowledge necessary to succeed in an ever-changing digital environment.

5.1 Incorporating Digital Design in Technical Education

The technological landscape is rapidly evolving, and educators must adapt their teaching methods to meet the needs of modern learners. One effective way to enhance technical education is by integrating digital design into the curriculum. Here are some ways in which digital tools can be utilized to enrich technical education and equip students with the skills they need to succeed in the digital age.

Digital tools empower students to think creatively, and problem-solve using technology. Whether it is through online coding courses and tutorials or virtual reality and augmented reality education tools, students can gain hands-on experience in designing and developing digital solutions.

Graphic arts education is an area where digital design can greatly benefit technical education. Students can learn how to use digital design software to create visually appealing and impactful designs, enhancing their artistic abilities and preparing them for careers in the digital marketing and advertising industries.

E-learning platforms are another valuable resource for technical skills development. These platforms provide students with the flexibility to learn at their own pace and access a wide range of courses and tutorials. Whether it is data science and analytics or web development and programming, e-learning platforms offer a comprehensive learning experience tailored to meet the specific needs of each student.

Online project management and collaboration tools play a vital role in technical education by enabling students to work together on projects, regardless of their geographical location. By simulating real-world scenarios, students gain valuable experience in working as part of a team and develop essential skills in communication, problem-solving, and time management.

Virtual laboratories and simulations are also revolutionizing science and engineering education. By providing students with a virtual environment to conduct experiments and simulations, teachers can enhance their understanding of complex concepts, save costs on expensive laboratory equipment, and ensure a safe learning environment for students.

The incorporation of digital design in technical education is essential for preparing students for the digital age. From online coding courses to virtual laboratories, there is a wide range of digital tools available to enhance technical education. Embracing these tools can help teachers provide students with the skills they need to succeed in today's rapidly changing world.

5.2 Introduction to Graphic Arts Education

In today's digital era, visual communication is becoming increasingly vital, which makes graphic arts education crucial. This article aims to introduce the significance of incorporating digital tools into teaching and learning processes for graphic arts education.

Graphic arts education is no longer limited to traditional mediums like painting and drawing. It now encompasses a wide range of skills, such as digital design, web development, animation, and multimedia production. With this knowledge, students can create visually appealing and engaging content that resonates with their target audience.

Digital tools have transformed graphic arts education, making it more accessible, interactive, and collaborative. For instance, online coding courses and tutorials have made learning programming languages and developing technical skills easier. Students can practice coding in a virtual environment, apply their knowledge to real-world projects, and gain hands-on experience.

Virtual reality (VR) and augmented reality (AR) tools have also been beneficial to graphic arts education. These tools provide immersive learning experiences that aid students in exploring three-dimensional spaces and interacting with virtual objects. They further enable students to design virtual environments, and develop their creativity, and problem-solving skills.

E-learning platforms have also been significant in enhancing technical skills development. These platforms offer a wide range of courses and programs in digital marketing, data science and analytics, web development, and project management. Students can access these courses at their convenience and pace, making learning flexible.

Online project management and collaboration tools have transformed technical education by enabling students to work collaboratively on projects, communicate effectively, and share resources regardless of location. This fosters teamwork, enhances problem-solving skills, and prepares students for real-world professional environments.

Lastly, virtual laboratories and simulations have greatly enhanced science and engineering education. These tools allow students to conduct experiments in a virtual environment, providing hands-on experience without the need for physical resources or equipment.

In conclusion, graphic arts education has evolved in the digital era, integrating various digital tools to enhance teaching and learning processes. Teachers can use online coding courses, digital design tools, VR and AR technologies, e-learning platforms, project management tools, and virtual laboratories to provide students with the necessary skills and knowledge to succeed in the modern digital world.

5.3 Digital Tools for Graphic Arts Education

With the fast-paced development of technology, the field of graphic arts education has undergone significant changes. In this subchapter, we explore the numerous digital tools that have revolutionized the way teachers impart knowledge and skills to their students.

Online coding courses and tutorials have emerged as one of the most prominent digital tools in graphic arts education. Programming languages like HTML, CSS, and JavaScript are essential for web design and development, and these courses offer students the opportunity to master these skills and create visually stunning websites and digital artwork.

Virtual reality (VR) and augmented reality (AR) education tools have significantly enhanced digital design and graphic arts education. These immersive technologies provide students with a more engaging and realistic learning experience, allowing them to visualize and interact with their creations in a virtual environment. With VR and AR, students can experiment with different design elements, explore 3D models, and gain a deeper understanding of spatial relationships.

E-learning platforms are a convenient and accessible way for students to learn technical skills in graphic arts. These platforms offer a wide range of courses and resources that cover various aspects of digital design, from graphic editing software to animation techniques. Students can learn at their own pace, access instructional materials, and receive feedback and guidance from industry professionals.

Digital marketing and analytics training programs are also valuable resources for graphic arts education. These programs provide students with insights into consumer behavior, data analysis, and marketing strategies, equipping them with the skills necessary to succeed in the digital marketplace.

Online project management and collaboration tools are essential for teamwork in graphic arts education. These tools enable students to collaborate effectively on group projects and share their work with peers and instructors. Through these tools, students develop essential skills in communication, organization, and time management, which are integral to success in the graphic arts industry.

Web development and programming boot camps provide students with an intensive and focused learning experience in graphic arts. These programs offer hands-on training in coding languages, web design principles, and user experience design, empowering students to create visually stunning and functional websites.

Lastly, virtual laboratories and simulations are valuable tools that simulate the printing process, allowing students to understand color management, image resolution, and other critical aspects of graphic design.

In conclusion, the integration of digital tools in graphic arts education has transformed the learning process, offering students immersive, interactive, and convenient learning experiences. As technology continues to advance, teachers and scholars in the field of graphic arts education need to embrace these digital tools and stay at the forefront of innovation.

Digital tools are an essential component of graphic arts education, giving students the chance to explore, create, and refine their design skills. Below are some of the digital tools commonly used in this field (See Table 5.1, Table 5.2, Table 5.3, Table 5.4, Table 5.6, Table 5.7, and Table 5.8).

Table 5.1 Graphic Design Software.

Tools	Description
Adobe Creative Cloud	• Photoshop: Image editing and manipulation. • Illustrator: Vector graphics and illustrations. • InDesign: Layout design for print and digital media. • XD: User experience and interface design.
CorelDRAW	• Vector illustration and page layout. • Supports photo editing and typography. • Popular among graphic designers and illustrators.
Affinity Designer	• Vector graphic design software. • Supports both raster and vector elements. • Affordable alternative to Adobe Illustrator.

Table 5.2 Online Design Platforms.

Platforms	Description
Canva	• User-friendly design platform. • Templates for various design projects. • Collaboration features for team projects.
Figma	• Collaborative design and prototyping tool. • Real-time collaboration for design teams. • Suitable for interface and user experience design.

Table 5.3 Digital Drawing and Illustration.

Tools	Description
Procreate	• Digital painting app for iPad. • Powerful drawing and illustration tools. • Supports high-resolution canvases.
Clip Studio Paint	• Digital drawing and painting software. • Ideal for manga and comic creation. • Offers advanced brush customization.

Table 5.4 Typography Tools.

Tools	Description
Font Forge	• Open-source font editor. • Allows users to create and edit fonts. • Supports various font formats.
Google Fonts	• Free and open-source fonts for web and print. • Easy integration into design projects. • Variety of font styles available.

Table 5.5 Photo Editing Tools.

Tools	Description
GIMP (GNU Image Manipulation Program)	• Free and open-source raster graphics editor. • Supports photo retouching and image editing. • Extensible with plugins.
Pixlr	• Online photo editing tool. • Offers both basic and advanced editing features. • Suitable for quick edits and enhancements.

Table 5.6 3D Modeling and Animation.

Tools	Description
Blender	• Open-source 3D creation suite. • Supports modeling, sculpting, animation, and more. • Extensive community and tutorials.
Autodesk Maya	• Professional 3D modeling and animation software. • Used in film, television, and game development. • Powerful tools for character animation.

Table 5.7 Color Management.

Tools	Description
Adobe Color Wheel	• Online color wheel for creating color schemes. • Helps with color harmony and combinations. • Integrated with Adobe Creative Cloud.
Coolors	• Color scheme generator. • Explore and create color palettes. • Suitable for web and graphic design projects.

Table 5.8 Interactive Prototyping.

Tools	Description
InVision	• Prototyping and collaboration platform. • Allows designers to create interactive mockups. • Real-time feedback and collaboration.
Sketch	• Vector-based design tool. • Popular among UI/UX designers. • Supports plugins for extended functionality.

These Digital tools offer a broad range of resources for graphic arts education, including image editing and 3D modeling. Educators can select tools that align with their teaching objectives and industry standards.

CHAPTER 6

Virtual Reality and Augmented Reality Education Tools

Virtual reality (VR) and Augmented Reality (AR) are revolutionizing the manner we study and train. Both technologies offer immersive and interactive stories that can decorate the conventional technique of schooling.

VR and AR schooling tools can offer college students a higher expertise of complicated standards by letting them visualize and interact with them in three-dimensional surroundings. For example, medical college students can use VR to have a look at the human frame and exercise surgical strategies in safe and managed surroundings. AR can also be used to beautify classroom experiences and make getting to know each other more engaging. For instance, records students can use AR to discover historic websites and artifacts, bringing the beyond to existence. AR can also be used to create interactive textbooks that permit students to discover standards more dynamically and attractively.

Overall, VR and AR schooling gear can transform the manner we study and teach. They offer students an extra immersive and interactive knowledge of experience, that could cause better information and retention of understanding. As the era continues to evolve, we will expect to look increasingly at more applications of VR and AR within the study room.

6.1 Introduction to Virtual Reality and Augmented Reality in Education

Recent years have seen the emergence of virtual reality (VR) and augmented reality (AR) as powerful tools in education, transforming the way students learn and engage with complex concepts This technology-driven this participation has the potential to provide an interactive and interesting experience that can greatly enhance engineering education. With the advancement of digital tools, teachers now have access to a wide range of VR and AR applications that they can incorporate into their teaching practices.

A key advantage of VR and AR in education is the ability to give students hands-on experience that would otherwise be difficult or impossible in a traditional classroom for example, students learning technology can now explore 3D models of design difficult and analyzed by those from different backgrounds, thus providing a deeper understanding of the subject.

Similarly, science students can conduct virtual experiments and simulations, giving them a safe, cost-effective way to practice and refine their skills. Coding courses and learning have also benefited greatly from VR and AR tools. Students can now write and test code in a virtual environment, allowing them to see the immediate impact of their design decisions. Digital design and picture arts training have additionally visible a significant transformation with the integration of VR and AR equipment. Students can now create and manipulate three-D fashions in digital environments, giving them a more realistic and immersive experience. This not simplest complements their creativity but also gives them valuable skills that are particularly fashionable within the virtual design industry.

E-studying platforms have also embraced VR and AR technologies to provide technical skills improvement packages. These systems offer interactive and tasty courses in areas that include digital advertising and analytics, recording technological know-how, net development, and programming. By incorporating VR and AR factors into their curriculum, these structures can provide students with an extra immersive and powerful studying level. Virtual laboratories and simulations have come to be worthwhile equipment in technological know-how and engineering education. Students can now perform behavior experiments and simulations in digital environments, letting them practice and refine their talents without the want for high-priced gadgets or bodily materials. This not only saves costs but also provides students with a safe and controlled environment to analyze and experiment. In the end, the combination of VR and AR tools in technical education has opened new opportunities for each teacher and college student. This virtual equipment offers immersive and interactive reports that substantially decorate getting to know and engagement. Whether it is through virtual laboratories, online coding publications, or digital layout training, VR and AR have emerged as essential tools within the present-day instructor's toolkit. Virtual Reality (VR) Education Tools and Platforms

Virtual Reality (VR) and Augmented Reality (AR) have become increasingly popular in the education sector, providing immersive and engaging experiences for students. Here are some of the most noteworthy tools and platforms for VR and AR in education.

Table 6.1 Noteworthy tools and platforms for VR in education.

Tools	Features
Google Expeditions	Google Expeditions allows teachers to take students on virtual field trips using VR. It provides a library of 360-degree photos and 3D objects to create immersive educational experiences.
AltspaceVR	AltspaceVR is a social VR platform that enables educators to conduct virtual classes, conferences, and events.
ClassVR	ClassVR is a complete VR and AR system designed for classroom use. It includes a variety of educational content, lesson plans, and a teacher management portal.
Unimersiv	Unimersiv offers educational VR experiences for various subjects. It covers topics such as history, science, and space exploration, providing a range of immersive learning opportunities.
Oculus Education	Oculus, owned by Facebook, has an education section that provides resources for educators interested in using Oculus VR headsets in the classroom. It includes apps, guides, and best practices.

Table 6.2 Noteworthy tools and platforms for AR in education.

Tools	Features
ARCore and ARKit	ARCore by Google and ARKit by Apple are software development kits (SDKs) that enable developers to create AR applications for Android and iOS devices, respectively.
Merge EDU	Merge EDU provides a range of AR experiences and applications for education. Their tools cover subjects like science, math, and anatomy, making learning more interactive.
Aurasma	Aurasma, now known as HP Reveal, allows users to create and share augmented reality experiences.
Suite	DAQRI offers an education suite that includes AR content for learning.
Zappar	Zappar is an AR platform that allows users to create interactive AR experiences. It has been used in education to enhance learning materials with augmented content.

CHAPTER 7

Enhancing Instructional Design with Digital Tools

In the past few years, digital tools have completely transformed how we design and deliver instruction. Instructional design has become more efficient, effective, and engaging thanks to technology. Here are some ways in which digital tools can enhance instructional design:

Interactive Learning: Digital tools allow instructional designers to create interactive learning experiences that are more engaging for learners. Quizzes, games, and simulations can be easily incorporated into online courses, making learning more enjoyable and effective.

Personalized Learning: Digital tools can be used to personalize learning experiences. Instructional designers can use analytics and data to track learner progress and create customized learning paths that cater to individual needs and preferences.

Collaborative Learning: Digital tools can facilitate collaboration and social learning. Discussion forums, chat rooms, and social media platforms can be incorporated into instructional design to create a collaborative learning environment where learners can connect and share ideas.

Mobile Learning: With the increasing use of mobile devices, instructional designers can create mobile-friendly courses that can be accessed anytime, anywhere. This allows learners to take their learning on the go and fit it into their busy schedules.

Gamification in Instructional Design with Digital Tools: The utilization of gamification in instructional design with digital tools has garnered significant attention due to its ability to integrate educational curriculum with game mechanics, ultimately amplifying motivation and engagement. This approach provides teachers the opportunity to incorporate a diverse set of interactive components such as games, quizzes, and challenges into their lesson plans resulting in an enjoyable yet fulfilling learning experience.

Interactive Simulations and Virtual Reality in Instructional Design: The utilization of interactive simulations and virtual reality in instructional design has introduced a novel approach to immersive learning experiences. These advancements allow for the creation of realistic scenarios that promote engagement and interaction with virtual environments, thereby facilitating deep comprehension and knowledge retention among students.

Social Media Integration in Instructional Design for Increased Engagement: The integration of social media within instructional design has become a fundamental element in enhancing student engagement. With the employment of various social media platforms, scholars can tap into collaborative opportunities and facilitate effective communication among students for better participation levels. Opportunities like discussion forums, live chats, or group-based learning provide active knowledge-sharing environments resulting in positive academic outcomes.

In conclusion, digital tools have opened new possibilities for instructional design. By leveraging technology, instructional designers can create more engaging, personalized, collaborative, and mobile-friendly learning experiences for learners.

7.1 The Role of Digital Tools in Instructional Design

As a professional in the instructional design field, it is imperative to remain current with advancements in technology and the potential enhancement of our skills. In contemporary times, digital tools have firmly established themselves as an integral component of instructional design by transforming how we produce and disseminate educational content. This chapter elucidates on diverse roles played by these cutting-edge digital tools within the ambit of instructional design whilst examining ways they can be utilized to generate more immersive and efficacious learning experiences.

Gamification constitutes a pivotal domain in which digital tools are heightening the efficacy of instructional design. Its essence involves integrating game-related features such as competition, rewards, and challenges throughout the phases of design instruction. The utilization of these technological resources allows for crafting interactive and immersive sessions that instill interest within learners, effectively stimulating their engagement with course material while enhancing retention levels thereof.

Digital tools are having a noteworthy influence on personalized learning, which is another area of educational development. By utilizing digital tools, instructional designers can customize the learning experiences to cater to individual preferences and requirements of learners. Such an approach not only allows students to learn at their own pace but also enables them to concentrate more easily on areas that they find challenging resulting in heightened efficiency and efficacy during the education process.

Interactive simulations and virtual reality are indispensable elements of instructional design. With the aid of these modern technologies, learners can acquire practical knowledge through realistic and immersive learning experiences in a safe and controlled environment. This hands-on approach greatly boosts engagement among students while helping them develop transferable practical skills that have applicability to real-world situations.

Digital tools are having a transformative effect on instructional design, particularly in the realm of mobile learning. The proliferation of smartphones and tablets has made educational content available to learners at any time and from anywhere. By taking advantage of this technology, instructional designers can create easily digestible and interactive learning modules that cater to individuals who are often on the go; offering flexibility and convenience without compromising substance or quality.

The integration of social media constitutes an additional means by which digital tools may enhance instructional design. By integrating various social media platforms into the learning process, instructional designers can foster a collaborative and communicative environment in which learners are encouraged to share knowledge. This form of integration serves to cultivate a sense of community and engagement amongst participants, thereby imbuing the learning experience with greater interactivity and dynamism initially absent from traditional pedagogical approaches.

The digitalization of the field has brought about transformative methods, including data-driven instructional design. This approach involves gathering and evaluating learner performance metrics for instructional designers to gain insights into their instruction's efficacy. The employment of this technique allows educators to continuously improve upon their strategies by optimizing them according to collected data; as a result, overall learning outcomes are enhanced.

Augmented reality represents a digital instrument that is transforming instructional design. By superimposing digital content onto the actual world, skilled designers have gained the ability to craft teaching experiences that are both immersive and interactive in nature. This method permits learners to navigate virtual objects and environments while interacting with them concurrently, thus elevating their grasp of information acquisition while promoting retention abilities as well.

Adaptive learning platforms are assuming a noteworthy function in the discipline of instructional design. Through their employment of algorithms, these platforms utilize personalized methods for learners' unique requirements, inclinations, and advancement stages as they navigate through any given subject matter or skill set. This adaptive content delivery system allows designers to manage individualized support mechanisms that quickly adapt to each learner's specific needs ensuring an optimal level of challenge leading towards ultimate success attainment rates amongst them all.

Digital tools are presently exerting a substantial influence on video-based learning. The integration of videos into instructional design enables educators to proficiently convey intricate concepts in an aesthetically appealing and accessible format. Additionally, such media can exemplify the application of practical skills and furnish concrete instances from real-world settings - thereby heightening knowledge translation for learners.

Collaborative learning presents an opportunity for the enhancement of instructional design through digital tools. By utilizing these collaboration tools, instructional designers can enable group work, foster discussions, and promote knowledge exchange amongst learners. Such a collaborative approach promotes active participation in the learning process while simultaneously enhancing interpersonal communication and teamwork skills within individuals.

Ultimately, digital tools have quickly become indispensable resources within the discipline of instructional design. With a wide-ranging array of functionalities that encompass gamification and customized learning modalities to interactive simulations and social media integration, they are fundamentally reshaping how we develop and provide instruction. This embrace of these technological innovations is arming educators with increased capabilities for crafting more captivating, potent educational environments geared towards diverse learner groups across assorted industries.

7.2 Benefits and Challenges of Integrating Digital Tools in Instructional Design

In the present era of digitization, incorporating digital tools in instructional design has gained significant significance. These sophisticated tools offer a plethora of advantages that enrich the learning process and foster novel prospects for both teachers and students alike. Nonetheless, there also exist impediments that necessitate being tackled to harness their full potential adequately. This subsection endeavors to expound on the merits as well as demerits associated with integrating digital tools into instructional design while delivering valuable inputs for scholars engaged across various dimensions of pedagogy designing practices.

The incorporation of digital tools in instructional design has emerged as a significant advantage, facilitating the enhancement of the learning experience.

Digital tools have created an interactive milieu with engaging and stimulating opportunities that capture learners' attention and pique their interest levels. The integration of gamification within such designs enables production akin to game-like experiences that are both enjoyable and educational, thereby promoting active participation among students while improving knowledge retention rates alongside comprehension abilities concerning course content.

An additional advantage lies in the capacity to individualize learning through digital mechanisms. The utilization of adaptive learning platforms enables instructional designers to customize the educational encounter, catering specifically to each learner's distinct requirements and preferences. This personalized methodology fosters self-directed education whilst guaranteeing learners receive appropriate levels of assistance and stimulation. In addition, modern advancements in technology have introduced digital tools such as interactive simulations and virtual reality that offer unparalleled immersive learning experiences not attainable through traditional instructional methods. By utilizing these resources, learners can engage with simulated environments that serve to enhance their comprehension of intricate concepts while simultaneously refining their abilities to solve problems effectively.

Nonetheless, the incorporation of digital tools within instructional design represents a set of obstacles. A predominant difficulty lies in educators' acquisition of essential competencies and knowledge to proficiently utilize such technology. To overcome this hurdle, it is recommended that training initiatives and professional development programs be established to ensure instructors acquire the necessary skills to fully leverage technological potentialities.

Moreover, the incorporation of social media into instructional design to enhance student engagement necessitates meticulous attention to privacy and ethical concerns. Educators must establish protocols for judicious and responsible utilization of these platforms to uphold a secure and all-encompassing learning atmosphere.

Considering the foregoing, it can be affirmed that integrating digital tools in instructional design confers a plethora of advantages, such as heightened learning experiences, tailored instruction, and immersive opportunities. Nevertheless, certain issues - namely educator training imperatives and privacy concerns- must be addressed to fully capitalize on these edifying technologies. Academics operating within niche fields inclusive of gamification paradigms, interactive simulation models or data-driven designs may significantly benefit from surmising both pros and cons germane to amalgamating technology insights into their pedagogical frameworks.

7.3 Creating Engaging Digital Lesson Plans

In today's digital age, utilizing technology in the classroom is essential. Teachers must embrace digital tools to meet the demands of the modern world. This subchapter aims to introduce digital tools for teachers and guide them in creating engaging digital lesson plans.

Digital lesson plans offer numerous benefits over traditional methods. They enhance student engagement, foster critical thinking skills, and provide a platform for collaboration and creativity. To create an engaging digital lesson plan, teachers must first understand the available tools and how to effectively utilize them.

Incorporating Interactive Elements: Teachers can captivate students' attention by utilizing multimedia resources such as videos, images, and interactive websites. Online quizzes, games, and simulations can promote active participation and enhance understanding.

Personalization: By using adaptive learning platforms, teachers can tailor their lessons to meet the diverse needs of students. This personalization fosters a sense of ownership and empowers students to take control of their learning journey.

Collaboration: Teachers can utilize platforms that allow students to work together on projects, share ideas, and provide peer feedback. This promotes teamwork and communication skills, essential for success in the modern world.

Creativity and Self-Expression: Encouraging students to create multimedia presentations, digital artwork, and videos enhances their creativity and develops their digital literacy skills.

Continuously Assess and Adapt: Regularly gathering feedback from students, analyzing data, and reflecting on the effectiveness of the tools used are all vital in improving the teaching and learning experience.

Embracing digital tools is not just a transformation from chalkboard to keyboard; it is a paradigm shift that prepares students for the digital world they will navigate. Creating engaging digital lesson plans is a crucial skill for teachers in the modern age. By incorporating interactive elements, personalizing instruction, promoting collaboration, encouraging creativity, and continuously assessing their plans, teachers can provide an enriching and effective learning experience for their students.

7.4 Customizing Online Learning Platforms for Effective Education

With the advent of the digital age, traditional teaching methods have evolved, and educators must adapt to engage students effectively. Online learning platforms have emerged as powerful tools that can enhance the learning experience and cater to the diverse needs of students. This subchapter delves into the concept of customizing online learning platforms to meet the specific needs of students, presenting teachers with valuable insights and strategies to create a personalized learning environment.

1. **Understanding Student Needs**

   To customize online learning platforms effectively, teachers must understand their students' needs. Every student has a unique learning style, pace, and preference. By conducting surveys, assessments, and discussions, teachers can gather valuable information to tailor the online platform accordingly.

2. **Adapting Content and Activities**

   Once teachers understand their students' specific requirements, they can begin customizing the online learning platform by adapting content and activities. This may involve selecting appropriate resources, modifying assignments, and creating interactive activities that cater to different learning styles. By doing so, teachers can ensure that students are engaged and motivated to learn.

3. **Utilizing Technology Tools**

   Online learning platforms offer a variety of technology tools that teachers can use to customize the learning experience. Interactive elements like videos, audio clips, and interactive simulations can enhance learning, while collaboration tools, discussion boards, and virtual classrooms can facilitate meaningful interactions and promote student engagement.

4. **Providing Individual Support**

   Customizing online learning platforms also involves providing individual support to students. Teachers can use chatbots, personalized feedback, and one-on-one virtual meetings to address specific concerns and provide timely assistance. This personalized support can create a sense of belonging and ensure that no student is left behind.

5. **Monitoring Progress and Adjusting**

   To ensure the effectiveness of the customized online learning platform, teachers must continuously monitor students' progress and make necessary adjustments. Analyzing data, tracking performance, and gathering feedback can help identify areas of improvement and refine the customization process. By being responsive to students' evolving needs, teachers can create a dynamic and effective learning environment.

Customizing online learning platforms is essential to meet the diverse needs of students in the digital era. By understanding student requirements, adapting content, utilizing technology tools, providing individual support, and monitoring progress, teachers can create a personalized learning experience that fosters engagement, motivation, and academic success. Embracing digital tools and customizing online learning platforms will empower teachers to navigate the modern educational landscape and prepare students for the challenges of the future.

7.5 The Importance of Integrating Digital Tools into Teaching Practice

In today's fast-paced digital age, teachers must incorporate digital tools to adapt to their students' needs and expectations. By effectively integrating digital tools into different teaching models, student engagement, collaboration, and overall learning outcomes can be enhanced.

This subchapter introduces teachers to a variety of digital tools and explores how they can be integrated into different teaching models. Teachers can create a more dynamic and interactive learning environment that caters to the modern student by utilizing these tools.

The traditional lecture-based approach can benefit from the integration of multimedia resources such as videos, interactive presentations, and online simulations. These digital tools provide visual and auditory stimuli, making complex concepts easier to comprehend and retain.

Project-based learning can be enhanced by using collaborative online platforms like Google Docs, Trello, and Padlet. Digital tools facilitate communication, organization, and document sharing, enabling effective collaboration even if students are not physically present.

Digital tools can also be integrated into the flipped classroom model, allowing teachers to assign pre-recorded video lectures or online readings for students to review at home. This approach frees up valuable class time for discussions, problem-solving, and hands-on activities. Teachers can use digital tools like learning management systems (LMS) and online quizzes to track student progress and provide immediate feedback.

In conclusion, integrating digital tools into different teaching models can revolutionize the educational experience. By embracing these tools, teachers can create a more engaging, collaborative, and personalized learning experience for their students. This subchapter introduces various digital tools to help inspire teachers to explore and incorporate them into their teaching practices. By doing so, we can empower ourselves as modern educators and equip our students with the necessary skills to thrive in the digital age.

7.6 Leveraging Learning Management Systems (LMS) for Modern Instructional Practices

In the digital age, teachers are constantly seeking innovative ways to engage students and improve their instruction. One such powerful tool is the Learning Management System (LMS), which has transformed the education landscape. In this subchapter, we'll explore how teachers can use LMS platforms to streamline their instructional practices and create a more effective learning environment.

An LMS provides a centralized platform where teachers can organize and deliver course content, communicate with students, track progress, and assess learning outcomes. With the right LMS, teachers can automate routine tasks such as grading and feedback, saving valuable time and energy. This allows them to focus on delivering high-quality instruction and supporting student learning.

Using an LMS allows teachers to create and deliver interactive multimedia content, including videos, audio files, presentations, and other resources. LMS platforms typically include built-in tools for creating quizzes, discussions, and collaborative projects, fostering active student participation and engagement.

Moreover, LMS communication features enable teachers to maintain a strong connection with their students beyond traditional classroom hours. Through discussion forums, messaging systems, and announcement boards, teachers can provide timely feedback, answer questions, and facilitate online discussions. This promotes a sense of community and engagement among students, ensuring that learning is not confined to the physical classroom space.

LMS platforms also provide teachers with valuable insights into student progress and performance. By analyzing data and generating analytics reports, teachers can identify areas where students may be struggling and tailor instruction accordingly. This data-driven approach to teaching allows for personalized learning experiences, ensuring that every student receives the individual support they need to succeed.

In conclusion, incorporating Learning Management Systems into instructional practices is essential for modern teachers seeking to leverage digital tools. LMS platforms streamline instruction, increase engagement, foster collaboration, and personalize learning experiences. With the right LMS, teachers can transform their classrooms into dynamic and efficient learning environments, benefiting both themselves and their students.

7.7 Adapting Instruction to Individual Student Needs with Personalized Learning Tools

In today's digital age, the role of teachers has expanded beyond traditional teaching methods. As educators, it's essential to embrace digital tools and personalized learning to cater to the diverse needs of students. This subchapter introduces the concept of personalized learning and how digital tools can support it.

Personalized learning acknowledges that each student has unique learning styles, abilities, and interests. Digital tools enable teachers to create customized learning experiences that engage students and promote active participation in their education. Immediate feedback allows teachers to track student progress and provide personalized guidance.

Digital tools provide a wealth of resources that cater to diverse learning styles. Students can explore concepts at their own pace, access supplementary materials, and collaborate with peers, creating a more student-centered and inclusive classroom environment.

While some teachers may be hesitant to integrate digital tools, this subchapter provides practical guidance on how to seamlessly incorporate them into lesson plans. It also addresses potential challenges and offers strategies to overcome them.

In conclusion, "Adapting Instruction to Individual Student Needs with Personalized Learning Tools" is a vital subchapter in the book "From Chalkboard to Keyboard: An Introduction to Digital Tools for Teachers." By embracing personalized learning and leveraging digital tools, teachers can create a more inclusive and engaging learning environment that empowers students to become active participants in their education.

7.7.1 The Concept of Personalized Learning

In the dynamic and constantly evolving field of education, personalized learning has emerged as a revolutionary instructional design approach. Thanks to state-of-the-art digital tools, educators can now cater their teaching strategies to meet every student's individual needs and preferences. This section aims to delve into the concept of personalized learning in greater detail while highlighting its efficient implementation through digital tools.

Personalized learning is founded on the premise that each student acquires knowledge at their rate and through means tailored to suit them. It acknowledges that customary, standardized methods of education have ceased to be competent in addressing contemporary learners' multifaceted requirements. By utilizing digital resources, instructors can establish individualized educational approaches attuned to pupils' strengths, fascinations, and distinct ways of assimilating information.

Personalized learning offers an essential advantage of heightened student engagement. Affording students greater autonomy in their educational journey augments their commitment to the process and encourages them to take ownership of it. Cutting-edge technologies, including but not limited to gamification techniques, interactive simulations, and virtual reality experiences are valuable resources available for optimizing immersive learning experiences that capture students' attention while promoting a more profound comprehension of relevant topics at hand.

Personalized learning facilitated by digital tools entails an additional essential advantage related to expeditious and targeted feedback provision. Through the utilization of data-oriented instructional design, educators can scrutinize students' performance in real time, leading to prompt interventions geared towards addressing potential comprehension deficits. This approach guarantees that learners obtain requisite support for achievement while simultaneously empowering educators with informed decision-making abilities concerning optimal teaching techniques.

Incorporating social media into instructional design can augment student engagement and collaboration. Utilizing the potential of social networks, educators can develop interactive and participatory learning practices that align with students' innate propensity for connection and communication. This not only fosters a communal sense but also creates avenues for peer-to-peer education, and knowledge dissemination, enhancing their overall academic experience.

Ultimately, personalized learning facilitated by digital tools holds the promise of a transformative impact on the realm of instructional design. With technology as its driving force, educators can curate bespoke educational experiences that cater to each student's idiosyncratic needs and predilections. Whether accomplished via gamification techniques, interactive simulations, social media assimilation, or data-informed course structuring strategies; personalized learning represents an avenue for amplified engagement levels resulting in enhanced comprehension outcomes within academic domains.

7.7.2 Implementing Personalized Learning with Digital Tools

Personalized learning is deemed a highly effective pedagogical approach that customizes education to cater to the specific academic requisites and inclinations of students. The emergence of digital toolkits has augmented educators' capacity for implementing personalized learning in their classrooms, providing them with an abundant range of resources at their disposal. This subchapter endeavors to delineate how various digital tools can be instrumental in enhancing instructional design and creating customized educational experiences for learners.

Digital tools in personalized learning offer a notable benefit, namely the capability to furnish adaptive learning platforms. These sophisticated systems leverage algorithms to scrutinize student data and supply tailored content as well as feedback predicated on their strengths and weaknesses. Consequently, pupils can advance through course material at an individualized pace while concentrating on areas where additional support is required.

Video-based learning is an additional digital tool that can effectively serve the purpose of individualized education. Utilizing videos to engage students and cater to their auditory and visual preferences enhances interactivity and immersion in the learning process. Educators have significant leverage while employing video content for presenting intricate concepts, illustrating experiments, or actual real-world applications relevant to the subjects being taught.

Digital tools have made substantial progress in delivering personalized instruction through mobile learning. With the pervasive presence of smartphones and tablets, educational resources are always readily accessible to students and locations. Mobile apps and online platforms facilitate engagement with course content, interactive simulations, as well as peer collaboration within a customized learning environment that meets individualized requirements.

Additionally, the integration of social media can serve to enhance student engagement in personalized learning. Educators can establish virtual communities where students can engage in substantive discussions about akin topics and exchange constructive feedback with peers and instructors alike. This approach cultivates an environment that facilitates collaborative learning while simultaneously permitting learners opportunities for customization by enabling connections with like-minded individuals possessing corresponding interests.

Digital tools facilitate data-driven instructional design, empowering educators to collect and scrutinize student performance data. By utilizing this information, instructors can glean valuable insights into students' progress while identifying specific points for improvement. Such analytics guide strategic educational decisions that allow pedagogues to customize their teaching approaches according to everyone's unique needs.

In conclusion, the implementation of personalized learning with digital tools presents several advantages for both educators and students. Through leveraging adaptive learning platforms, video-based instruction, mobile teaching techniques, social media integration practices, data-centric instructional design strategies, and other similar technologies or mechanisms; instructors can curate immersive educational experiences that are tailored to individual student needs while stimulating ownership in their education. Embracing these powerful resources at disposal including scholars in Instructional Design disciplines could revolutionize conventional approaches to academic progress thereby fostering a more dynamic environment primed towards student-centered learning paradigms.

7.7.3 Case Studies: Personalized Learning Approaches in Instructional Design

Personalized learning is deemed a highly effective pedagogical approach that customizes education to cater to the specific academic requisites and inclinations of students. The emergence of digital toolkits has augmented educators' capacity for implementing personalized learning in their classrooms, providing them with an abundant range of resources at their disposal. This subchapter endeavors to delineate how various digital tools can be instrumental in enhancing instructional design and creating customized educational experiences for learners.

Digital tools in personalized learning offer a notable benefit, namely the capability to furnish adaptive learning platforms. These sophisticated systems leverage algorithms to scrutinize student data and supply tailored content as well as feedback predicated on their strengths and weaknesses. Consequently, pupils can advance through course material at an individualized pace while concentrating on areas where additional support is required.

Video-based learning is an additional digital tool that can effectively serve the purpose of individualized education. Utilizing videos to engage students and cater to their auditory and visual preferences enhances interactivity and immersion in the learning process. Educators have significant leverage while employing video content for presenting intricate concepts, illustrating experiments, or actual real-world applications relevant to the subjects being taught.

Digital tools have made substantial progress in delivering personalized instruction through mobile learning. With the pervasive presence of smartphones and tablets, educational resources are always readily accessible to students and locations. Mobile apps and online platforms facilitate engagement with course content, interactive simulations, as well as peer collaboration within a customized learning environment that meets individualized requirements.

Additionally, the integration of social media can serve to enhance student engagement in personalized learning. Educators can establish virtual communities where students can engage in substantive discussions about akin topics and exchange constructive feedback with peers and instructors alike. This approach cultivates an environment that facilitates collaborative learning while simultaneously permitting learners opportunities for customization by enabling connections with like-minded individuals possessing corresponding interests.

Digital tools facilitate data-driven instructional design, empowering educators to collect and scrutinize student performance data. By utilizing this information, instructors can glean valuable insights into students' progress while identifying specific points for improvement. Such analytics guide strategic educational decisions that allow pedagogues to customize their teaching approaches according to everyone's unique needs.

In conclusion, the implementation of personalized learning with digital tools presents several advantages for both educators and students. Through leveraging adaptive learning platforms, video-based instruction, mobile teaching techniques, social media integration practices, data-centric instructional design strategies, and other similar technologies or mechanisms; instructors can curate immersive educational experiences that are tailored to individual student needs while stimulating ownership in their education. Embracing these powerful resources at disposal including scholars in Instructional Design disciplines could revolutionize conventional approaches to academic progress thereby fostering a more dynamic environment primed towards student-centered learning paradigms.

7.8 The Power of Interactive Simulations in Instructional Design

Over the past few years, instructional design has undergone a significant transformation due to the impact of digital tools. Among these resources, interactive simulations have become particularly popular and are driving major advancements in scholarly approaches toward instructional design practices. These dynamic virtual scenarios offer a wide variety of benefits that significantly enhance learning experiences across diverse niches ranging from gamification and personalized learning to virtual reality and mobile learning. Primarily, interactive simulations offer a practical and immersive educational encounter. Scholars can actively engage in the content by conducting research on virtual laboratories, resolving intricate problems within gamified surroundings, or examining a simulated world. This degree of interaction stimulates active learning practices alongside enhancing essential thinking abilities and augmenting problem-solving skills thereby transforming into an invaluable instrument for advancing pedagogical designs with digital technologies.

Furthermore, interactive simulations afford opportunities for customized learning experiences. Customization enables learners to advance according to their requirements and predilections by concentrating on those areas that require more attention while bypassing previously mastered concepts. Such a tailored approach guarantees personalized instruction for every scholar, optimizing their capacity to acquire knowledge.

In addition, interactive simulations provide a platform for social interaction and cooperation. Academicians may engage with their colleagues and mentors in digital spheres where they can exchange ideas, deliberate on topics of interest, as well as collaborate toward problem resolution. By integrating social media into pedagogical design practices, heightened engagement levels are induced while fostering an environment that boosts community bonding; thus, creating a supportive learning milieu infused with interactivity.

One notable advantage of interactive simulations is their capacity to offer instantaneous feedback and performance evaluation. Using a data-driven instructional design approach, educators can monitor the progress of learners, pinpoint areas for enhancement, and deliver prompt feedback. This type of analysis serves as an informed basis for devising effective teaching strategies that cater specifically to each scholar's needs to ensure optimal learning outcomes.

Moreover, interactive simulations possess the capacity to provide immersive learning experiences through augmented reality. By superimposing digital information onto real-world settings, learners can investigate and engage with their surroundings in novel and intriguing ways. This method of instructional design captures students' interest while increasing comprehension of intricate notions and cultivating greater participation levels.

In summation, the potential of interactive simulations within instructional design holds significant value. By incorporating gamification features, personalized learning experiences, virtual reality integration, and leveraging social media and data-driven strategies - scholars across various specialties can reap multifarious benefits from these digital tools. Such an approach has transformative implications for learners by offering a more enriched experience that is both dynamic in nature as well as highly effective at facilitating engagement with course material.

7.8.1 Incorporating Virtual Reality into Instructional Design

The use of virtual reality (VR) is swiftly revolutionizing the instructional design space by introducing novel and compelling prospects to enrich learning encounters. Through the fabrication of immersive and interactive simulations, VR can captivate learners in manner that conventional instructional techniques cannot replicate. The present subchapter examines the potential benefits associated with integrating VR technology into educational settings for effective instructional design practices while also furnishing practical strategies regarding its application. Virtual Reality (VR) offers a significant advantage in being able to produce authentic and engaging simulations. By immersing learners within virtual environments, educators are empowered with the ability to furnish practical training experiences that may have been previously impractical or unfeasible for classroom settings. This technology provides immense benefit as medical students can conduct simulated surgical procedures within sanitized VR domains, thereby proffering an optimal platform for practice before embarking upon actual patients - delivering improved levels of expertise through experiential learning techniques augmented by advanced technologies such as VR.

VR presents an additional advantage in its capacity to facilitate personalized learning experiences. Through VR, educators can fashion tailored scenarios that cater specifically and singularly to individual learners' idiosyncratic needs and inclinations. This customized approach has been found by research studies conducted on education technology as a means of increasing both student engagement levels and motivation towards course content primarily through attuning lesson material according to each learner's preferred modality for comprehending new concepts.

Moreover, Virtual Reality (VR) has the potential to enable collaborative learning experiences. Through connecting learners in a unified virtual space, educators can encourage cooperation and group work amongst individuals even when they are geographically dispersed. This feature holds particular significance in distance education contexts where face-to-face interaction may not be possible for all participants involved.

The incorporation of Virtual Reality (VR) in the context of instructional design presents significant opportunities for data-driven analysis. The tracking and monitoring of learners' interactions within virtual environments provides educators with valuable insights into their performance, as well as progress over time. This information facilitates informed decision-making regarding learning interventions that best support individual students' needs to enhance student success rates effectively.

To sum up, the integration of virtual reality into instructional design exhibits immense potential for enriching learning experiences. By devising immersive and interactive simulations, personalizing pedagogy encounters, enabling cooperation between learners, as well as incorporating data-driven analysis techniques; educators could harness VR technology in a way that engages and empowers those undergoing instruction. Given our scholarly pursuits in this domain of educational training programs' creation process, we ought to explore what possibilities may accompany such an approach diligently. In doing so we must carefully consider how this technological invention can be adeptly integrated within academic environments to produce a transformative effect on conventional instructional designs - creating innovative teaching methods with resonating impact across diverse learning cohorts.'

7.8.2 Case Studies: Using Interactive Simulations and Virtual Reality in Instructional Design

In the past few years, there has been a notable evolution in the discipline of instructional design precipitated by advancements in digital tools. Of particular interest are interactive simulations and virtual reality (VR) which have received substantial attention within this field. These innovative technologies provide an unparalleled potential for developing captivating learning experiences that can substantially optimize pedagogical outcomes through their immersive nature.

An illustrative example of the potency of interactive simulations in instructional design is evident through the utilization of flight simulators for pilot training. Previously, such preparation would involve amalgamating classroom tutelage with practical sessions aboard real aircraft, which was not only exorbitant but also restricted in exposure to varied scenarios. However, integrating interactive flight simulators into this process facilitates trainee pilots' practice within a secure and supervised world that encompasses an array of simulated situations; thus augmenting their skills while optimizing efficiency as well as reducing expenses incurred during training procedures.

A further case study that accentuates the advantages of virtual reality in instructional design pertains to its application within medical education. Typically, aspiring physicians encounter difficulties acquiring practical expertise in surgical techniques as a consequence of limited access to cadavers and potential hazards associated with actual procedures. However, through the implementation of VR technology, students are enabled to engage in realistic simulations replicating surgical scenarios wherein they can hone their abilities without exposure to any detrimental outcomes. Resultantly, this not only refines proficiency but likewise enhances patient safety over time.

The presented case studies clearly illustrate the immense potential of interactive simulations and virtual reality for instructional design purposes. By incorporating these innovative technologies into their pedagogical strategies, educators may effectively enhance student engagement levels while promoting an immersive learning environment that bolsters academic outcomes. The versatile nature of such tools allows various fields to benefit from them - be it within aviation or medical education contexts- with transformative implications regarding educational processes at large; thus, providing learners with valuable experiences that are both authentic and unprecedented in standard practice.

As academic experts in the realm of instructional design, it is essential to investigate and adopt digital tools that have emerged as game-changers. The utilization of interactive simulations and virtual reality can augment educators' abilities to create bespoke, captivating, and efficacious learning encounters for their pupils. The potentialities are boundless; therefore, as scholars within this field, we must harness the potency of these innovative technologies to revolutionize instruction design positively.

7.9 Mobile Learning and Instructional Design with Digital Tools

M-learning, or mobile learning, is an educational method that employs smartphones and tablets to transmit instructional information. It enables students to obtain academic resources at any time and place, offering them versatility and ease during their education exploration. As digital tools continue being incorporated into teaching models on a large scale, m-learning has gained greater accessibility and efficacy.

The use of digital tools in instructional design is critical to crafting captivating and interactive mobile learning lessons. By integrating multimedia presentations, videos, gamified quizzes, and augmented reality simulations into the curriculum, educational professionals can amplify learners' engagement while accommodating their unique styles of instruction delivery. Additionally, these technologies furnish instructive experts with insightful analytics which enable them to monitor each student's advancement and recognize subjects where supplemental aid might be necessary. The synergy between mobile education bolstered by digitally enabled instructional design empowers individuals pursuing knowledge with personalized pedagogies that are immersive as well as aligned with personal interests or requirements.

7.9.1 Mobile Learning: Definition and Benefits

In the present era of digital technology, mobile learning represents a potent tool for augmenting instructional design. Thanks to the ubiquitous presence of smartphones and tablets, learners now enjoy unfettered access to educational resources at any time or place. This subchapter endeavors to furnish scholars with an exhaustive grasp of mobile learning as well as its definition and myriad advantages it bestows within the domain of instructional design.

Mobile learning, commonly referred to as m-learning, pertains to the utilization of mobile devices for facilitating educational experiences and acquiring knowledge. It encompasses imparting education through digital platforms such as websites or mobile applications. In contrast with conventional classroom-style pedagogy, m-learning offers learners greater personalization in their pursuit of academic goals by way of its flexibility and convenience features.

Mobile learning offers a crucial advantage in terms of improving instructional design using digital technologies. Through seamless integration with mobile devices, educators can create dynamic and interactive learning experiences that captivate their students' attention. This approach allows for innovative techniques such as gamification and personalized instruction to be employed effectively, resulting in more enjoyable and effective outcomes for learners. Gamification is an instructional design tactic that assimilates game elements into the educational progression. With mobile applications and games, trainees can be involved in interactive exercises, gather points, and contend with others to foster motivation while enhancing knowledge retention.

Moreover, mobile learning fosters tailored and customized educational experiences by catering to the unique requirements and preferences of individual learners. This is made possible using digital tools that aid educators in providing adaptive learning platforms capable of adapting content difficulty levels based on learners' progress, thereby ensuring optimal knowledge acquisition outcomes.

In the realm of instructional design for mobile learning, there exist interactive simulations and virtual reality (VR) as digital tools that can be effectively incorporated. These educational resources enable immersive experiences wherein learners are exposed to intricate concepts both visually and through hands-on activities; thereby enriching their comprehension and memorization capabilities.

Furthermore, the implementation of mobile learning provides an opportunity to integrate social media into instructional design. This approach bolsters learner engagement and collaboration by incorporating various social media platforms in the process. It enables educators to establish communities of learners that promote peer-to-peer interaction and knowledge sharing through strategically designed lessons.

Utilizing digital tools for data-driven instructional design is also facilitated by mobile learning. Through the collection and analysis of learners' performance data, educators can detect areas in need of improvement and adapt their instructional approaches accordingly to optimize teaching efficacy and promote active knowledge acquisition.

In summary, mobile learning has brought about a revolutionary change in the realm of instructional design by leveraging digital tools. Through its capacity to augment engagement, customization, cooperation, and data-based decision-making processes; it proves itself an indispensable resource for educators working within this domain. By embracing mobile learning methodologies and technologies, trainers can facilitate transformative educational experiences that enable students to meeting present-day needs dictated by advancements made in technology.

7.9.2 Designing Mobile Learning Experiences with Digital Tools

In the contemporary era of advancing technologies, mobile devices have seamlessly integrated into our quotidian routine. The burgeoning demand and ease of use pertaining to smartphones and tablets emphasize the indispensability for instructional designers to account for mobile learning experiences whilst devising educational materials. This subsection expounds on diverse digital mechanisms that can be employed to augment instruction design specifically targeted towards mobile-based learning environments.

The utilization of mobile learning presents a multitude of advantages. It provides learners with unrestricted access to academic content, enabling convenient and flexible acquisition anywhere at any time. Targeted digital resources can engender engaging and interactive educational opportunities that are tailored to the distinctive demands and predilections specified by mobile scholars.

An essential component of mobile learning experience design concerns the incorporation of gamification. When digital tools are harnessed in instructional design, learners can be stimulated, and their engagement levels elevated resulting in enhanced outcomes. By utilizing game elements including leaderboards, badges, and points an immersive and pleasurable learning environment may be established for those pursuing knowledge on a mobile platform under the guidance of skilled designers. Personalized learning is a pivotal characteristic of mobile learning. Utilizing digital tools in instructional design, learners have access to tailored content and activities that cater to their unique requirements and educational progress. Such an individualistic approach fosters self-directed study, enabling students to concentrate on areas where they require the most improvement.

Interactive simulations and virtual reality (VR) are robust instructional aids that can be seamlessly embedded into mobile learning modules. The employment of digital tools empowers training experts to craft authentic simulations, alongside engaging and immersive VR environments. These platforms significantly aid learners in exercising their understanding using practical applications within a safe environment that is controllable explicitly for this purpose. This method's implicit benefit improves knowledge retention through active participation by boosting the learner's overall skillset effectively while enhancing their educational experience holistically inclusive of hands-on exposure throughout the journey towards comprehensive subject mastery attainment.

Incorporating social media integration into the mobile learning experience is a highly efficacious tactic for boosting learner engagement. By seamlessly integrating popular social platforms into instructional design, learners acquire opportunities to engage in collaborative pursuits, and exchange viewpoints and insights with their peers and instructors alike while receiving constructive feedback. This interactive dynamic promotes a sense of solidarity within the group whilst equally advancing active participation across various stages of the student's learning journey.

Within the arena of data-centric instructional design, digital tools offer indispensable insights into learners' performance and advancement. Through an examination of the data gathered from mobile learning platforms, educational designers can pinpoint growth opportunities, monitor learner accomplishments, and execute informed determinations to refine and optimize the overall pedagogical experience.

Augmented reality (AR) is a swiftly developing technology that has the potential to considerably transform mobile learning. Through its ability to superimpose digital content onto tangible surroundings, AR can create instructive and interactive experiences for learners. Instructional designers have the opportunity to utilize AR as an effective tool in furnishing contextual information, simulating practical situations, and providing engaging hands-on training opportunities.

Adaptive learning platforms refer to digital tools that endeavor to personalize the learning experience by taking into consideration learners' individual needs and progress. Utilizing data-driven algorithms, these cutting-edge technologies are capable of gauging strengths and weaknesses amongst students thereby affording them appropriate content as well as recommended activities geared towards enhancing their mobile-learning experiences. This adaptive approach is instrumental in amplifying learner engagement whilst fostering significant improvements in various domains of student's academic performance.

Utilizing video-based learning is deemed an efficacious approach to mobile education. By integrating videos into the instructional design, learners can acquire both visual and auditory content that enriches their grasp of knowledge retention. The incorporation of videos may be utilized in exhibiting intricate notions, presenting tangible scenarios from daily life, and promoting learner engagement through a narrative structure.

Finally, collaborative learning constitutes a potent instructional design methodology that can be augmented through the utilization of digital tools. Through leveraging mobile devices and online platforms, learners possess the capability to cooperate with their peers by exchanging ideas and collaborating on assignments. This approach towards collaboration inspires engaged learning, and facilitates critical thinking ability development as well as problem-solving skills sharpening.

Ultimately, in contemporary times dictated by digital advancements and trends, it is vital to design mobile learning experiences with the aid of cutting-edge tools. Through integrating an array of features such as gamification elements, customized instructional approaches, interactive simulation techniques along with social media incorporation coupled with data-derived insights leveraging augmented reality technology supported through adaptive platforms for knowledge transfer supplemented by visual-based practices whilst maintaining highly collaborative environments; proficient professionals within this domain can craft truly immersive mobile vernaculars that consistently engage learners at a much higher level while also effectively addressing their individualized educational needs alongside personal predilections.

7.9.3 Case Studies: Successful Integration of Mobile Learning in Instructional Design

In recent times, mobile learning has emerged as a highly favored strategy in instructional design by harnessing the capabilities of digital tools to augment the learning process. This segment will expound upon multiple case studies that manifest the successful assimilation of mobile learning into instructional design, highlighting its efficacy across diverse domains.

This case study centers on the optimization of instructional design through digital tools, in which a university employed mobile learning to complement conventional classroom instruction. By offering students access to course materials, interactive quizzes, and discussion forums via a mobile application, the university registered an elevation in student engagement levels alongside better academic achievements.

A further examination reveals the utilization of gamification in instructional design using digital tools. A mobile learning platform, featuring leaderboards and badges akin to typical gaming elements, was executed within a corporate training scheme as an incentive for employee involvement. The efficacy of this program manifested not only through amplified levels of staff motivation and engagement but also via heightened preservation rates concerning commensurate knowledge transfer activities during said instruction.

The application of digital tools in instructional design, aimed at facilitating personalized learning, represents a promising area that increasingly benefits from mobile learning. An exemplary instance is the adoption by a K-12 school district of an innovative mobile learning platform enabling students to access customized educational modules aligned with their distinct needs and interests. This approach fostered enhanced learner autonomy and yielded noticeable academic improvements among participating students.

Interactive simulations and virtual reality have a significant presence in instructional design regarding mobile learning. A medical school has effectively integrated virtual reality simulations into its curriculum to instruct students on surgical procedures using mobile platforms. This innovative approach is highly immersive, producing an improved understanding of the subject matter, while simultaneously reducing reliance on costly physical equipment.

The presented case studies exemplify the triumphant incorporation of mobile learning into instructional design, spanning diverse sectors. These illustrate the prospective ability of utilizing digital tools such as gamification, personalized instruction techniques, interactive simulations, and virtual reality to elevate instructional design with mobile learning.

Academics specializing in instructional design will find great value in these case studies, as they offer a comprehensive insight into the practical applications and advantages of mobile learning. The findings presented are based on empirical evidence that can serve to inform decisions regarding the formulation and execution of mobile learning strategies across various educational and training contexts.

Embracing mobile learning and harnessing the potential of digital tools presents an opportunity for scholars to delve deeper into adaptive learning platforms, collaborative pedagogy, data-driven instructional design, augmented reality applications, video-based education, and social media integration. The realm of augmenting instructional design through mobile technology is vast with myriad possibilities that are substantiated by compelling case studies in this regard.

7.10 Gamification in Instructional Design with Digital Tools

The utilization of digital tools to enhance the learning experience is a strong instructional design technique referred to as gamification. Integrating game aspects like challenges, leaderboards, badges, and points into educational content, not only makes the process more captivating but also motivates learners to remain actively engaged while retaining information.

The use of digital tools in instructional design allows for endless opportunities to incorporate gamified strategies. By incorporating game-like features such as timed questions and bonus rounds into interactive quizzes, learners can experience a sense of excitement and competition. Additionally, the immersive experiences provided by virtual reality simulations allow them to apply their knowledge in a realistic setting. These technological advances enable designers to create customized learning environments that cater specifically to different learning styles while fostering engagement among participants resulting in better retention over time. Gamification using digital technology has been recognized in various educational settings as an innovative approach leading to increased motivation, participation, comprehension, and application of acquired information creating an effective platform for enhancing learning outcomes through progressive methodologies.

7.10.1 Understanding Gamification in Education

Gamification involves incorporating game-like features and mechanisms into non-gaming scenarios, such as education. It serves the purpose of engaging learners and motivating them to excel in their studies. Within the realm of instructional design, gamification has become a highly effective instrument for elevating the quality of learning experiences while also enhancing learner achievements. This section aims to delve deeper into how gamification can revolutionize educational practices by discussing its concept and potential impact on instructional design.

Due to its ability to harness learners' intrinsic motivation, gamification has become increasingly popular in recent years. By including features like challenges, leaderboards, badges, and points into educational tasks/games; gamification instills a sense of progress and achievement which aids learner engagement and incentives for them. Scholars who specialize in instructional design have observed that creating immersive education environments is within the potentiality of this technique thereby promoting interactive learning systems with better outcomes.

The personalization of learning is a significant advantage provided by gamification in instructional design. Utilizing digital tools, educators can customize educational content and exercises according to individual learners' needs and preferences. Gamification enables self-paced progression, instant feedback receipt, and the monitoring of progress; all these facets foster a culture of autonomous learning resulting in ownership over their learning process being instilled within learners themselves.

Interactive simulations and virtual reality offer a prime example of the intersection between digital tools and gamification. These advanced resources afford learners authentic, engaging educational encounters that can help them gain proficiency in applying knowledge in safe, controlled settings. Through integrating gamification features into these learning environments rewards for completing objectives or reaching milestones, say - students are inspired to interact with and fully explore this immersive world.

The rising trend of mobile learning has paved the way for gamification to enrich this mode of education. Mobile learning applications can be infused with game-inspired features like interactive quizzes, challenges, and stories which enable learners to access educative content at their convenience while simultaneously enjoying an engaging and playful experience on the go.

Gamification can improve instructional design by integrating social media. Educational activities that include sharing achievements or collaborating with peers foster a sense of community and connectedness for learners. This, in turn, boosts motivation and engagement levels during the learning process.

The increased use of data-driven instructional design in education has made gamification a vital tool to facilitate the process. Through gathering and assessing learner data, educators can pinpoint areas that require improvement, tweak their teaching methods accordingly, and offer individualized feedback. By incorporating game-like components such as performance-based incentives or progress monitoring tools into the learning environment, crucial information about learners' achievements can be gathered and analyzed for valuable insights into their overall performance.

Moreover, immersive, and personalized learning experiences can be achieved through augmented reality and adaptive learning platforms. By incorporating gamification features, these technologies foster a dynamic interaction between learners and the subject matter. This results in an enhanced immersive experience that ultimately improves comprehension of the content as well as retention over time.

To sum up, the integration of gamification into education can revolutionize instructional design by captivating and inspiring students, tailoring their learning experience towards individual needs, and providing engaging interactive platforms for learning. Through leveraging digital resources at hand educators can put forth new innovative means of teaching that better serve varied preferences across learners' spectrum; judicious implementation of gamified elements will positively impact enhancing instructional designs leading to improved academic results among pupils.

7.10.2 Gamification Techniques and Strategies for Instructional Design

Incorporating game elements and mechanics into non-game contexts, also known as gamification, has become increasingly popular in recent times. In the realm of instructional design specifically, educators have found that using this process can be highly advantageous for engaging learners and enhancing their overall learning experience. Consequently, integrating various techniques and strategies related to gamification into instructional design is an effective way to create interactive environments conducive to active participation which ultimately improves learning outcomes.

The utilization of rewards and incentives is a powerful gamification approach that can fuel learner motivation. By assigning points, badges, or virtual currency for task completion or milestone achievement, educators prompt students to actively engage with learning materials and progress through them. These awards should align with relevant educational goals to stimulate learners' acquisition of the necessary knowledge and skills.

An additional tactic involves incorporating competition and leaderboards. By promoting a friendly rivalry among learners, educators can cultivate a feeling of accomplishment and motivate individuals to pursue excellence. The use of leaderboards showcasing everyone's progress and standings further instills drive while also encouraging healthy competition.

Integrating storytelling and narrative elements into instructional design is made possible by gamification. Educators can create a captivating story that leads learners through their learning journey, resulting in an experience that's more engaging and memorable. By connecting with content emotionally, using storytelling techniques helps boost motivation and retention for learners.

In addition, the utilization of gamification strategies can aid in bolstering problem-solving and critical-thinking abilities. By integrating challenges, puzzles, and simulations into instructional planning, tutors can grant learners chances to exercise their competencies within practical scenarios. These dynamic experiences not only amplify education but also cultivate inventiveness and originality.

Moreover, digital tools can aid instructional designers in delivering tailored learning experiences. With the help of adaptive learning platforms, learners' performance data are analyzed to provide individualized recommendations and feedback based on their unique needs and preferences. Learners might also access study materials remotely via mobile devices or collaborate with peers through social media integration for improved engagement and knowledge-sharing opportunities.

7.10.3 Case Studies: Successful Implementation of Gamification in Instructional Design

Gamification techniques and strategies have great potential to enhance digital instructional design. With the help of gamification, educators can develop interactive and personalized learning experiences that encourage active participation, leading to better outcomes in education overall. Gamification has increasingly garnered attention as a potent instrument in instructional design, revolutionizing the mode of learners' interaction with content and augmenting their overall learning achievements. This subsection examines several case studies that exemplify efficacious applications of gamification within instructional design. Such instances showcase how digital resources can be effectively leveraged to develop immersive, captivating, and custom-tailored educational experiences.

7.10.3.1 Case Study 1: Advancing Instructional Design using Digital Tools

This case study delves into the process by which a university revamped its online course using gamification principles. By integrating game elements such as badges, leaderboards, and progress bars, instructors recorded remarkable enhancements in student motivation and engagement levels.

Students were galvanized to accomplish tasks collaboratively with peers whilst accomplishing learning objectives resulting in discernible advances in course completion rates coupled with elevated satisfaction among students.

7.10.3.2 Case Study 2: The Implementation of Gamification in Instructional Design through Digital Tools

The present case study directs attention towards a corporate training program that incorporated the pedagogical approach of gamification in delivering instructional content to employees, specifically concerning elaborate software systems. Through utilization of role-play circumstances, interactive assessments and incentives were made available for employee participation. This enabled learners to experience an enhanced learning process which contributed positively toward their understanding and retention capacity thereby leading them towards increased output efficiency as well as achievement of fewer errors while performing tasks related with the system at hand.

7.10.3.3 Case Study 3: The Implementation of Personalized Learning Utilizing Digital Tools in the Field of Instructional Design

In the present case study, we investigate how a primary school successfully incorporated gamification within its personalized learning curriculum. This involved tailoring educational material to suit individual student requirements and offering self-directed studies to foster an enhanced sense of accountability among pupils toward their learning journey. The institution further introduced digital tools that enabled teachers to monitor scholastic advancement while allowing for prompt corrective feedback and alteration in instructional methods where necessary. This strategic integration resulted in notable increments in academic performance alongside constructive modifications regarding pupil attitudes relating to education.

The presented case studies effectively demonstrate the transformative impact of gamification in instructional design. Leveraging digital tools, skilled instructional designers are empowered to develop engaging and tailored learning experiences that inspire motivation, foster collaboration, and facilitate achievement. In all education settings including K-12 programs and corporate training or higher educational institutions alike, the potential for revolutionizing instruction through gamification is apparent with its ability to advance learner outcomes significantly. As scholars committed to advancing effective pedagogical practice within this field's bounds particularly instructed design development it lies at our core responsibility towards embracing innovative technologies such as digital tools along with integrating those platforms in a complementary manner featuring game-based incentive structures too without undermining prevailing academic standards hence enabling future generations success by empowering them thoroughly while elevating current teaching practices' efficacy level using these methodologies meaningfully constitutes an inseparable aspect imperative aiming forward progressiveness concerning holistic upskilling through enhanced edifying systems.

7.11 Social Media Integration in Instructional Design for Increased Engagement

The use of social media in instructional design has gained immense popularity owing to its effectiveness in enhancing student engagement. By integrating platforms like Facebook, Twitter and Instagram into the learning process, educators can establish an interactive environment that captures students' attention. In place of traditional discussion boards, teachers can employ hashtags or groups on various social media channels for enriching classroom debates while encouraging collaborative learning among their learners. This innovative approach not only complements comprehension but also fosters creativity and critical thinking amongst pupils who become active participants rather than passive listeners in class discussions. Furthermore, the integration of social media enables instant communication and feedback between students and teachers. Via these platforms, educators can share valuable resources such as articles or videos that spark meaningful discussions beyond traditional classroom settings. Simultaneously, learners can approach instructors for clarification on assignments through direct messaging systems or comment sections within posts at any time. As a result of this heightened accessibility to one another's messages in real-time online environments via their respective devices - mobiles phones etc., inclusive learning is being fostered among all participants who feel equally valued by having access into each other’s lives outside physical classrooms' spaces but still remain connected digitally speaking globally regardless borders around us geographically situated across different regions worldwide without constraints imposed from either timezone differences nor limited bandwidth capabilities available easily accessed unresrictively now possible with technological advancement rapidly improving overtime significantly surely Ultimately integrating social media usage aptly designed instructional materials endows unique opportunities fostering active learner engagement empowering their self-discovery journeys while promoting authentic senses belongingness encouraging group cohesion conducive comfortable positive educational milieu where everyone thrives beautifully amid shared cultural values shaping multi-faceted international experiences noteworthy witnessed during today modern era thanks largely achieved major strides made towards edtech inventions enhancing our pedagogy practices sustainability solidified we see reflecting reality mirrored back affirming progress assured moving forward steadily marching intelligently together forging better future aligned squarely benefitting humankind more than ever before much broader scope envisaged.

7.11.1 Leveraging Social Media in Instructional Design

In contemporary society, social media has assumed a crucial role in shaping our daily routines by affecting the nature of communication, information dissemination and collaborative activities. In regard to instructional design practices, leveraging this powerful tool can significantly enrich students' learning experiences. The present section examines multiple methods through which social media platforms may be incorporated within teaching strategies aimed at augmenting participation levels while promoting an interactive educational atmosphere that prioritizes mutual collaboration among learners.

One of the principal advantages that come with utilizing social media within instructional design is its capacity to foster a community among learners. The integration of platforms such as Facebook, Twitter or LinkedIn in educational activities allows academics to interconnect and explore diverse viewpoints whilst simultaneously collaborating on various projects. This approach not only enriches the student learning experience but also equips them for participation within contemporary workforce environments where collaboration stands crucial.

In addition, social media imbues a platform for personalized education. Targeted ads, customized content and tailored feedback enable scholars to partake in an individualized learning experience that precisely caters to their specific requisites and interests. This degree of customization cultivates insightful comprehension of the subject matter, alongside heightened student engagement.

Incorporating social media in the instructional design alongside personalized learning gives rise to interactive simulations and virtual reality experiences. In this context, scholars are presented with opportunities for conducting experiments within safe and controlled environments as well as partaking in engaging virtual field trips. Through such immersive simulations, complex concepts can be explored effectively which enhances comprehension while simultaneously rendering the learning experience more enjoyable and memorable through a hands-on approach.

Social media has the potential to enhance instructional design in the field of mobile learning. Given that a significant number of academics rely on smartphones or tablets, integration of social media platforms into this domain always facilitates unparalleled access to educational content and locations. This flexibility enables learners to acquire knowledge at their own pace while simultaneously offering prospects for continuous education outside conventional classroom settings.

To conclude, the utilization of social media in instructional design provides numerous advantages to scholars. Social media integration offers a means to augment instructional design with digital tools and facilitate personalized learning, interactive simulations, as well as collaborative learning. This potential reinforces an innovative way of educating our students by revolutionizing their educational experiences through embracing the power of social media. By doing so, scholarly practitioners can create engaging and immersive opportunities that afford success for learners within this era's digitally driven society.

7.11.2 Strategies for Integrating Social Media into Instructional Design

In the current digital era, social media has assumed an indispensable role in our routine, proffering novel opportunities for communication, cooperation and participation. As erudite savants within instructional design academia, it behooves us to not only appreciate but also harness this powerful tool with respect towards enhancing learning experiences through its integration into systematic pedagogical strategies. This subsection examines numerous efficacious approaches of optimally incorporating social media into instructional design paradigms aimed at bolstering user involvement whilst fostering a communal platform conducive for acquiring knowledge collaboratively.

An effective approach towards integrating social media with instructional design involves utilizing various social media platforms as a medium for communication and collaboration. By establishing exclusive groups or pages on prominent platforms like Facebook or LinkedIn, educators could potentially spur discourse and exchange of information amongst learners while simultaneously promoting peer-to-peer learning within the academic community. Apart from enhancing engagement among learners, incorporating dedicated online spaces helps to cultivate an atmosphere conducive to knowledge sharing thereby enriching overall pedagogy efforts.

An additional approach is to integrate social media tools into the learning curricula directly. Educators may utilize Twitter as a means of promoting real-time discussions during lectures or leverage Instagram for inspiring learners in generating visual depictions of course concepts. Through leveraging both familiarity and popularity with these platforms, instructional designers have an opportunity to harness their innate engagement and interactivity levels towards crafting meaningful educational experiences.

In addition, social media presents an opportunity to foster personalized learning. Educators have the ability to utilize platforms such as YouTube or Pinterest in order to compile and disseminate resources that are customized for each learner's specific interests and requirements. This approach encourages individuals to engage with content that aligns with their individual preferences thereby enabling self-directed education while also accommodating diverse learning styles through instructional design techniques.

Furthermore, social media can serve as a potent instrument for formative evaluation and feedback. Educators may construct digital tests or surveys via platforms such as Kahoot or Mentimeter to enable learners to promptly assess their grasp of the course materials. Additionally, social media channels facilitate prompt delivery of constructive critiques and motivational support that endorse continuous learning opportunities.

In conclusion, the integration of social media into instructional design presents a host of advantages for both academics and learners. By employing social media platforms as communication tools, integrating them within learning activities, fostering personalized education experiences through their use, and utilizing such technology to facilitate feedback provision in assessment processes – educational leaders are empowered with an approach which enables engaging collaboration alongside optimal effectiveness across pedagogical initiatives.

7.11.3 Case Studies: Enhancing Engagement through Social Media Integration

In the contemporary digital era, social media has increasingly gained prominence as a crucial component of our routine existence. It has brought about significant transformation in our communication processes and mode of interaction while facilitating seamless information exchange. Design professionals have recognized its vast potential in augmenting learner engagement, resulting in a growing trend where instructional designers are incorporating these platforms into their design frameworks. This subchapter delves into multiple illustrative case studies that underscore the efficaciousness of integrating social media within instructional design to enrich the engagement quotient.

A case study has been conducted to investigate the potential benefits of integrating digital tools, specifically social media platforms such as Facebook and Twitter, in enhancing instructional design. Through the creation of dedicated groups and hashtags, learners are empowered to take an active part in discussions concerning course materials, share useful resources amongst themselves while fostering peer collaboration. The findings underscore how this integration not only stimulates deepened engagement among learners but also cultivates a sense of community within their academic environment.

An additional investigation examines the utilization of gamification in instructional design using digital tools. The unification of social media attributes, such as leaderboards and badges, facilitates a competitive environment amongst learners wherein rewards can be earned while their accomplishments are shared on various social media platforms. This study presents noteworthy evidence supporting the notion that gamification combined with integration to several forms of social media can substantially enhance learner motivation and engagement levels. Furthermore, this subchapter delves into the notion of personalized learning employing digital tools within instructional design. Through strategic utilization of social media platforms, instructional designers have the opportunity to generate tailored and customized learning experiences catered specifically according to individual learners' necessities and inclinations. The case study highlights how incorporation with leading social media channels enables learners not only access bespoke content but also obtain swift feedback while fostering connections with subject matter authorities in their fields of interest.

In addition, the present subchapter explores the application of interactive simulations and virtual reality within instructional design. Through inclusion of social media functionalities, learners are afforded opportunities to partake in real-time collaboration with peers while sharing perspectives and seeking feedback on their experiences. Our case study provides evidence that such integration enhances immersion levels associated with simulated as well as virtually real environments; consequently enhancing learner engagement along increased knowledge retention rates.

This particular section of the text delves into the significance of mobile learning in instructional design, specifically with regards to digital tools. The incorporation of social media platforms provides learners with uninterrupted access to educational materials as well as opportunities for collaborative activities alongside their peers regardless of location or time. Through a case study analysis, it is demonstrated how integrating social media within mobile learning leads to heightened learner engagement and an ongoing drive towards knowledge acquisition.

In summary, social media integration has emerged as a potent instrument for augmenting engagement in instructional design. The present subchapter presents several case studies that showcase the effectiveness of integrating social media in redefining pedagogical strategies and generating immersive learning opportunities. Aspiring to furnish valuable insights and practical examples thereof, this section will serve as an indispensable reference resource for scholars specializing across diverse niches such as gamification, personalized learning, interactive simulations, mobile learning, and collaborative instruction.

7.12 Augmented Reality in Instructional Design for Immersive Learning Experiences

Immersive learning experiences in instructional design have been revolutionized by augmented reality (AR). With the ability to superimpose digital objects onto physical surroundings, AR facilitates interactive and enriching engagement with educational content. The technology offers limitless potential for crafting stimulating and captivating pedagogical settings. AR can greatly benefit instructional design by boosting students' comprehension and retention of intricate concepts. Specifically, in the realm of science education, AR technology has the power to illustrate perplexing ideas such as molecular structures or astronomical phenomena. By presenting these notions through engaging 3D models that enable interaction and exploration, learners are better equipped to grasp even challenging theories. Moreover, AR offers experiential learning opportunities where pupils can undertake digital experiments or simulations replicating real-life situations building a deep understanding along with critical thinking and problem-solving skills concurrently.

In addition, AR fosters personalized and adjustable learning encounters by customizing content to meet the specific needs of each learner. By monitoring performance data and employing analytics, AR systems can collect information on individual progress and supply immediate feedback as well as guidance. This accommodating function guarantees that every learner gains unique instruction tailored according to their strengths, weaknesses, or favored learning approaches. Furthermore, inculcating an inclusive setting for learners with varying disabilities is easier thanks to AR which offers visual aids or audio signals suitable for people having hearing impairments or dyslexia alike.

Conclusively, augmented reality possesses immense potential to revolutionize instructional design for immersive learning experiences. By merging virtual elements with the tangible world, AR amplifies the assimilation of intricate concepts while promoting involvement and customization. The continual progressions in this technology will undeniably reinvent education by providing innovative approaches toward effective teaching and learning methodologies.

7.12.1 Exploring Augmented Reality in Education

The technology known as augmented reality (AR) presents a promising opportunity to revolutionize the field of education. This cutting-edge approach superimposes digital information onto real-world environments, thereby elevating instructional design and affording students immersive and interactive learning experiences. Within this subchapter, we aim to explore AR's diverse educational applications while analyzing its potential for transforming overall instructional design practices.

One of the principal advantages afforded by Augmented Reality (AR) technology within education lies in its capacity to augment instructional design processes through digital tools. In this regard, conventional approaches to instructive strategies regularly confront challenges besetting learner engagement levels; however, AR presents an innovative remedy that allows for highly interactive and immersive content-based learning experiences. By way of illustration, students may leverage AR-enabled devices as a means of exploring historical landmarks or dissecting virtual organisms with heightened realism - thereby imparting an artifice-proof quality unavailable from even the most sophisticate textbooks.

One domain in which AR technology can be applied is the integration of gamification into instructional design. By infusing game elements within educational activities, AR has demonstrated its potential to enhance student motivation and engagement levels. To illustrate this point further, one can create an AR-based game that educates students on mathematical or scientific concepts, thereby transforming education into a delightful and interactive practice.

Augmented Reality (AR) also facilitates customized learning through the implementation of digital tools in instructional design. By specifically tailoring educational content to meet individual student's needs and preferences, AR technology can provide a bespoke learning experience. For instance, it can adjust simulation difficulty levels based on students' performance records so that they remain adequately challenged throughout their studies.

In addition, Augmented Reality (AR) can serve as a tool for crafting immersive simulations and virtual reality encounters in the context of instructional design. AR enables learners to immerse themselves into simulated environments that would be either inaccessible or unsafe otherwise. A case in point is medical students who may rehearse intricate surgical procedures within an augmented operating room environment thereby bolstering their dexterity and self-assurance levels.

Augmented Reality (AR) presents a significant potential impact on instructional design in the domain of mobile learning. Considering the proliferation of smartphones and tablets, students can conveniently avail themselves of AR anytime and anywhere they prefer to learn. The exceptional flexibility this feature provides enables learners with opportunities for continuous development beyond conventional classroom settings, thus promoting self-paced education practices effectively.

In instructional design, social media integration has emerged as a potent instrument for enhancing engagement levels. Augmented reality technology can be effectively coalesced with diverse social platforms to produce interactive and collaborative learning opportunities. The confluence of these innovative tools allows students to exchange their augmented reality artifacts amongst themselves thereby fostering an enhanced sense of camaraderie and cooperation within the academic community.

The utilization of data-driven instructional design techniques with the assistance of augmented reality (AR) affords educators an opportunity to meticulously analyze student performance, enabling them to arrive at decisions that are grounded in empirical evidence. AR technology is especially effective for gathering rich and comprehensive information about students' interactions as well as their progress throughout the learning process, offering valuable insights into key facets such as methodological efficiencies or course content ineffectiveness. By leveraging these insights, pedagogues can identify areas in need of improvement while simultaneously tailoring instruction precisely according to everyone's needs.

In summary, it is apparent that augmented reality holds significant promise in revolutionizing instructional design through its capabilities to heighten engagement levels, facilitate personalization and interactivity. The seamless fusion of AR technology with educational programs can effectively create immersive learning environments conducive for enhanced comprehension and retention of knowledge. In this era characterized by technologically driven advancements, scholars are obligated to fully exploit the potential benefits accorded by AR advances towards education.

7.12.2 Designing Immersive Learning Experiences with Augmented Reality

The utilization of Augmented Reality (AR) is presently transforming the landscape of instructional design, presenting academics with prospects to conceive interactive learning encounters that inspire and engage learners beyond conventional means. This segment scrutinizes AR's potential in conducting modern-day educational practices and provides pertinent guidance for devising progressive AR-grounded immersive education experiences bestowed with efficacy and impactfulness.

Augmented reality (AR) entails superimposing digital assets onto the physical world, thereby amplifying learners' discernment and engagement with their surroundings. By assimilating computer-generated components like 3D models, videos, and interactive simulations into learning activities AR has a radical capacity to revolutionize conventional instructional design techniques. One of the primary advantages that augmented reality (AR) offers in instructional design is its capacity to furnish learners with active, experiential learning opportunities. Through enabling interaction with virtual objects and environments, AR serves as a connecting force between theoretical knowledge and practical skills; it enables students to apply what they have learned within authentic settings. To exemplify this use case: medical trainees can hone surgical techniques by practicing on simulated patients via AR technology while engineering pupils could manipulate digital prototypes for better comprehension of intricate concepts.

One of the advantageous features offered by augmented reality (AR) technology is its capability to provide personalized and tailor-made learning experiences. The use of digital tools enables instructional designers to create customized AR content that best suits individual learners' expected outcomes, preferences as well as abilities. Consequently, this method allows learners to independently navigate through course material at their own pace while tracking progress with flexible feedback mechanisms resulting in better overall academic performance outcomes.

Moreover, Augmented Reality (AR) can augment cooperation and interpersonal communication within learners. Through the integration of social media functionality, instructional designers may facilitate peer-to-peer learning and knowledge dissemination. In this way, learners are able to cooperate on AR initiatives, exchange experiences with one another as well provide feedback in order to nurture a sense of community whilst promoting engagement amongst them all.

The creation of successful augmented reality (AR) learning experiences necessitates a methodical approach to instructional design principles. It is incumbent upon the instructional designers to ensure that AR materials are congruent with educational aims, user-friendly and deliver stimulating learning outcomes. Additionally, those involved must factor in technical requirements as well as limitations inherent within devices or platforms utilized for AR applications.

To conclude, the incorporation of augmented reality (AR) into instructional design possesses significant potential for revolutionizing immersive learning experiences. AR offers a powerful mechanism to enhance instruction design practices, customize educational deliveries and facilitate collaboration while maximizing learner engagement. As augmented reality continues its evolutionary trajectory, scholars must proactively embrace this innovative technology as they seek to unlock its full potency in instructional methodologies.

7.12.3 Case Studies: Augmented Reality Applications in Instructional Design

The utilization of Augmented Reality (AR) is presently transforming the landscape of instructional design, presenting academics with prospects to conceive interactive learning encounters that inspire and engage learners beyond conventional means. This segment scrutinizes AR's potential in conducting modern-day educational practices and provides pertinent guidance for devising progressive AR-grounded immersive education experiences bestowed with efficacy and impactfulness.

Augmented reality (AR) entails superimposing digital assets onto the physical world, thereby amplifying learners' discernment and engagement with their surroundings. By assimilating computer-generated components like 3D models, videos, and interactive simulations into learning activities AR has a radical capacity to revolutionize conventional instructional design techniques. One of the primary advantages that augmented reality (AR) offers in instructional design is its capacity to furnish learners with active, experiential learning opportunities. Through enabling interaction with virtual objects and environments, AR serves as a connecting force between theoretical knowledge and practical skills; it enables students to apply what they have learned within authentic settings. To exemplify this use case: medical trainees can hone surgical techniques by practicing on simulated patients via AR technology while engineering pupils could manipulate digital prototypes for better comprehension of intricate concepts.

One of the advantageous features offered by augmented reality (AR) technology is its capability to provide personalized and tailor-made learning experiences. The use of digital tools enables instructional designers to create customized AR content that best suits individual learners' expected outcomes, preferences as well as abilities. Consequently, this method allows learners to independently navigate through course material at their own pace while tracking progress with flexible feedback mechanisms resulting in better overall academic performance outcomes.

Moreover, Augmented Reality (AR) can augment cooperation and interpersonal communication within learners. Through the integration of social media functionality, instructional designers may facilitate peer-to-peer learning and knowledge dissemination. In this way, learners can cooperate on AR initiatives, exchange experiences with one another as well provide feedback in order to nurture a sense of community whilst promoting engagement amongst them all.

The creation of successful augmented reality (AR) learning experiences necessitates a methodical approach to instructional design principles. It is incumbent upon the instructional designers to ensure that AR materials are congruent with educational aims, user-friendly and deliver stimulating learning outcomes. Additionally, those involved must factor in technical requirements as well as limitations inherent within devices or platforms utilized for AR applications.

To conclude, the incorporation of augmented reality (AR) into instructional design possesses significant potential for revolutionizing immersive learning experiences. AR offers a powerful mechanism to enhance instruction design practices, customize educational deliveries and facilitate collaboration while maximizing learner engagement. As augmented reality continues its evolutionary trajectory, scholars must proactively embrace this innovative technology as they seek to unlock its full potency in instructional methodologies.

7.13 Interactive Simulations and Virtual Reality in Instructional Design

Instructional design has been transformed through the adoption of interactive simulations and virtual reality (VR), enabling immersive and captivating learning experiences. These innovative technologies enable learners to participate actively, leading to better comprehension retention. Interactive simulations take a tangible approach by providing opportunities for hands-on manipulation of variables with real-time observation on consequences; science classes offer students an excellent opportunity to conduct virtual experiments equivalent or akin in actual situations without fearing for their safety while practicing problem-solving skills. On the other hand, VR allows people's immersion into environments that might not be practical otherwise impossible concerning realistic life limitations, such as surgical procedures or flight stimulations where complex skill sets can easily translate from within safe controlled conditions during training purposes.

Furthermore, various learning styles and preferences are addressed by interactive simulations and VR. They provide a multi-sensory encounter that resonates with visual, auditory, and kinesthetic learners alike as they can explore ideas through a mix of images, sound explanations, and physical interactions within the simulated environment. This advances their understanding while engaging them in ways outstripping conventional pedagogical methods stressing lecturing or written materials only. Additionally, these tools further offer tailored experiences for each learner via personalized settings based on individual needs alongside progress prompts to alter content suited to skill levels thus ensuring precise targeted direction is received by every student utilizing interactive simulations or VR technology.

To sum up, through immersive learning experiences that boost comprehension, engagement and personalization of knowledge acquisition, interactive simulations and virtual reality have revolutionized instructional design. By facilitating learners' active participation in hands-on activities and digital settings while acquiring information, these highly-effective technologies represent a remarkable pedagogical tool for diverse academic contexts. As technology continues to evolve rapidly there is no doubt that interactive simulations and VR will become increasingly prevalent within education even further as they continue to offer an innovative approach catering specifically toward the needs of every type of learner imaginable.

7.13.1 The Power of Interactive Simulations in Instructional Design

Over the last few years, instructional design has experienced a radical change as digital tools have become more prevalent. Among these tools, interactive simulations are gaining traction and transforming how teachers approach instructional design. These simulations offer numerous advantages that improve learning experiences in different fields like gamification, personalized learning, virtual reality technology, or mobile-based education to name but a few examples.

Interactive simulations offer a prime opportunity for scholars to engage in hands-on and immersive learning. By experimenting with virtual labs, tackling complex challenges within gamified environments, or exploring digital worlds, active participation is promoted which leads to the development of vital skills such as problem-solving abilities and critical thinking. As an effective tool for enhancing instructional designs through digital methods, this interactivity offers great value.

The use of interactive simulations results in customized educational experiences by catering to the unique requirements and preferences of each learner. This adaptable approach enables scholars to advance at their preferred speed and concentrate on topics that require further improvement while skipping over subjects they have already mastered. The result is individualized instruction for every student leading to an optimal learning outcome.

Additionally, interactive simulations provide a chance for scholarly individuals to engage socially and collaborate. They can connect with their instructors and peers in virtual settings, which encourages meaningful conversations, idea-sharing sessions as well as teamwork aimed at tackling problems together. By incorporating social media into instructional design through such means of simulation, student involvement is enhanced alongside the fostering of an encouragingly interactive environment that nurtures a sense of community amongst learners.

Interactive simulations offer the added benefit of supplying instantaneous feedback and performance analysis. By utilizing data-driven teaching techniques, educators can examine students' advancement, pinpoint areas for growth, and deliver prompt responses. This scrutiny enables the adaptation of instructive approaches to guarantee that pupils receive personalized instruction that yields positive results.

Moreover, immersive learning experiences using augmented reality can be achieved through interactive simulations. Teachers can engage with their surroundings in novel and innovative ways by superimposing digital content onto reality. This captivating instructional design strategy not only enhances scholars' comprehension of intricate concepts but also fosters a deeper sense of engagement.

The significance of interactive simulations in instructional design cannot be overlooked. They have tremendous potential to improve learning by incorporating gamification, personalization, virtual reality integration, and data-driven strategies. Irrespective of the field or discipline, these digital tools offer many advantages for scholars and can transform the educational experience into an engaging and effective one if used effectively.

7.13.2 Incorporating Virtual Reality into Instructional Design

Instructional design in education is undergoing a major transformation through the emergence of virtual reality (VR). This innovative technology presents exciting prospects for crafting immersive and interactive simulations, which can engage learners in ways that are not possible with traditional instructional methods. Through this subchapter, we delve into VR's potential as an instructional tool and offer useful techniques to incorporate it within educational settings.

VR's capacity to produce authentic and engaging simulations is one of its primary benefits. By immersing learners in digital settings, instructors can offer practical learning opportunities that would otherwise be arduous or unachievable within the confines of a standard classroom. The use case for medical students who wish to train on surgical protocols serves as an excellent illustration; VR enables them to practice procedures confidently in safe conditions before commencing with live patients, thereby gaining indispensable exposure beforehand.

VR's potential to customize learning experiences is another advantage. By using VR, teachers can develop tailored scenarios that cater to the unique requirements and preferences of every learner. This customized strategy enhances engagement and enthusiasm since students are more likely to be invested in content that fits their learning styles.

In addition, VR has the potential to enhance collaborative learning by bringing learners together in a shared virtual space. This can promote teamwork and collaboration among students, regardless of their physical location, which is particularly advantageous for those participating in remote education programs where they might not have access to traditional face-to-face interactions.

The inclusion of virtual reality in instructional design expands the scope for data-driven analysis. By observing how learners engage with virtual environments, educators can gain valuable insights into their progress and performance. The acquired information is then utilized to make informed decisions regarding instruction that lead to provision of appropriate support and resources required by learners towards success.

To sum up, the integration of virtual reality in instructional design presents a tremendous opportunity to enhance learning experiences. Through creating captivating simulations that promote interactivity and personalization, encouraging collaborative efforts between students as well as leveraging data analytics capabilities; educators can effectively engage learners by tapping into the potential of VR technology. As practitioners within this field, it's critical for us to explore its possibilities and evaluate how we might successfully incorporate VR technologies within educational environments. Embracing digital tools including but not limited to VR is crucial if transformational opportunities are sought after regarding innovative teaching methods aimed at making an impact on all types of learners alike.

7.13.3 Case Studies: Using Interactive Simulations and Virtual Reality in Instructional Design

The domain of instructional design has undergone a notable metamorphosis in recent times, primarily due to the emergence of digital tools. Of particular significance is the utilization of interactive simulations and virtual reality (VR) within this discipline, which have generated profound interest. These technologies present distinctive possibilities for crafting captivating and immersive learning encounters that can efficaciously elevate instruction efficacy.

One illustrative example of the efficacy of interactive simulations in instructional design pertains to the utilization of flight simulators for pilot training. Historically, this style involved a blend involving classroom instruction and legitimate flying experience; however, glaring limitations persisted with regards to cost-inefficiency compounded by restricted opportunities for imaginative learning experiences. In light thereof, immersive flight simulation technologies have been integrated into contemporary trainee pilots' curricula as acknowledged facilitators that enable extensive practice under varying conditions within controlled environments which subsequently foster heightened professional proficiencies attendant on efficient and economically feasible certification procedures.

An additional case study that illuminates the advantages of virtual reality technology in instructional design is its implementation within medical education. Certain difficulties arise for students pursuing a career in medicine who attempt to acquire hands-on experience with surgical procedures due to highly restricted cadaver availability and potential hazards associated with live surgeries. By employing VR simulated environments, it becomes possible for such individuals to become fully immersed in realistic scenarios which facilitate practice and skill development without any risk involved and consequently enhancing their proficiency over time while also bolstering long-term patient safety measures.

The following case studies present evidence for the significant potential of interactive simulations and virtual reality in instructional design. By blending these advanced technologies into educational practices, educators can fashion captivating and immersive experiences that magnify student learning outcomes exceptionally well. There is no denying that employing interactive simulations and virtual reality platforms has vast implications across various fields such as pilot training or medical education – marking a pivotal moment to revamp conventional models of instruction while providing learners with exceptional opportunities to acquire specialized knowledge through unique, invaluable experiences.

As professionals engaged in the study of instructional design, it is imperative to investigate and adopt digital tools as a means of remaining at the forefront of educational practice. By integrating interactive simulations and virtual reality into our designs, we can foster individually tailored learning experiences that are immersive, engaging, and efficacious for learners. The potential applications are manifold; thus, we must make use of these technological advancements by harnessing their transformative power towards improving instructional design outcomes.

7.14 Social Media Integration in Instructional Design for Increased Engagement

The integration of social media into instructional design has gained traction in recent years as educators acknowledge its potential for amplifying student engagement. With the inclusion of prominent platforms including Twitter, Facebook and Instagram in teaching practices, instructors can craft a more dynamic learning environment that is interactive by nature. In real-time communication scenarios fostered via social media usage during classes or seminars enables students to share ideas openly while also enabling robust collaboration between peers enhancing their critical thinking capabilities through analysis and response stimulation from diverse perspectives presented within these discussions.

Moreover, the integration of social media into instructional design presents prospects for tailored learning experiences. Educators can customize their instruction to accommodate the diverse needs and inclinations of individual learners by utilizing assorted social media tools. Examples include tasking students with multimedia projects that demand video or podcast creation via platforms such as YouTube or SoundCloud. This approach not only stimulates student engagement through creative expression but also enables them to exhibit their comprehension in a manner suited to their unique proficiencies and abilities. Furthermore, integrating social media provides an avenue for authentic evaluation where pupils can manifest knowledge transferal through blog entries or online deliberations.

To summarize, the convergence of social media with instructional design represents a potent approach to enhance student engagement within classroom settings. Through harnessing the functional capabilities of various online platforms, educators can facilitate effective collaboration among learners while also accentuating critical thinking abilities and delivering bespoke learning experiences calibrated towards individualized student needs. Considering advancing technological innovations, it's vital for instructional designers to proactively incorporate these digital tools in their educational blueprints as part of an overarching ambition to optimize pedagogical outcomes holistically.

7.14.1 Leveraging Social Media in Instructional Design

Social media has evolved as an indispensable part of our everyday existence, impacting the way we interact with each other, exchange information and undertake cooperative endeavors. In the realm of instructional design, leveraging social media's potential can effectively magnify learners' educational encounter. The present section sheds light on diverse methods for blending various forms of social media into instruction designing that aids in intensifying learner engagement while fostering a learning milieu promoting collaboration among peers.

An essential advantage of utilizing social media within the context of instructional design is its capacity to foster a sense of community amongst learners. By integrating platforms such as Facebook, Twitter or LinkedIn into the learning process, students are able to interact with each other in myriad ways: exchanging ideas and working collaboratively on projects. Such an approach not only enriches their overall educational experience but also better prepares them for collaboration-based ventures pervasive throughout real-world scenarios which demand effective teamwork participation.

Moreover, social media affords an opportunity for customized and personalized learning. By utilizing targeted advertising, individualized feedback mechanisms and tailored content delivery methods, learners can enjoy a bespoke educational experience that is uniquely attuned to their specific needs and interests. This high degree of personalization engenders improved comprehension of the material being studied whilst also amplifying student engagement levels.

Apart from customized education, the integration of social media in instructional design facilitates interactive simulations and virtual reality experiences. Scholars can indulge in simulated field excursions, execute experiments under safe conditions, and delve into intricate ideas by means of immersive simulations. This experiential methodology towards learning amplifies understanding while also rendering the overall process more engaging and enduring.

The utilization of social media in enhancing instructional design is a feasible option for mobile learning. Given the widespread usage of smartphones and tablets among scholars, incorporation of social media platforms into this method can provide accessibility to educational content around the clock and across different locations. This level of convenience accommodates individualized pacing for learners while also rendering continuous learning chances beyond traditional classroom arrangements.

To conclude, the utilization of social media in instructional design provides numerous advantages for educators. This includes enhancing instructional methodologies with digital tools as well as promoting personalized learning, interactive simulations, and collaborative education. The integration of social media has a tremendous potential to transform contemporary pedagogy wherein scholars can incorporate captivating and comprehensive teaching techniques that equip students with skills necessary for their success in an increasingly digitized world.

7.14.2 Strategies for Integrating Social Media into Instructional Design

In the contemporary digital era, social media has emerged as a pivotal component of our day-to-day existence by presenting fresh prospects for communication, teamwork and participation. It is critical that we as experts within instructional design make adept use of the potency embedded in social media and embed it into our pedagogical tactics to augment learning experiences. This chapter delves into multiple methodologies aimed at effectively integrating social media elements with instructional designs leading to increased involvement among students whilst instilling an environment conducive towards collaborative study practices.

An effective approach to incorporating social media into instructional design is by leveraging social media platforms as a mechanism for communication and collaboration. By establishing exclusive groups or pages on mediums like Facebook or LinkedIn, educators can facilitate discourse, disseminate pertinent educational materials, and cultivate an atmosphere of connectedness amongst learners. This not only amplifies involvement but also incites peer-to-peer learning initiatives whilst encouraging information exchange between learners.

An additional approach is to integrate social media tools into the instructional activities, wherein educators may utilize Twitter for moderating real-time discussions amidst a lecture or make use of Instagram so as to encourage learners in creating visual representations concerning course concepts. By capitalizing on the recognition and prominence of these social media platforms, instructional designers can harness their natural interactivity and interest thereby leading towards valuable learning experiences.

Moreover, social media has the potential to foster personalized learning. Teachers and educators can capitalize on platforms such as YouTube or Pinterest in order to compile and distribute resources that are customized according to each learner's unique interests or requirements. By empowering learners with opportunities for independent exploration of materials that align with their personal affinities, instructional designers have a means by which they can encourage self-guided education while accommodating various modes of comprehension.

Furthermore, social media platforms can serve as a potent instrument for formative assessment and feedback in the realm of education. Educators are able to fabricate online quizzes or polls via Kahoot or Mentimeter, thereby enabling learners to promptly assess their comprehension of course material. In addition to that, these same social media channels also grant an opportunity for providing timely feedback and words of encouragement which promote continuous learning and improvement among students.

To summarize, the incorporation of social media into instructional design presents a multitude of advantages for both educators and students. Employing social media platforms as communication conduits and integrating them within learning activities facilitates personalized instruction implementation while enabling collaborative engagement among learners. Moreover, using these platforms in assessment yields valuable evaluative feedback which enhances overall effectiveness of the educational experience crafted by designers vested with such innovative prowess.

7.14.3 Case Studies: Enhancing Engagement through Social Media Integration

In contemporary times, the advent of digitization has necessitated an increased reliance on social media platforms for daily communication and information sharing. This phenomenon has positively impacted our connection with others in society, revolutionizing traditional practices significantly. As instructional designers have become cognizant of social media's potential to enhance engagement levels among learners, they are increasingly integrating such platforms into their design strategies. This subchapter serves to examine several case studies that demonstrate how effective this integration can be at elevating learner engagement during instructional activities through leveraging various aspects offered by social media channels.

The presented case study centers on augmenting instructional design with digital tools through the integration of social media platforms such as Facebook and Twitter. This is achieved by establishing unique discussion groups and hashtags, which facilitate learner engagement by enabling them to actively participate in discourse, share educational resources, and engage collaboratively with peers. The comprehensively analyzed case underscores how this interactive fusion not only stimulates active learning but also engenders a sense of community among learners.

A further examination revolves around the utilization of gamification in instructional design utilizing digital tools. Through incorporation of social media attributes like leaderboards and badges, reap rewards and publicize their accomplishments on diverse platforms of social media while partaking in learning activities. This case study serves as a testament illuminating that integration between gamification and social media is linked with notable enhancement towards learner motivation levels alongside engagement rates.

Furthermore, this subchapter delves into the notion of customized learning via digital tools incorporated in instructional design. Through utilization of social media platforms as a tool, instructional designers are empowered to create bespoke educational experiences that cater towards all learner's individualized requirements and inclinations. The case study exemplifies how integration with various social media outlets provides learners an avenue for accessing personalized content; acquire specific feedback on their performances along with connecting them to professionals aligned within their field of interest.

Moreover, this subsection endeavors to explore the application of interactive simulations and virtual reality within instructional design. By assimilating social media attributes, students can exchange their experiences, solicit critique and work collectively with peers in a live setting. The empirical study clearly illustrates how incorporation of social media facilitates heightened engagement levels among learners participating in simulations or utilizing virtual reality technology; consequently, leading towards an increased retention rate for acquired knowledge.

This subchapter delves into the role of mobile learning in instructional design using digital tools. The utilization of social media platforms enables learners to access educational resources at any time and from anywhere, subsequently encouraging their participation in collaborative activities alongside fellow students. The case study presented therein demonstrates how incorporating social media within mobile learning undertakings heightens learner engagement while simultaneously facilitating continuous education.

In summary, the integration of social media has demonstrated a remarkable impact on engagement levels within instructional design practices. Drawing from multiple case studies as evidence, this subsection underscores the efficacy of incorporating social media in transforming traditional models and fostering meaningful learning experiences. Valuable insights and practical examples are available within this subchapter for professionals such as instructional designers and academics specializing in fields like gamification, collaborative learning environments or mobile education who aim to enhance their understanding regarding advanced approaches to designing effective instruction programs that facilitate personalized interactive simulations with diverse audiences.

7.15 Video-Based Learning and Instructional Design Using Digital Tools

Utilizing digital tools to enhance instructional design, video-based learning is a contemporary approach to education. The proliferation of technology has made videos an efficacious medium for delivering educational content in an engaging and interactive manner. Educators can create high-quality videos that cater to various learning styles with the help of digital tools like animation programs, video editing software, and online platforms.

The prime advantage of video-based education is its potential to seize and detain learners' focus. As opposed to conventional text-centered resources, videos engage students by encompassing audiovisual effects that arouse multiple senses. By conveying information through a dynamic and captivating medium, videos facilitate the comprehension of intricate ideas, leading to longer retention periods. Moreover, digital platforms enable educators to incorporate interactive components like quizzes or discussion forums within the videos themselves; this boosts student participation while fostering communal learning environments.

To sum up, the integration of video-based learning and digital instructional design has transformed modern-day education. Its incorporation provides multiple ways of catering to diverse learning styles through an interactive multimedia experience that heightens student involvement. The advancement in technology suggests a growing significance for video-based teaching as it paves innovative paths towards delivering information effectively and enhancing educational outcomes.

7.15.1 The Power of Video-Based Learning in Instructional Design

The advent of video-based learning has significantly transformed the domain of instructional design, providing a potent means to captivate learners and augment their educational journey. Within this section, we will delve into the diverse avenues through which video-based learning can be leveraged in instructional design and appraise its advantages for optimizing the pedagogical process.

Video-based learning offers a significant advantage in its capacity to accommodate diverse learning styles. Especially relevant for visual learners, video content generates dynamic and captivating presentations of information that prove highly beneficial. By integrating multimedia elements, animations, and visuals into their designs, instructional designers can produce interactive and immersive educational experiences which captivate learners' attention while promoting comprehension as well as retention of the material at hand.

In addition, the utilization of video-based learning enables tailored and individualized educational experiences. Through digital resources, instructional designers are empowered to craft targeted videos that cater precisely to the unique needs and learning objectives of each learner. This customized methodology enhances involvement with course material while simultaneously affording learners opportunities to advance at their preferred pace and concentrate on facets in which additional support or challenge is required.

An additional influential application of video-based learning resides within the domain of simulations and virtual reality. Through a fusion between videos, interactive components and virtual environments, instructional designers can produce authentic yet engrossing educational experiences that enable learners to exercise abilities effectively while applying acquired knowledge in an environment characterized by safety and precision. This not only amplifies the educational process but also cultivates skill preparedness among learners for dilemmas encountered in realistic conditions outside academic settings.

Video-based learning proves to be effective in the realm of mobile education. As smartphones and tablets remain prevalent, individuals have ample access to video content whenever they desire or wherever their location may be. Such flexibility enables autonomous learning and permits learners individually engage with subject material hence promoting motivation and optimized educational results.

Additionally, the incorporation of social media platforms into instructional design has significant potential to augment learner engagement and collaboration. Videos can be effortlessly circulated among learners for discussion purposes which enhances community building capability fostering peer-to-peer learning experiences. By leveraging social media as a virtual toolset, instructional designers are empowered to devise interactive and collaborative-based educational programs that harness collective intelligence towards newfound knowledge acquisition opportunities.

To conclude, video-based learning presents significant potential in the realm of instructional design. Its capacity to accommodate diverse learning styles, furnish personalized instruction opportunities and foster engagement through facilitating collaboration renders it an invaluable resource for scholars practicing within this discipline. By harnessing the enormous capabilities inherent in video-based learning, instructional designers possess a means by which they can fashion highly impactful educational experiences that empower learners while advancing higher quality outcomes across all measurements of successful course completion.

7.15.2 Designing Effective Video-Based Learning Experiences

The employment of video-based learning in instructional design has gained significant traction owing to its capacity to captivate learners and deliver content that is dynamic. When created meticulously, video-based learning can be remarkably beneficial in fortifying knowledge retention and augmenting the general experience of education. This subchapter aims at delving into the fundamental principles and strategies required for fabricating efficacious video-based learning experiences.

An initial factor to consider when designing video-based learning experiences pertains to the duration of the videos. Researchers have established that shorter videos, generally spanning a maximum length of 10 minutes, are more conducive in terms of attracting and retaining learners' attention than lengthy ones; prolonged recordings can result in lower engagement levels and reduced capacity for knowledge absorption. Consequently, it is imperative to divide intricate concepts into smaller units that can be easily processed by students through short-sized clips.

One crucial consideration in creating video-based learning experiences is the effective utilization of visuals and graphics. Visuals play a vital role in fortifying conveyed information, rendering it more enduring for learners' memory retention. This can encompass diverse visual aids such as diagrams, charts, and animations to elaborate on significant concepts. Moreover, integrating subtitles and captions fostered accessibility for hearing-impaired individuals or those who prefer following along with text when viewing videos.

The inclusion of interactive elements is a critical component when developing efficacious video-based learning experiences. The integration of quizzes or knowledge checks, for instance, can serve to strengthen and solidify the acquisition of knowledge while also providing learners with real-time feedback on their comprehension. This approach not only fosters active participation in the learning process but equally facilitates reflective self-assessment amongst learners regarding their ability to grasp course material.

In video-based learning experiences, it is imperative to offer opportunities for contemplation and discourse. To this end, the implementation of discussion forums or chat features allows learners to partake in meaningful exchange and share valuable reflections with their fellow students. This approach towards collaborative learning promotes a sense of community whilst encouraging enhanced levels of comprehension.

Finally, it is crucial to ensure that the learning experiences delivered through videos are readily accessible across various devices and platforms. Given the proliferating usage of mobile gadgets, optimizing videos for effective delivery on such a platform has become essential in enhancing access to content by learners irrespective of time or location constraints.

To sum up, the creation of effective learning experiences focused on video necessitates a meticulous evaluation of various factors such as duration and format of visual materials utilized, interactivity, opportunities for introspection and discourse. By adhering to these prescribed principles and strategies experts can develop immersive educational interventions that augment instructional design while fostering positive outcomes in learners' academic progress.

7.15.3 Case Studies: Successful Implementation of Video-Based Learning in Instructional Design

Video-based learning is an influential instructional design technique that offers learners compelling and interactive content, augmenting their comprehension and retention of knowledge. Within this subchapter, numerous case studies are presented to emphasize the successful utilization of video-based learning in diverse educational environments, effectively showcasing its efficacy within these contexts.

In the initial case study, a cohort of academics employed video-based learning to advance instructional design incorporating digital tools. They produced a sequence of educational videos that incorporated animations and graphics as an aid in visually expounding intricate concepts. The outcomes demonstrated marked progressions in both student engagement and comprehension, affirming the efficacy of videotape training on enriching instructional design.

A further investigation was conducted on the incorporation of gamification in instructional design through digital tools. The academic researchers developed interactive videos that included game-infused components like quizzes and challenges to encourage engagement among learners for enhanced active participation. Findings indicated a heightened degree of learner motivation and improved knowledge retention, thus verifying the effectiveness of video-based learning within gamified instructionally designed environments.

The primary subject of the third case study was personalized learning through digital tools. Learned scholars devised video-based modules, which enabled learners to tailor their individualized learning experience in accordance with their specific needs and preferences. The research revealed that video-based instruction helps foster a more customized approach to education, catering adeptly towards variegated styles of learning while simultaneously resulting in superior educational outcomes.

In an additional case inquiry, the scholars investigated the utilization of interactive simulations and virtual reality within instructional design. They created immersive video-based simulations to provide learners with real-life situations that encouraged problem-solving skill development. The research exhibited a notable enhancement in learner engagement along with improved performance on practical tasks; underscoring the potential effectiveness of implementing video-based learning as platforms for authentic educational experiences.

The following case study focuses predominantly on the concept of mobile learning. Scholars formulated a series of video-based educational modules that were intentionally designed for accessibility through various mobile devices, empowering learners with round-the-clock academic resources and enduring pedagogical experiences. The research findings unveiled an upsurge in learner accessibilities alongside enhanced flexibility within this inventive approach to instructional design via mobile technology- further highlighting the categorical advantages offered exclusively by utilization of video-spawned interactive techniques whilst devising such courses.

The aforementioned subchapter explores the utilization of social media in instructional design to promote heightened engagement. Through scholarly investigation, it was revealed that video-based learning can be amplified by integrating various social media platforms, which facilitate collaboration and interaction amongst students. Furthermore, a case study illustrated how video-based learning has the potential to establish an interactive and communal educational environment.

Moreover, a case study investigated the application of data-driven instructional design through digital tools. Scholars employed video-based learning and integrated data analytics to comprehensively scrutinize learner performance towards tailoring instruction accordingly. The outcomes presented an enhanced level of educational attainment achieved via personalized and meticulous approaches rooted in data-driven instructional principles.

The subchapter further elaborates on the integration of augmented reality in instructional design to facilitate immersive learning experiences. Academics have devised video-based modules that leverage augmented reality technology to offer learners interactive and lifelike educational sessions. A case study was conducted highlighting how such an approach can effectively engender engaging and pedagogically robust content for education purposes.

A different case study was conducted to investigate adaptive learning platforms and instructional design leveraging digital tools. The scholars implemented a combination of video-based learning and adaptive learning platforms to deliver tailored instruction to learners. The outcomes demonstrated the advantages of incorporating video-based learning into an adaptive instructional approach, leading to enhanced learner performance.

The final segment of the chapter is centered on collaborative learning and instructional design employing digital tools. Academicians have investigated strategies for harnessing video-based instruction to establish interactive, peer-to-peer learning modalities that foster knowledge exchange among learners.

The case study reveals conclusive evidence suggesting that leveraging such an approach not only stimulates better collaboration but also enhances student engagement levels significantly.

In summary, this subchapter presents a collection of case studies that demonstrate the triumphant utilization of video-based learning in instructional design. The broad spectrum of investigations highlights the potency of incorporating digital tools like video-based learning to augment instructional design and fulfill specific scholarly needs while addressing diverse niches inherent within such training frameworks.

CHAPTER 8

Data-Driven Teaching with Digital Tools

In today's digital age, collecting, analyzing, and utilizing data has become an essential part of effective teaching practices. The practice of data-driven teaching with digital tools involves the utilization of technology to acquire, scrutinize, and decipher information for educational purposes. This methodology enables educators to make carefully considered decisions about their pedagogical techniques as well as ascertain the outcomes achieved by students in learning activities. Through the implementation of online evaluations or e-learning systems accompanied by other suitable technological instruments, instructors can instantly obtain statistical facts on student advancement and academic accomplishment. Such findings facilitate personalization in instructional delivery that caters uniquely towards each learner's distinctive demands while also availing channels for identifying growth opportunities and enhancing overall development among all students alike. One of the primary advantages associated with data-driven teaching utilizing digital tools is its ability to offer educators a comprehensive grasp on their students' skillsets and challenges. Conventional assessment techniques often furnish restricted insights into student learning, whereas digital technologies allow for thorough analysis of individual performance. A prime example being online quizzes or assignments whereby evaluation results provide teachers an opportunity to decipher where pupils are struggling regarding specific concepts or skills so that modifications can be made accordingly in instruction delivery. Moreover, these resources function as real-time feedback mechanisms allowing learners to cogitate over areas needing improvement and take ownerships towards enhancing their education themselves actively. Ultimately adopting this approach reinforces both instructors' & scholars' confidence while making informed decisions based upon empirical evidence promoting academic growth inevitably without ambiguity thereof. This chapter delves into how educators can harness digital tools to enhance their teaching strategies through a data-driven approach.

8.1 Understanding the Role of Data in Education

In the current era of digitalization, data plays a significant role in diverse industries including education. The emergence and accessibility of ample digital tools and technologies allow educators to collect and evaluate extensive amounts of information to augment their teaching methodologies as well as enhance student achievements. The primary objective behind this subchapter is to furnish teachers with an all-inclusive perspective on how data can contribute towards revolutionizing their pedagogical approaches in educational settings.

The utilization of digital tools in data-driven teaching is a robust methodology that empowers educators to make evidence-based and real-time informed decisions. Through the gathering of student performance, participation, and assimilation style data, teachers are equipped with effective means for personalized instruction tailored towards individualized student necessities. The potency of this technique is especially observable within STEM disciplines wherein analysis instruments can pinpoint areas requiring sustained improvement or reinforcement allowing instructors to apply interventions constructively.

The utilization of data analysis tools for personalized learning is an essential component of teaching driven by data. Such instruments enable educators to monitor students' progress, pinpoint their weaknesses and provide prompt feedback. By harnessing the power of information, teachers can design individualized educational strategies that cater to each student's distinct style, rate-of-pace as well as interests in order to yield favorable outcomes coupled with heightened involvement from students.

In addition, data-driven evaluation and response are integral components of education. Conventional methods for assessment frequently furnish a restricted understanding of students' comprehension and advancement. Yet, through the utilization of digital resources, educators can compile information on student achievement to recognize trends and provide expedient feedback that enhances learning outcomes. This methodology not only enables learners to comprehend their competencies alongside areas requiring further attention but also informs instructors' pedagogical tactics.

Data visualization tools serve as valuable resources for educators, enabling the presentation of intricate data in a visually captivating and easily comprehensible format. Integration of these tools into classroom instruction enables teachers to encourage students' engagement in activities such as data analysis, building critical thinking skills while facilitating enhanced comprehension of key concepts.

Furthermore, employing data-driven methodologies provides an avenue for customizing instruction to suit students with unique educational requirements. Thoroughly evaluating individual student progress and learning preferences enables instructors to tailor their instructional approaches in a manner that accommodates diverse academic necessities, thereby guaranteeing equal opportunities for every learner's success.

Furthermore, instructional methodologies based on data analysis have the potential to enhance student engagement and bolster their motivation. Through exploitation of advanced analytics techniques, educators can apprehend determinants that essentially promote pupil disinterest; subsequently adopting a focused strategy for rekindling learner participation. Such an approach culminates in establishing an encouraging milieu aptly suited to fostering educational growth consequently resulting in better academic accomplishments by pupils.

Finally, leveraging data-driven education yields not only advantages for individual classrooms but also for scientific inquiry and examination in the field of academia. Through comprehensive gathering and analysis on a grander scale, experts can accurately identify prevalent patterns, appraise pedagogical methods' efficiency as well as mold educational doctrines and improvements accordingly.

In conclusion, comprehension of the significance of data in education is paramount for educators endeavoring to elevate their pedagogical techniques and ameliorate academic achievements among students. By embracing data-centric teaching approaches along with digital tools as learning aids, teachers can customize instructional processes, provide focused interventions tailored according to student-specific requirements, facilitate better engagement levels amongst learners while also contributing towards educational research and analysis endeavors.

8.2 Benefits of Data-Driven Teaching

In the present era of digital technology, there has been an upsurge in the widespread employment of data-driven pedagogical approaches within global classrooms. Educators have come to appreciate the myriad benefits that arise from leveraging data resources for refining and augmenting their instructional methodologies. This section delves into a thorough examination of diverse advantages attributable to data-informed teaching paradigms as well as how digitized tools could exponentially reform education standards through such methods.

Data-driven teaching presents a vital advantage of enabling the customization of learning for students. Through meticulous analysis and evaluation of student performance data, teachers can identify individual areas requiring improvement or that exhibit exceptional strength, facilitating tailored instructions to fulfill unique requirements in each pupil effectively. This personalized approach enhances students' progress at their own pace while ultimately culminating into improved academic outcomes.

Data analysis tools play a pivotal role in data-based instruction, particularly with regards to STEM subjects. Such instruments empower teachers to collate and scrutinize voluminous amounts of information, thereby facilitating comprehension of learners' progress as well as highlighting patterns and trends. Utilizing this knowledge base, educators can effectuate informed determinations about course structuring methods, pedagogical approaches and allocation of resources- ultimately guaranteeing that students reap optimal benefits from an immersive educational experience imbued with efficacy.

Moreover, data-driven assessment and feedback have demonstrated their efficacy as potent instruments in the realm of education. Through the implementation of data-based evaluation techniques to appraise student progress, educators can discern areas warranting attention that require advancement while furnishing personalized criticism that is definitive and practical. Such prompt assessments empower pupils with insight into both their strengths and weaknesses, thereby enabling them to assume responsibility for their intellectual growth by making adequate alterations to enhance academic performance levels.

The presence of digital tools in the classroom has contributed to an improvement in data visualization, consequently promoting more accessible and engaging comprehension for students regarding intricate concepts. Through visually pleasing mediums such as graphs and charts, educators can augment pupil's understanding while encouraging connections between various data points. This display assists with developing vital cognitive skills including critical thinking abilities necessary within current society's dependency on information interpretation.

Data-informed pedagogical methods are not confined solely to mainstream educational settings; they can also prove efficacious in benefiting students with special needs. By carefully scrutinizing data pertaining to the personalized learning goals and academic progress of each student, educators may generate contemporary methodologies that address their specific requirements. This approach guarantees equitable support for every student's individualized path toward academic success, irrespective of inherent aptitudes or impairments.

Furthermore, the incorporation of data-driven teaching methodology possesses a significant capability to enhance student engagement and motivation in educational processes. Through timely provision of feedback as well as progress reports, educators can successfully cultivate accountability and ownership among students regarding their own learning experiences. Consequently, this leads to increased motivation levels amongst pupils who are inspired to take an active role within their academic pursuits whilst striving towards continual development and improvement.

Furthermore, the implementation of data analytics can facilitate the monitoring and enhancement of student progress over an extended period. The analysis of longitudinal datasets enables educators to identify prevalent patterns and trends in academic performance, enabling them to take informed decisions on interventions and teaching methods. This preemptive approach towards tracking student progress guarantees timely support is provided when necessary whilst simultaneously mitigating any exacerbation or widening of educational disparities among learners.

Data-driven education goes beyond the classroom context and can extend to educational research as well as analysis. Extensive datasets serve useful insights for researchers, unveiling prevalent trends within the field while identifying areas that require attention by informing policymaking decisions. Adopting such a data-centric approach guarantees evidence-based teaching methods that continuously adjust and evolve in response to students' changing requirements. To conclude, data-supported pedagogy utilizing digital tools provides a plethora of advantages to educators and scholars. The application of data-driven instructional techniques has the potential to transform education by facilitating customized learning and augmenting assessment procedures through enhanced feedback mechanisms. By leveraging the power vested in analytics and metrics, instructors can optimize their teaching practices resulting in amplified academic achievements for learners, thereby establishing more effective educational settings that are both interesting as well as stimulating.

8.3 Challenges and Limitations of Data-Driven Teaching

The challenges and limitations inherent in employing data-driven teaching strategies are a topic of significant professional interest. Such an approach relies upon the use of collected information to shape instruction, but consistently encountering obstacles presents concerns for educators seeking optimal student outcomes. Thus, it is imperative that these difficulties be thoroughly examined and addressed within the context of classroom practice in order to achieve success with this methodological framework.

In the swiftly advancing domain of education, data-driven pedagogy has come forth as a potent mechanism to transform teachers' approaches towards instruction. Employing digital apparatuses and techniques for scrutinizing data renders educators with useful insights regarding student learning styles that permit personalized ways of teaching. This approach contributes significantly in fostering enhanced levels of engagement and accomplishment amongst students holistically. Yet, despite its manifold benefits, leveraging on structured analytical processes vis-a-vis educational datasets retails various difficulties presenting salient concerns related to which instructors must exercise cognizance commensurate with their professional responsibilities.

One of the foremost obstacles in implementing data-driven instruction is associated with obtaining adequate and accurate information. Teachers frequently confront complexity gaining access to pertinent student performance indicators that are both timely and refined. This challenge may stem from insufficiencies within restricted resources, inadequate management infrastructure for collecting or processing data concerning a students' progress, insufficiently integrated technological platforms designed specifically for education purposes amongst others reasons. Within this context, unreliable instructional inputs could hinder teachers' ability to design informed decisions regarding any necessary modifications of teaching approaches needed tailored individually towards specific learners-group sequences.

Moreover, the implementation of data-driven teaching necessitates that educators possess a robust comprehension in data analysis tools and techniques. However, several instructors may not have obtained adequate training to interpret and employ these insights effectively. Besides this challenge, continuous advancements in technology and subsequent developments in analytical approaches emphasize the need for teachers to regularly update their skill set maintaining current applicability within this rapidly changing educational landscape.

One additional constraint of data-focused teaching approach is the likelihood for excessive dependence on data to detrimentally impact other critical factors. Although information derived from data can furnish useful understandings, it must not exclusively dictate instructional determinations. Educators are required to contemplate other facets like students' level of motivation, social and emotional welfare as well as their individual learning preferences when establishing instructional methodologies. Failure to consider these aspects may lead educators towards a narrow-minded outlook that caters only the generalization at the expense of recognizing each student's distinct needs and capabilities.

Furthermore, the implementation of data-driven teaching methodologies may encounter opposition from instructors who harbor reservations regarding its efficiency or possible manipulation of information. It is vital to acknowledge these concerns and equip teachers with adequate resources and instruction necessary for the adoption of data-informed pedagogy. The cultivation of a climate built upon mutual confidence and cooperation remains paramount in guaranteeing that student outcomes are enhanced through ethical utilization of collected data.

As a final point, it is important to acknowledge that although the utilization of data-driven teaching methods presents invaluable possibilities for revolutionizing education, there exist certain obstacles and constraints which must be considered. Amongst these concerns are matters concerning access to reliable and coherent data sets as well as proficiency in interpreting such information. Moreover, excessive dependence on collected statistics may represent an additional challenge alongside resistance towards adopting innovative approaches within educational systems. By comprehensively assessing these issues at hand and aptly responding through applicable measures, educators can effectively draw upon the advantages inherent in incorporating empirical insights into pedagogical practices thereby facilitating progress toward meaningful scholastic outcomes for learners.

8.4 Data-Driven Teaching Methods for STEM Subjects

The utilization of data-driven teaching techniques for science, technology, engineering, and mathematics (STEM) subjects has been deemed a potent tool in education. These methods enable the analysis of students' performance results to inform educational decisions effectively. This approach allows educators to identify knowledge gaps easily and adjust their pedagogical strategies accordingly by altering lesson plans or employing alternative instructional approaches when necessary. Consequently, individualized instruction is tailored towards each student's needs leading to enhanced academic outcomes promoting an advanced grasp on topics taught within these areas of study.

In addition, the implementation of data-driven teaching approaches enables educators to conduct ongoing assessment and evaluation of student progress. Through interactive assessments such as quizzes, tests, and assignments in real-time settings, teachers can consistently monitor individual performance throughout the learning process. This helps them trace developmental growth over time while also recognizing trends or patterns in educational outcomes. Equipped with this critical information at an early stage allows for timely recognition of underperformance or reduced engagement among students on specific topics which offers opportunities for targeted intervention by instructors. Moreover, data-driven methodology encourages accountability amongst learners through enabling self-reflection leading students towards acceptance of responsibility regarding their own development journey. By incorporating a data-oriented instructional approach into STEM education curriculum, personalization customizes study experiences cultivating vital skills including scientific experimentation and cognitive processing necessary ingredients required by 21st century global citizens ready to contribute positively towards socio-economic advancements within human civilization.

8.4.1 Implementing Data-Driven Approaches in Science Education

In recent times, the utilization of data-driven approaches has significantly transformed the domain of education by equipping instructors with robust resources to augment student learning and accomplishments. The ensuing segment delves into an investigation of how data-driven methods can be implemented within science education. It is imperative for educators to embrace these techniques actively and leverage digital tools proficiently towards establishing a more immersive educational environment tailored specifically to meet their students' personalized learning needs.

Data-driven pedagogy offers a significant advantage for instructing STEM disciplines, especially science. It enables data analysis tools to customize teaching methods actively that foster personalized learning experiences by collecting and scrutinizing student progress indicators. Such an approach benefits greatly from recognizing students' individual strengths and limitations, thereby permitting targeted interventions directed towards efficacious academic outcomes while simultaneously improving overall learner engagement levels as well as motivation to succeed in these fields of study.

The utilization of digital tools for data visualization in the classroom is an additional critical component within data-driven teaching. Visual depictions of information can prove exceedingly influential when it comes to aiding students' understanding of intricate scientific concepts and processes. By employing interactive graphs, charts, and simulations, instructors may furnish pupils with a more engaging learning experience that fosters enhanced comprehension and better retention rates regarding fundamental scientific principles.

Moreover, data-driven methodologies can prove to be particularly advantageous for students with exceptional learning requirements. By compiling and scrutinizing academic information pertaining to these pupils' advancement and cognitive trends, educators can devise custom-made curricula that cater precisely to their distinct necessities. This customized modus operandi has the potential of drastically enhancing their educational accomplishments whilst simultaneously augmenting their overall scholarly journey.

In the sphere of science education, data-driven evaluation and feedback assume a critical function. Employing analytical tools to monitor student advancement enables instructors to furnish prompt and specific advice that can steer students towards improvement and expansion. Furthermore, data analytics assists in recognizing trends pertaining to misconceptions or cognitive lacunae amongst pupils; this potentially valuable information empowers teachers with the ability to address these problem areas more effectively.

Ultimately, data-oriented teaching methods serve as a crucial factor in educational investigation and analysis. Through the collection and scrutiny of extensive sets of data, analysts can acquire invaluable perspectives on the efficacy of varying instructional approaches and measures undertaken. Such observations could subsequently inform policies firmly grounded upon evidence-based standards aimed to enhance pedagogical practices holistically.

To summarize, the adoption of data-driven methodologies in science education holds great promise to transform pedagogical practices. Through utilization of digital resources for tasks such as scrutinizing and visualizing data, evaluating performance levels, offering assessments and furnishing feedback; instructors are well-positioned to craft more bespoke learning experiences that captivate students' interests effectively. This section delves into diverse data-based approaches while imparting pragmatic guidance aimed at enhancing educators' capacity for providing exemplary scientific instruction along with betterment of learners' outcomes.

8.4.2 Utilizing Data Analysis Tools in Mathematics Instruction

In the present era of digital technology, incorporating data analysis tools within mathematics instruction has emerged as a significant aspect. These aids not only elevate the quality of teaching and learning but also furnish critical facts related to student performance and advancement. Adopting pedagogical techniques guided by empirical evidence can transform conventional methods employed in math education and ultimately augment learners' achievements.

One of the significant advantages associated with employing analytical instruments in teaching mathematics is its capacity to provide customized learning. Such tools facilitate educators' ability to collect and analyze real-time data on individual students' academic performance, enabling them to pinpoint areas where learners excel or struggle. Accessing such insights allows teachers to customize instruction for each student according to specific needs, providing tailored interventions as required. This personalized approach ensures that pupils receive appropriate levels of support and challenge which thereby enhances their educational outcomes considerably.

The implementation of data-driven evaluation and feedback mechanisms is a fundamental requirement for efficient math instruction. The utilization of analysis tools enables educators to promptly appraise student comprehension levels, discern errors in understanding and take corrective actions as required. This process facilitates the provision of specific advice aimed at aiding students' remediation activities leading towards an improved grasp on mathematics concepts. Additionally, such instruments offer instructors a panoramic insight into learners' progress; serving as helpful resources in making informed instructional choices while also monitoring academic growth over time.

Data analysis tools can serve a dual purpose in the classroom, not only for assessment but also for data visualization. Leveraging visual representations of mathematical concepts has been demonstrated to improve comprehension and attentiveness among students, thereby increasing accessibility to complex topics. From graphing functions and examining geometric transformations to evaluating statistical information, these interactive and dynamic resources offer an animated approach that breathes life into mathematical education.

Moreover, incorporating data-driven methodologies in mathematics education can facilitate customized instruction. By meticulously scrutinizing student information, educators can pinpoint personalized learning profiles and accordingly tailor their modes of pedagogy. Employing techniques such as small group mentoring sessions or tailored coursework through individualized assignments or alternative educational paths is rendered less intricate with the aid of advanced data analysis tools that guarantee a comprehensive approach towards catering for each scholar's distinct needs whilst avoiding any instances of underachievement by providing equitable opportunities for all students to excel academically.

The implementation of pedagogical techniques informed by data analysis is particularly advantageous for students receiving special education services.

Through the utilization of quantitative measures detailing their aptitudes and difficulties, educators can formulate bespoke interventions and accommodations to best serve these pupils' educational needs. The tailored approach grants exceptional learners an improved opportunity to surmount obstacles encountered in mathematical instruction and realize accomplishments commensurate with peers not requiring such specialized instruction.

Furthermore, the incorporation of data analytics has the potential to enhance student engagement and motivation within academic contexts. Through offering students immediate feedback on their progression, these resources empower learners to assume responsibility for their education. Additionally, gamification components like leaderboards and badges present an opportunity to incentivize student participation whilst cultivating a supportive learning milieu.

The adoption of data-driven teaching techniques bears advantages not singularly to pupils but extends also towards educational research and analysis. Through the collection and investigation of instructional practices alongside student results, scholars can pinpoint successful pedagogical strategies in addition to informing education through evidence-based decision making.

To sum up, the integration of data analysis tools in mathematics education carries significant potential for educational transformation. With features like customized learning experiences, prompt evaluation and feedback mechanisms, visualization aids for mathematical concepts, individualized instruction methodologies that cater to diverse student needs alongside improved engagement levels; these sophisticated technologies can significantly enhance both teaching and learning processes. Additionally, the implementation of data-driven approaches may prove advantageous towards special needs learners as well as foster scientific research on educative practices while adequately elevating students' academic achievement rates within the domain of Mathematics. Thus by wholeheartedly embracing digital facilitations into their pedagogical blueprint educators are warranted an opportunity to unlock a wide array availed through insights offered by inclusive studies based upon empirical evidence; thus revolutionizing traditional classroom methods pertaining exclusively to mathematics instructions.

8.4.3 Enhancing Technology Integration in Engineering and Technology Classes

In the current era of rapid progress, technology has assumed a central role in human existence. From handheld devices to autonomous vehicles, technological innovations have revolutionized numerous domains such as education. Particularly within engineering and technology specializations, it is imperative for educators to incorporate technological solutions into their teaching methods so that students are adequately equipped with relevant skills and knowledge necessary to navigate through the complex digital landscape they will encounter in future endeavors.

The integration of technology in engineering and technology courses surpasses the mere utilization of digital tools and resources. It encompasses incorporating technological aspects into the syllabus that enhance pedagogy, facilitate critical thinking, and foster creativity among learners. The objective of this subchapter is to furnish teachers with pragmatic knowledge on how they can promote augmented levels of technology fusion within their classroom settings.

An optimal means of elevating technology integration is through the implementation of data-driven instructional strategies. Utilizing digital resources and analytical techniques, educators can acquire advantageous perspectives concerning student academic progress while pinpointing areas that may require further development - experience leading to custom-tailored instruction accommodating individual needs for each learner. Such an approach enables students to achieve superior educational outcomes and affords educators with foundations upon which they can make well-informed decisions in refining their pedagogical practices based on gathered empirical evidence thereof.

In addition, leveraging data analysis tools to cater personalized learning can yield substantial advantages for engineering and technology courses. These instruments enable instructors to monitor students' advancement, ascertain their aptitudes and inadequacies, and deliver individualized feedback. Through data analysis techniques, educators have the capacity of customizing lesson delivery in line with each student's distinct requirements that fosters an enhanced educational experience empower a more tailored approach towards teaching which consequently enhances efficacy in instructionally catering every learner's unique needs leading towards a refined pedagogical involvement as well as outcomes.

Furthermore, technology has the potential to facilitate data visualization within academic settings. The implementation of digital tools for this purpose can allow educators to effectively communicate intricate engineering and technological ideas in an engaging and comprehensible manner. Through visual depictions of information, students are better equipped to comprehend abstract concepts, establish correlations between different notions, as well as attain a more profound comprehension of course material.

Furthermore, the integration of technology has remarkable potential to fortify differentiated instruction methodologies within engineering and technology courses. By adopting data-driven teaching techniques, educators can identify personalized learning styles, preferences and requirements tailored specifically towards students with special educational needs effectively addressing individualized challenges in a comprehensive approach that ensures equal opportunities for academic success among all sets of pupils regardless their capacity levels.

Finally, technology can be utilized to enhance student engagement and motivation. Through the integration of interactive digital tools, gamified learning experiences, as well as real-world applications relevant to engineering and technological concepts, educators possess the means of fashioning a more comprehensive and stimulating educational setting. This method stimulates curiosity amongst students while nurturing their creativity by instilling an eagerness for the topic at hand.

To conclude, the integration of technology into engineering and technology classes is imperative for adequately equipping students with necessary skills in this digital era. Educators can facilitate an optimal learning process by adopting data-driven teaching methodologies, leveraging personalized learning through advanced data analysis tools, implementing differentiated instruction tactics to tailor lessons suited to individual student requirements while utilizing effective techniques for visualization that promote engagement and motivation among learners. These combined efforts yield a dynamic classroom environment where students are empowered towards becoming proficient engineers or technologists prepared to succeed in future careers.

8.5 Using Data Analysis Tools for Personalized Learning

In the dynamic milieu of education, personalized learning has emerged as a potent instrument for augmenting student engagement and academic accomplishment. Proficient comprehension of the description and significance of personalized learning is imperative for educators since it holds transformative potential in delivering education to meet heterogeneous student needs.

Personalized learning pertains to an instructional methodology that customizes teaching and learning engagements accordingly based on the distinctive requirements, preferences, and aptitudes of each student. It acknowledges individual differences among students as regards their preferred modes of learning, areas of strength or challenge. Embracing personalized learning enables educators to establish a more inclusive classroom atmosphere with a focus on empowering each student individually.

The significance of personalized learning cannot be overstressed. Primarily, it facilitates a more profound comprehension and proficiency in fundamental concepts. Through individualized instruction, students can advance at their own preferred pace while receiving tailored assistance when necessary. This customized methodology guarantees mastery and internalization of critical ideas before progressing to other topics, culminating in enhanced academic achievements.

Additionally, individualized learning fosters student engagement and motivation. To caters the specific needs and interests of each learner, there is an increased likelihood that they will actively participate in their educational pursuits. As a result, students are more inclined to take ownership of their academic progress which contributes to elevated levels of motivation throughout the learning process.

Moreover, customized education boosts the acquisition of imperative 21st-century competencies. Through customizing pedagogy to suit individual students' needs, instructors can furnish occasions for autonomous learning, troubleshooting capabilities, and collaborative as well as creative thinking. These aptitudes are indispensably crucial for triumph in the digital era where flexibility and inventiveness hold weighty significance.

Finally, personalized learning facilitates the integration of students with varied learning needs. By utilizing digital resources and evidence-based methods, educators can ascertain and attend to individualized disparities in knowledge acquisition through tailored interventions and reinforcement. This technique is particularly advantageous for those who require special educational provisions since it guarantees that their singular prerequisites will be accounted for comprehensively and efficiently.

As educators, we must embrace and leverage the potential of personalized learning. Employing data-informed pedagogical approaches and technological resources, we can cultivate a classroom ambiance tailored to individual learners' distinct requirements. This practice will enhance their engagement levels while cultivating motivation as well as promoting critical 21st-century skill acquisition. Personalized education offers an opportunity for transformative change empowering students to realize their highest potential in academic pursuits effectively.

8.5.1 Leveraging Data Analysis Tools to Tailor Instruction

Within the current era of digitization, there has been a marked rise in the utilization of data analysis tools pertaining to education. A wide spectrum of information is presently accessible by educators that can render crucial insights into student performance and learning patterns. This subchapter delves into "Leveraging Data Analysis Tools to Tailor Instruction" and expounds upon how teachers may avail themselves of these resources for improved personalization and enhancement their pedagogical methodologies.

The utilization of digital tools in data-driven instruction has brought about a revolutionizing impact on education. With the application of statistical analysis to student performance metrics, educators can obtain concrete evidence that informs responsive teaching practices tailored towards specific areas where students may require additional support or challenging activities depending on their strengths. In STEM-based subjects, such analytical instruments furnish teachers with an insightful comprehension into learners' problem-solving capabilities and inform the creation and implementation of targeted lesson plans as well as instructional materials designed to mitigate potential learning gaps which could hinder optimal academic outcomes for each learner.

One of the notable advantages of employing data analysis tools for personalized learning is its capability to offer tailored feedback. By scrutinizing student data, educators can determine areas that require improvement and deliver timely guidance towards academic development. This specific form of feedback does not only aid in comprehending one's strengths and weaknesses but also promotes eagerness amongst students to enhance their performance.

Data visualization tools play a pivotal role in the classroom by rendering intricate data more obtainable and captivating for students. Through presenting data via charts, diagrams, and infographics, educators can aid pupils' comprehension of information while enhancing their analytical faculties and fortifying critical thinking skills. Consequently, this approach advances not just scholars' literacy regarding data but also supports lasting intellectual growth within multiple academic domains as well.

Data analysis tools can prove to be highly efficacious in the implementation of differentiated instruction. A thorough examination and evaluation of student data enables teachers to isolate individual learning requirements, thereby facilitating the amendment and tailoring of their teaching methods accordingly. This technique affords a personalized educational experience that ensures students receive adequate support geared toward their attainment of academic success.

The application of data-driven teaching techniques can prove beneficial for students receiving special education. Through the analysis of relevant data, educators can pinpoint specific domains that require improvement and personalize instructional strategies accordingly. This methodology serves to empower such learners towards realizing their maximum academic potential and attaining success in their studies.

In addition, the utilization of data analysis tools may enhance student engagement and motivation. Effective tracking of students' academic progress coupled with prompt feedback provision creates a sense of responsibility within learners, thereby promoting ownership in their learning processes. The adoption of this meticulous practice fosters a growth-oriented mindset that inspires consistent betterment among students through continuous improvement initiatives.

To summarize, data analysis tools hold significant promise for customizing instruction to cater to the varied requirements of contemporary learners. By utilizing such tools, educators can personalize their instructional techniques and offer well-directed feedback while enhancing student participation and dedication. The application of data-driven approaches in pedagogical practices is transforming education as we know it by empowering academic advancement across STEM disciplines, special needs domains as well as general curriculum settings.

8.5.2 Strategies for Implementing Personalized Learning with Data Analysis Tools

Amid the dynamically evolving educational environment nowadays, educators are persistently searching for pioneering techniques to captivate and reinforce their pupils. A potent method that has emerged is personalized learning that caters to student requirements and interests on an individual basis. Utilizing tools for data analysis allows teachers access to crucial revelations into learner achievement, inclinations, as well as advancement progress; thus providing them with opportunities to design tailored learning experiences fostering improved comprehension levels and engrossment of learners. This subchapter delves into pragmatic approaches of implementing customized instruction through utilization of analytical instruments empowering instructors towards a transformative impact in the classroom setting or education sector at large.

An imperative tactic involves utilizing data analysis tools to identify the specific requirements and inclinations of individual students. Through acquisition and scrutiny of student performance metrics, educators can obtain a holistic comprehension of each pupil's aptitudes, deficiencies, as well as learning predilections. Subsequently, this information can be utilized to customize instructions as well resources exclusively catering towards fulfilling each scholar's distinct necessities thereby facilitating an individually tailored education that is conducive for effective learning outcomes.

A crucial approach in education is utilizing data analysis tools for persistent evaluation and feedback purposes. Through consistent collection and examination of student progress information, educators can furnish timely and personalized advice that facilitates students' comprehension of their areas of strength as well as the ones requiring further improvement. Consequently, this constructive assessment can guide subsequent instructions while also ensuring perpetual challenges along with efficient support provision throughout each student's learning process.

Moreover, the application of data analysis tools can effectively facilitate the monitoring and enhancement of student engagement and motivation. Teachers are able to track variables such as task time duration, participation percentages, and interest levels in order to recognize obstacles inhibiting active involvement; this subsequently allows for targeted intervention-based initiatives aimed at augmenting motivation and facilitating learning immersion among students.

Moreover, data analysis tools can facilitate differentiated instruction by imparting valuable insights about individual students' readiness levels, learning styles and preferences to educators. With this knowledge at hand, teachers can design and implement instructional strategies that cater to each student's distinctive requirements with utmost efficacy. This helps in guaranteeing the holistic development of every learner without any exception.

Finally, the implementation of data-driven teaching methodologies can prove advantageous for students enrolled in special education programs. Through utilization of analytical tools to monitor academic progress and pinpoint areas requiring greater attention, educators are empowered with customizable instructional strategies tailored specifically toward individual needs resulting in more efficient and comprehensive instruction inclusive to all learners involved.

To summarize, the incorporation of personalized learning utilizing data analysis tools offers educators potent techniques to transform education within their classrooms. By utilizing apparatuses as a means to gain comprehension on student necessities, offer tailored remarks and enrichment activities, stimulate involvement and incentive enhancement protocols in addition providing differentiated pedagogy; not excluding support for students within specialized education programs- teachers are able to administer truly bespoke educational experiences that cater towards the unique requirements/specificities affecting each particular pupil. Engaging with data-oriented teaching strategies enables tutors access full efficacy yielded from digital resources which will enhance academic achievements thus shaping forthcoming trends impacting academia indefinitely.

8.6 Data-Driven Assessment and Feedback in Education

Assessment is a pivotal component in the realm of education, as it aids educators in comprehending their students' advancement and discerning areas that necessitate enhancement. In modern times, data has emerged as an instrumental instrument within assessment practice, significantly transforming how instructors gauge student progress. By utilizing data-centered pedagogical approaches, teachers can yield informative perspectives into individual learning requirements whilst furnishing tailored guidance which facilitates academic development.

The integration of digital tools into STEM education has initiated a paradigm shift in teaching methodologies and assessment practices. With the aid of data analysis technology, educators can amass voluminous amounts of information regarding their pupils' academic performance to extrapolate useful trends and patterns which may have otherwise remained undetected. This allows for an individualized pedagogical approach conducive to personalized instruction targeting specific shortcomings or advanced subject matter suitable for gifted learners.

Data-driven assessment offers a significant advantage in providing personalized feedback to students. With the aid of digital tools, educators can track student progress in real-time and deliver prompt feedback that assists them in recognizing their strengths and areas for development. This form of tailored feedback has the potential to improve learning outcomes as it enables learners to make necessary modifications while aiming for continued improvement.

In addition to individualized feedback, data-driven instruction also employs tools of visualization in order to enrich the classroom experience. By graphically representing relevant information and insights, instructors are able to foster a more dynamic and purposeful educational interaction that enables abstract notions readily accessible for pupils. For instance, diagrams or charts serve as illustrative devices demonstrating trends and patterns effectively aiding students' comprehension of intricate concepts with ease."

The application of data-driven teaching methodologies is applicable not only to conventional learning settings but also holds relevance in catering to the education needs of individuals with special educational requirements. Analyzing pertinent statistical insights pertaining to students' progress and their unique demands, educators can devise individualized lesson plans that essentially cater towards addressing their distinct academic requisites. Such an informed approach guarantees access for special education students towards essential resources and support mechanisms vital for optimal scholastic outcomes.

In addition, empirical evidence suggests that utilizing data-driven teaching methodologies can enhance student engagement and motivation. Through employing techniques in data analytics to observe students' academic advancement, instructors may detect any disengagement or difficulty within specific subject matters. By proactively addressing these concerns through prompt interventions and necessary support measures provided by educators, students can be re-engaged with the educational material while being motivated towards their ultimate achievement of learning objectives.

The incorporation of data-driven teaching methodologies extends beyond the classroom setting and holds significant implications for educational research and analysis. Through analytical examination of vast volumes of information, researchers can glean critical insights into the efficacy levels associated with various pedagogical practices while concurrently singling out areas in need of improvement. Leveraging this unparalleled approach to academic inquiry facilitates a continuous refinement process that fosters optimal instructional techniques resulting in enhanced student outcomes.

To conclude, data assumes an integral role in the realm of assessment. By leveraging the potency of data-centered pedagogical methods and technological resources, instructors can acquire worthwhile perspectives regarding their pupils' learning imperatives. This enables them to dispense targeted education that caters individually to each student's requirements while enhancing engagement levels and motivational drive within students themselves. Data-driven teaching harbors extraordinary potential for effecting a transformative impact on educational paradigms at large by empowering educators with informed decision-making capabilities aimed at nurturing academic advancement amongst students and optimizing scholastic outcomes accordingly.

8.6.1 Using Data for Formative Assessment

The application of formative assessment is a pivotal element in promoting efficacy within teaching and learning. It offers educators the opportunity to acquire comprehensive feedback on students' comprehension, recognize areas necessitating improvement, and finely tune instruction correspondingly. Notably, teachers can now tap into a broad range of digital tools and data analysis techniques that furnish them with an abundant source of information capable of enhancing the effectiveness inherent in the process they employ during their formative assessments.

The employment of data-driven teaching techniques in STEM subjects has been demonstrated to be immensely efficacious in advancing student engagement and comprehension. With the incorporation of digital instruments and analytical tools, instructors can effortlessly monitor pupils' advancement as it happens, discern any misconceptions they may have developed about a given topic or concept, and furnish timely feedback instantaneously. This approach not only ensures that learners stay on course but also empowers educators with the capacity to implement prompt interventions while executing adjustments to their instruction strategies accordingly. Utilizing data analysis tools for personalized learning confers a significant benefit in terms of the ability to customize instruction according to individual student requirements. Through an examination of students' informational metrics, educators can discern patterns, trends and opportunities for improvement on an individual basis leading them towards targeted interventions, instructional material modification as well as affording tailor-made educational experiences that align with each learner's specific strengths and weaknesses.

Moreover, data-driven assessment and feedback have the potential to significantly augment student learning outcomes in addition to personalized education. By utilizing digital means, educators can collect and scrutinize information pertaining to students' academic progress; consequently identifying areas of difficulty which may require additional focus. Subsequently offering timely responses fosters a sense of ownership over their own development amongst learners by not only enabling them track their advancement but also empowering them with requisite tools for self-improvement.

The utilization of data visualization presents a formidable technique that can bolster the efficacy of formative assessment. By incorporating digital tools for visualizing information in an educational environment, teachers are empowered to present intricate material through visually attractive and easily comprehensible formats. Such an approach imbues students with discerning capabilities as they become more adept at identifying patterns, making connections, and deepening their insights related to their learning experiences.

The utilization of data-driven techniques for implementing personalized instruction proves to be highly advantageous for students with exceptional educational requirements. Upon scrutinizing individual learners' strengths, weaknesses and learning preferences using statistical analysis tools, educators are able to optimize instructional strategies accordingly. This not only guarantees that every student is furnished with the appropriate academic assistance but also facilitates their ability to thrive academically on a customized level.

Furthermore, teaching methodologies facilitated by data analysis can augment student engagement and motivation. Through diligent evaluations of pupil information regarding their level of involvement in the learning process, inclination to participate actively as well as preferences related to educational methods employed; educators are able create more engaging instructional plans that align with students' interests. This approach fosters an environment conducive for effective learning whilst encouraging learners to own and drive their academic growth journey.

Moreover, the implementation of data analytics can aid educators in monitoring and enhancing student progress. Through gathering comprehensive information and scrutinizing behavioral patterns concerning academic performance during a specific period, teachers can distinguish tendencies, establish objectives, and precisely supervise advancement towards proficient learning achievements. This empirical methodology guarantees that students are perpetually advancing while also receiving adequate assistance needed to excel academically.

Finally, implementing data-driven teaching practices can have a significant impact on educational research and analysis. Through the examination of extensive datasets, researchers can access pivotal information regarding pedagogical trends, instructional approaches as well as student progressions. Such insightful observations enable educators to make informed decisions based upon empirical evidence and consequently improve their teaching methodologies at a larger scale.

To summarize, utilizing data for formative assessment presents a plethora of advantages to educators. These benefits encompass tailoring instruction to individual students' needs, delivering prompt feedback, augmenting student engagement levels, and bringing meaningful contributions towards educational research. Data-informed teaching methodologies are reshaping the education sector by empowering teachers in making informed decisions within their classrooms. By adopting digital tools and implementing rigorous data analysis techniques, instructors can unleash pupils' full potential while establishing an all-encompassing learning milieu that caters to diverse backgrounds better ensuring effectiveness uniformly across varied learners' profiles.

8.6.2 Providing Timely and Actionable Feedback with Data

In the rapidly changing field of education, educators are continuously striving to enhance their pedagogical techniques and elevate academic outcomes for students. One potent strategy that has emerged in recent times is data-driven instruction, a methodology employing digital tools to amass and scrutinize information with the aim of guiding teaching decisions. By leveraging insights derived from such analytics, instructors can deliver prompt feedback to learners which helps drive interest levels up, bolsters enthusiasm towards learning objectives thereby leading ultimately better grades and improved educational results overall.

The implementation of data-driven teaching methods has yielded noteworthy outcomes, especially in STEM subjects. The utilization of analytical tools for scrutinizing student information can provide a customized learning experience catered to individual needs and abilities. By amassing and evaluating performance metrics along with comprehension levels, educators can identify aptitudes as well as deficiencies which enable them to modify their instructional technique accordingly. This outcome not only accelerates the potentiality for optimal academic achievement but also instills accountability within students by encouraging active participation in their educational journey.

One of the principal advantages attributed to data-driven teaching is offering prompt feedback to students. The conventional lag times in grading papers or returning assessments are no longer a concern due to the availability of digital tools that permit an immediate evaluation of student work. Hence, teachers can instantaneously assess learning achievements and furnish constructive insights on areas for improvement that align with specific learning objectives, enabling continuous growth and progress toward academic goals through actionable recommendations provided by this critical feedback loop.

One of the benefits of utilizing digital tools for data visualization in academic settings is their capacity to present information in an engaging and easily digestible format. Through charts, graphs, interactive displays, complex concepts as well as trends can be effectively represented facilitating a meaningful assimilation by students fostering deeper comprehension levels on particular topics. This visual mode not only augments student learning but also nurtures critical thinking abilities coupled with adeptness at interpreting data - skills that assume greater significance given today's preoccupation with analytics-driven insights.

The integration of data-driven teaching methodologies can extend to differentiated instruction, thereby offering appropriate support and challenges for all students, including individuals with exceptional educational requirements. The analysis of student performance statistics by educators enables the identification of specific areas requiring intervention or accommodation tailored to individual needs. This personalized approach not only advances education outcomes but also advocates inclusiveness and equity within the learning environment.

Moreover, data analytics can be utilized as a monitoring tool to enhance the progress of students over an extended period. The visualization and analysis of student performance-based information enable teachers to recognize consistent patterns, trends along with critical areas that require attention for informed instructional decisions. This continual assessment approach assists in keeping pupils on track while also providing them with necessary support towards achieving success at their level best.

In summary, the implementation of data-driven teaching methodology holds significant promise for elevating education to new heights by facilitating teachers' access to valuable insights that enrich their instructional methods. By leveraging digital tools designed specifically for analyzing inputted data, educators are empowered with timely and impactful student feedback which is custom-tailored to corresponding individual learning experiences in order to differentiate instruction effectively while boosting overall levels of engagement and motivation among students. The potential unlocked through such a powerful approach can enable teachers impart comprehensive knowledge tailored towards harnessing the full range of abilities present within each pupil whilst preparing them adequately for success amid an increasingly prevailing culture emphasizing highly sophisticated analytical methodologies based on aggregated information streams from diverse sources across multiple platforms in our current world today.

8.7 Using Digital Tools for Data Visualization in the Classroom

In the present era of digitization, data-centric pedagogical approaches have brought about a fundamental transformation in the domain of education. With access to digital means and methods for analyzing student behavior, educators now possess an invaluable vantage point from which they can grasp pupils' learning tendencies as well as their strengths and areas requiring enhancement. One particularly essential facet that has emerged with data-driven instruction is visualization techniques since these play an integral part in effectively conveying intricate information flow while enabling informed decision-making procedures.

In education, data visualization pertains to the graphical representation of data through means such as charts, graphs and infographics. This goes beyond conventional spreadsheets and reports by presenting raw information in aesthetically engaging formats that are comprehensible for both teachers and students alike. Through this methodical approach, educators can identify recurrent themes, patterns or anomalies that enable them to customize teaching strategies accordingly with greater precision.

Data visualization plays a pivotal role in education by affording the possibility of personalized learning. Visualizing students' progress empowers educators to discern individual strengths and weaknesses, allowing them to tailor instruction according to specific needs. For instance, the depiction of a graph showcasing their performance over time serves as an effective tool for highlighting areas where they excel or struggle, thereby enabling teachers to offer targeted interventions or enrichment activities accordingly.

Furthermore, the utilization of data visualization considerably contributes to enhancing student engagement and motivation. The presentation of information through visual means is more attractive and readily understood by students in comparison with conventional numerical data display techniques. By employing methods such as infographics or interactive dashboards, an inherent curiosity for exploring and analyzing data is evoked within students which further fosters their capacity for independent inquiry whilst simultaneously nurturing critical thinking skills essential for effective problem-solving abilities that equip them to take greater control over their own education trajectory.

In addition, the implementation of data visualization greatly enables systematic evaluations and feedback based on reliable information in education. The utilization of visual representations presenting assessment outcomes can furnish prompt and practical reviews for both educators and students alike. Specifically for instructors, employing data visualization assists in recognizing deficiencies within student comprehension, assessing the efficacy of instructional approaches utilized, as well as determining informed resolutions towards future pedagogical techniques to employ. Alternatively speaking from a learner's perspective; pupils have access to track their developmental advancement throughout educational modules using this technique while also owning responsibility over regulating personal progress by setting attainable objectives along one's own learning path.

To conclude, data visualization serves as a potent instrument in promoting teaching based on data and positively impacting both teachers and students through its various benefits. Through the use of visual representations for information, educators can tailor learning experiences to individual learners' needs, increase their engagement levels effectively while simultaneously making informed decisions about curricular methods. As advancements continue progressing technology further mandates exploring ways of incorporating such techniques into classroom settings to aid better student outcomes holistically and transform educational systems altogether.

8.7.1 Types of Data Visualization Tools for Educators

In today's era of technology, educators are privy to a significant amount of data which can aid them in making insightful decisions pertaining to their teaching methodologies. The complexity and magnitude of said data may prove overwhelming when it comes time for interpretation. This is where the utility of data visualization tools presents itself; by rendering these complex datasets into visually appealing representations that facilitate understanding and comprehension amongst stakeholders. This subchapter aims at exploring several types of such intelligent visualization tools available across different platforms catering specifically towards educators aspiring to enhance overall learning outcomes for students under their guidance.

Graphing and Charting Tools: Graphing and charting tools are a fundamental prerequisite for rendering numerical data, including but not limited to test scores, attendance rates, or students' academic progression over the course of time. Educators can make use of these robust analytical instruments in producing various visualizations such as bar graphs, line graphs and pie charts among others; thereby enabling them to efficiently detect patterns and trends latent within their datasets.

Interactive Dashboards: The use of interactive dashboards serves as a dynamic tool to assist educators in visualizing and exploring important data metrics. These advanced tools offer customizable options for teachers, enabling the display and interaction with specific sets of chosen information. In turn, these dashboards can be implemented by educators to closely track students' progress over time, recognize any prevalent areas requiring attention or improvement, thereby empowering informed decision-making processes based on reliable quantitative insights.

Geospatial Mapping Tools: Geospatial mapping tools serve as a valuable resource for educators, providing them with the ability to visually represent data on maps. This functionality facilitates comprehension regarding spatial distribution of educational elements such as student demographics, school performance and regional allocation of resources. As an illustration, teachers can apply these instruments to scrutinize information relative to any region in order that they might draw conclusions about various criteria therein mentioned earlier.

Infographic and Presentation Tools: Infographic and presentation tools are valuable resources for condensing intricate data into visually comprehensible content. These instruments can be utilized by educators to craft stimulating presentations, posters or handouts that facilitate increased understanding of pertinent knowledge among students. Ultimately contributing towards better retention of crucial concepts using compelling visuals.

Simulation and Gamification Tools: Simulation and gamification tools offer educators the opportunity to generate interactive and immersive learning opportunities for their pupils. These techniques have the capacity to represent information in a manner that engrosses students, thereby inspiring active engagement with the educational process.

Through the strategic utilization of data visualization tools, educators are able to convert unprocessed information into meaningful insights and make informed decisions aimed at improving their instructional practices. Whether they are scrutinizing student performance or tracking progress while identifying weaknesses, these cutting-edge instruments furnish teachers with a potent resource for enhancing their data-centric pedagogical approach; ultimately bringing about revolutionary change within education.

8.7.2 Integrating Data Visualization into Instructional Practices

In the present era of digitization, data-driven teaching has emerged as a crucial component in modern education. As educators, we are consistently striving to discover avant-garde techniques for engaging our students and tailoring their learning journeys. The employment of visualization tools pertaining to digital information can prove transformative with respect to instructional practices within this domain.

The graphical depiction of data, commonly known as data visualization, facilitates comprehension, analysis and interpretation. By incorporating this methodology in our pedagogical approach, we can aid students in comprehending intricate concepts, recognize patterns and establish affiliations which may have otherwise remained elusive.

Regarding STEM subjects, the application of data-driven teaching methodologies can significantly augment students' comprehension and academic attainments. Implementation of analytical tools empowers instructors to customize learning experiences in accordance with individual strengths and weaknesses at both group as well as personal levels. The utilization of these effective instruments facilitates monitoring student progress, detecting opportunities for improvement as well as giving specific feedback that stimulates development.

Utilizing data-driven assessment and feedback holds utmost significance in ensuring impactful teaching. Employing digital tools to visualize vital statistics allows educators to present pertinent information with clarity and visual richness, not only enabling students to comprehend their own performance better but also allowing teachers to meticulously monitor student progress while making informed decisions based on the data available at hand.

One of the most significant advantages offered by data visualization is its capacity to interest and invigorate students. The presentation of information through visual representations has the potential to capture pupils' attention, arouse their inquisitiveness, inspire productive dialogue among them, as well as encourage dynamic involvement within the educational experience.

Data-driven techniques can play a pivotal role in the realm of differentiated instruction. Through thorough analysis of student data, educators are equipped to identify individual learning needs and correspondingly tailor their pedagogical approaches while delivering precise interventions. This practice ensures that no learner is neglected or left behind; rather, it guarantees each pupil's access to personalized support aimed towards realizing academic success.

Data-informed educational practices are not restricted to conventional learning environments. They can be equally applied in specialized education settings where the provision of tailored lessons is vital. By harnessing data analytics, educators have the ability to closely monitor and evaluate advancements made by students with specific needs; thereby identifying areas requiring enhancement while adjusting teaching methodologies accordingly.

In addition, instructional methods that are grounded in data analysis can enhance student engagement and motivation. Assessment of students' interests, preferences, and learning styles enables educators to customize instruction according to their individual requirements whilst fostering curiosity towards the subject matter; ultimately resulting in a heightened drive for academic achievement.

The utilization of data-driven teaching can be applied towards educational research and analysis. Through the accumulation and scrutiny of student performance data, educators as well as researchers may attain noteworthy viewpoints regarding instructional techniques' efficacy. Furthermore, this process enables identification of areas requiring enhancement whilst contributing to a wider pool of knowledge in educational research.

In summary, the incorporation of data visualization techniques in educational instruction has the potential to revolutionize and improve teaching practices. The utilization of data-driven methods empowers educators with personalized instructional abilities, superior assessment feedback capabilities and a more impactful engagement approach that enhances student motivation while facilitating differentiated instruction opportunities. Additionally, embracing digital technologies for this purpose is not simply fashionable but an essential requirement towards promoting meaningful advances within education as we know it today.

8.8 Applying Data-Driven Techniques for Differentiated Instruction

The pedagogical approach of differentiated instruction acknowledges and honors the diversity among learners within a classroom setting. This technique is founded on the fundamental premise that students exhibit varying learning styles, aptitudes, and passions; consequently, requiring distinct instructional methods coupled with appropriate resources to facilitate their academic attainment. The focus of this section aims at furnishing educators an all-encompassing appreciation of differentiated instruction alongside data-informed methodologies for its effective implementation in educational settings.

The integration of digital tools in teaching to analyze data has become a critical element in supporting differentiated instruction. The collection and analysis of learning metrics, including student preferences, progress reports, and specific needs provide the basis for creating custom-tailored lesson plans aligned with individual students' requirements. Such insights garnered from data analytics facilitate effective selection by teachers of appropriate instructional materials as well as deployment strategies suitable for strengths or weaknesses exhibited by learners.

One of the primary advantages of utilizing data analysis tools for personalized education is its capacity to identify areas that require improvement per learner. Through thoroughly studying students' performance records, educators can pinpoint any knowledge gaps or misunderstandings and subsequently craft tailor-made interventions specifically designed to resolve these issues. This highly individualized approach guarantees that each student receives ample support required in reaching their learning objectives.

The incorporation of data-driven assessment and feedback is a crucial aspect required for differentiated instruction. Through utilization of digital instruments to gather and scrutinize evaluation-related information, instructors can attain an in-depth understanding regarding the progression made by their students, thus enabling them to make appropriate modifications before disseminating academic content. Furthermore, timely and explicit appraisal that stems from this analytical process aids pupils in recognizing areas wherein they excel as well as those where improvement is necessary-endorsing developmental thought-processes whilst augmenting their motivation towards acquiring knowledge.

Data visualization tools can prove to be highly advantageous in the classroom, given their ability to assist teachers and students in comprehending complex sets of data. By leveraging digital tools for data visualization purposes, educators gain access to a means for presenting information that is visually engaging and readily graspable by learners. Moreover, visual representations of information allow instructors greater flexibility when it comes time to personalize lessons based on individual learning styles or needs among students.

Utilizing data-driven techniques to implement differentiated instruction can greatly benefit students who require special attention. By gathering and evaluating data pertaining to these learners' aptitudes and preferences, educators can devise personalized education plans that address their distinctive requirements. This individualized approach is essential for ensuring the provision of adequate support and accommodation required by students with special needs for them achieve academic success.

In summary, comprehending the concept of differentiated instruction and integrating data-driven methodologies into pedagogical approaches have the capacity to significantly transform education. By valuing individual differences among students in a learning environment and leveraging digital platforms for information gathering and evaluation, educators can facilitate personalized teaching that caters to each student's distinct requirements. The utilization of such analytical tools could benefit various educational domains ranging from STEM disciplines to special needs learners or even enhance learner participation levels alongside motivation.

Therefore, it is apparent that employing data-dependent techniques holds tremendous potential towards elevating academic achievements amongst pupils within diverse settings.

8.8.1 Using Data to Identify Student Needs and Preferences

With the advent of technology, information has acquired immense significance as a resource for educators in comprehending their students' requirements and proclivities. By leveraging data analytics, teachers can access enlightening perspectives that enable them to customize their teachings while fostering an immersive learning milieu.

One of the pivotal advantages associated with data-driven teaching methods is its potential to pinpoint specific student requirements. Through systematic collection and analytical interpretation of performance-based information, instructors can identify areas where students face difficulties and modify their instructional approach accordingly. As an illustration, upon discovering that some learners are encountering challenges in comprehending a concept particular to STEM subjects based on gathered metrics, educators may provide focused interventions or supplementary resources custom-tailored towards addressing such lapses in learning.

Data analysis tools provide teachers with the ability to identify student preferences and interests. Through gathering data on student engagement and motivation, educators are able to discern which subjects or activities resonate most effectively with their pupils. This valuable information can then be utilized in order to develop instructional materials and coursework that is more applicable and captivating for students, thereby ultimately enhancing both participation levels as well as overall success rates.

Moreover, the usage of data-driven evaluation and responsiveness forms a vital aspect of efficient pedagogy. With aid from technological devices, educators can assemble and scrutinize information concerning student performance to proffer prompt feedback that is explicit and implementable. This approach enables students to comprehend their proficiencies as well as inadequacies, thus making improvements accordingly. Conversely, educators can employ gathered data for monitoring progress over time while also pinpointing patterns evident therein which may inform instructional decisions they take thereafter.

Data visualization applications are also of fundamental significance in educational settings. The utilization of digital tools for data representation allows instructors to present intricate concepts more efficiently and stimulate students' interest effectively. Data rendered visually assists learners in comprehending trends, patterns, and correlations; thus promoting profound learning experiences and development of critical thinking abilities among them.

The application of data-driven techniques in the area of differentiated instruction is noteworthy. By scrutinizing the metrics on student performance and preferences, educators can aptly customize their pedagogy to address individual requirements. Such an approach guarantees that students receive appropriate support and challenges suiting their abilities for them to realize maximal potential.

Employing data-centered teaching methodologies is especially advantageous for pupils in special education. Through gathering and scrutinizing information tailored to their circumstances, educators can create personalized intervention strategies that cater to their distinctive requirements while fostering both academic and socio-emotional development.

To conclude, data-driven teaching methodologies have the capacity to revolutionize education by granting teachers the ability to customize instruction, cater to specific student requirements, and develop dynamic learning environments. Through advanced techniques in data analysis tools and digital visualization technologies, classroom utilization of such statistics holds tremendous potential for reshaping pedagogical practices across diverse educational settings. By embracing this innovative approach towards instructional design through a focus on analytical insights obtained from collected datasets; educators can drive superior academic performance amongst students while enhancing their engagement levels leading them toward personal fulfillment with maximized outcomes arising from untapped potentials.

8.8.2 Customizing Instruction with Data-Driven Differentiation Strategies

In the current era of digital technology, data-driven pedagogical practices have gained significant prevalence in education. Through utilization of digital tools and analysis techniques, educators are empowered to identify valuable insights into their students' learning preferences and requirements for customized instruction leading towards more effective outcomes. One potent technique employed by teachers these days is utilizing differentiation strategies underpinned by data analytics within their classrooms.

Data-driven differentiation pertains to adapting instruction in accordance with the specific requirements of each student. Through scrutinizing data on individual students' performance, inclinations and advancement, educators may recognize established aptitudes as well as knowledge gaps for effective customization of teaching methods that cater to their needs. Employing this distinct approach guarantees tailored support and guidance for every learner towards outstanding educational achievement within their capabilities.

Data-driven differentiation holds a significant advantage in augmenting STEM (Science, Technology, Engineering and Mathematics) education. By leveraging data analysis tools judiciously, educators can discern patterns pertaining to students' performance and understanding of these subjects. This facilitates the development of tailored curricula that cater to individual learning requirements while addressing areas requiring improvement which nurtures an optimal foundation for mastering crucial disciplines encompassed by this category.

Furthermore, the utilization of data-driven differentiation strategies can prove to be highly advantageous for students with special education needs. With a thorough examination and analysis of individual learning profiles, educators are capable of pinpointing distinctive requirements for each student in order to devise customized educational plans that cater appropriately toward these demands. Through this approach, it is ensured that pupils who require specific accommodations or support receive what they need in regards to their academic success.

The implementation of data-supported differentiation is an essential factor in enhancing student engagement and motivation. Through the analysis of students' interests and preferences, educators can devise customized learning models that resonate with their pupils on a personal level while promoting feelings of ownership and relevance within their studies. This approach leads to more meaningful educational experiences for learners that boost overall enjoyment levels.

Moreover, utilizing data-based differentiation is a valuable method for monitoring and enhancing student advancement. Consistently scrutinizing performance metrics empowers educators to pinpoint potential areas of development while modifying their pedagogy appropriately. This cyclic protocol guarantees that pupils are persistently stimulated and aided, ultimately resulting in sustained progression and refinement.

In conclusion, data-driven differentiation strategies possess the revolutionary capability to customize instruction in meeting individual students' distinct educational needs. These impactful methods are applicable for STEM subjects, special education programs, student engagement means, and progress monitoring techniques. Data-oriented teaching procedures offer valuable insights and tools that serve as indispensable aids for educators. By leveraging digital technologies along with pertinent analytical frameworks, teachers can fabricate personalized learning experiences optimized towards bolstering successful outcomes among their pupils while fostering a deep appreciation for the art of scholarly pursuits.

8.9 Data-Driven Approaches to Improve Student Engagement and Motivation

Ensuring student engagement and motivation is an essential element of proficient teaching. As pedagogues, we recognize that active involvement in the learning process significantly enhances students' comprehension and retention of information. Additionally, incentivized learners are inclined to set high objectives for themselves and persevere through adversities. The ensuing subchapter shall examine the significance of stimulating student engagement and motivation while outlining how data-guided instruction can revolutionize education on this front.

The implementation of Data-Driven Teaching with Digital Tools presents teachers with a notable prospect to optimize the use of technology for amplifying student engagement and motivation. Through systematic examination and analysis of student data, educators can efficiently assimilate pertinent information on everyone's learning preferences, competencies as well as areas where improvement is required. Such knowledge provides an opportunity for personalization in instruction, customization in study materials coupled with targeted intervention aimed at sustaining students' interest while encouraging their active participation throughout academic tasks.

The implementation of data-driven teaching methods can significantly enhance the effectiveness and efficiency of STEM subjects. These fields frequently necessitate a practical, interactive approach to learning complex concepts. The utilization of digital technologies permits instructors to obtain real-time empirical evidence during experiments, simulations or coding exercises that enables learners to scrutinize and interpret findings expeditiously. This prompt feedback fosters an appreciation for the applicability and utility of such skills among pupils while also augmenting their motivation levels substantially towards achieving academic excellence in these areas.

Employing data analysis tools to facilitate personalized learning is an efficacious method. By monitoring student progress, educators can identify areas where individuals may encounter difficulties and offer customized assistance correspondingly. This approach guarantees that students receive the requisite support promptly, thereby averting frustration and disinterest from potentially arising. Additionally, utilizing feedback generated through data-driven evaluation empowers teachers to provide timely responses while reinforcing constructive learned behaviors for their pupils to achieve improvement holistically.

The utilization of data visualization tools can effectively elevate student engagement within the classroom setting. With an aid in visual depictions of complex concepts and interrelated topics, students can better comprehend information presented to them. This approach fosters interactive learning opportunities through the manipulation and exploration of data leading towards an enhanced sense of curiosity coupled with a deeper understanding by learners themselves.

The utilization of differentiated instruction constitutes a fundamental element in proficient pedagogy. The strategic employment of data-driven techniques can significantly supplement this method. Through the assessment and analysis of student data, educators are able to discern personalized learning requirements for each individual pupil, consequently facilitating custom-fit teaching styles that correspond with specific needs. This meticulous approach guarantees optimal engagement and motivation whilst ensuring that students receive tailored guidance apposite to their respective levels adeptly fostering academic growth within the classroom setting. Students enrolled in special education programs necessitate tailored instruction and support services. Utilizing data-driven pedagogical techniques, educators can aptly ascertain the requirements of these students, offering targeted interventions to tackle their distinctive academic obstacles. By skillfully tracking student advancement through precise analytics mechanisms, teachers may refine instructional approaches and individual accommodations for optimal levels of participation and progress among learners with disabilities.

Enhancing student engagement and motivation constitutes an ongoing endeavor. Through a meticulous evaluation of data and vigilantly monitoring the academic progression of students, educators can discern recurrent patterns as well as trends which enable them to make judicious decisions about their instructive methodologies. This empirically informed approach ensures seamless advancement while equipping teachers with the flexibility required in adjusting instructional techniques congruent with emerging pedagogical demands posed by learners.

In summary, the significance of student engagement and motivation cannot be overemphasized in effective pedagogy. The utilization of data-driven teaching methodologies coupled with digital tools equip educators with ample resources for personalizing instruction, exponentially boosting engagement levels whilst providing necessary support mechanisms to enhance students' academic progressions. By optimizing the use of available data sources via technology-assisted techniques, teachers have an opportunity to revolutionize educational practice by transfiguring learning environments into dynamic and invigorating spaces that encourage all learners towards excellence.

8.9.1 Using Data to Identify Factors Affecting Engagement and Motivation

In the current era of digital advancements, educators have at their disposal copious amounts of data that hold immense potential in transforming educational practices. By optimizing the technique of data-driven teaching, teachers can gain critical knowledge regarding the level and extent to which learners are engrossed or motivated throughout instructional periods. This perspective ultimately enables customized instruction coupled with efficient support strategies aligned towards unique individual needs for optimal academic achievement outcomes. The ensuing section delves into how analytical tools designed for scrutinizing student motivation levels and engagement propensities could be operationalized to identify determinant factors geared towards improving education output generally.

One of the principal advantages associated with data-driven teaching rests on its capability to enable real-time tracking and monitoring of students' engagement. Leveraging digital tools that gather and evaluate data empowers educators to gain a thorough comprehension concerning how pupils are interacting with curricula, thus disclosing patterns pertaining thereto. Such information permits them to identify variables instrumental in precipitating higher degrees of involvement like interactive activities or project-based learning while pinpointing those features undermining motivation such as inadequate personalization or relevance.

Data analysis software applications can yield valuable insights into the motivation levels of students. By scrutinizing data related to student behaviors, such as time allocation for assorted tasks, completion statistics and participation rates in classroom discussions, educators may gain a more profound comprehension regarding what drives their pupils. For instance, if a specific individual consistently excels on assignments that entail experiential learning practices or practical application methods; then instructors might consider integrating additional activities of this sort within the curriculum - thereby augmenting overall interest levels among pupils.

Moreover, data-driven pedagogical techniques can prove to be exceptionally successful when applied in STEM subjects. Through the utilization of sophisticated tools for data analysis aimed at evaluating student performance in these domains, educators have the capability to discern zones where their students excel or struggle and thus provide them with customized support and resources accordingly. By adopting this targeted approach towards instruction, learners often feel more invested and encouraged as it aligns seamlessly with their individual needs.

Aside from individualized instruction, data-informed teaching methodologies can also contribute to diverse instructional strategies. Through the examination of student performance and involvement metrics, educators may identify clusters of learners who stand to gain from alternate learning approaches. For example, if evidence indicates that a particular set of pupils is experiencing difficulties with regards to an idea or concept in question, instructors could provide supplementary materials or tailor their methods for more optimal efficacy towards these students' needs.

Through the utilization of data analytics tools, educators can obtain important insights into student engagement and motivation. This affords them the ability to make informed decisions regarding instructional strategies and support. Furthermore, classroom approaches founded on empirical evidence not only led to enhanced individual academic performance but also collectively improve educational outcomes overall. Empowering instructors toward harnessing analytical power is transformative for education prospects; thereby assuring every learner has equal opportunity towards success.

8.9.2 Strategies for Increasing Student Engagement and Motivation with Data

In the current era of technology, education has undergone a significant transformation through data-driven teaching approaches that furnish instructors with valuable knowledge regarding student performance and advancement. By leveraging digital instruments and employing analytical techniques on datasets, educators can not only enhance students' engagement but also elevate their motivation levels inside classrooms significantly. This section aims to delve into diverse methodologies for effectively utilizing information sets in creating an interactive and tailored learning setting.

An efficacious approach would involve utilizing data analysis tools to facilitate personalized learning. Through analyzing performance metrics, educators can discern the strengths, areas requiring improvement and individualized modes of comprehension for each student. Employing this knowledge, instructors may then customize their teaching methodology with a view towards meeting every learner's unique needs which in turn produces an enriched and stimulating academic environment.

An additional approach is to utilize data-driven assessment and feedback. Through consistent evaluation of students' advancement, coupled with prompt feedback derived from thorough analysis, educators can facilitate an enhanced comprehension amongst their pupils regarding areas where progress has been made or attention should still be focused upon. This structured cycle instills within the students a sense of accountability towards their learning journey which acts as motivation for them in striving consistently for excellence.

Data visualization tools are essential in enhancing student engagement. These tools effectively present data sets through visually appealing and interactive mediums, enabling teachers to facilitate comprehension of complex concepts and patterns within students. Visual depictions of statistics stimulate curiosity amongst learners, prompting deeper analysis and exploration of information presented before them.

The implementation of differentiated instruction is an efficacious approach that can be further strengthened through utilization of data-driven methodologies. Utilizing data to determine the unique academic requirements and educational preferences of students enables teachers to customize their pedagogy to suit diverse learning modes. This approach confers the dual benefits of heightened student engagement as well as instilling a sense of inclusivity and empowerment within learners.

Data-driven teaching techniques can be significantly advantageous for special education students. Teachers can make informed decisions about instructional strategies and interventions by gathering and analyzing data pertaining to their individualized educational plans (IEPs) and progress. By employing a data-driven approach, it is ensured that these students receive the support required to maintain engagement levels, as well as foster motivation towards achieving success throughout their unique learning journeys.

In addition, the utilization of data analytics holds potential for monitoring and enhancing student progress. Periodic scrutiny of students' performance metrics to identify patterns or trends enables teachers to take swift remedial action in case any concerns arise. Such a preemptive measure results in keeping motivated students on track towards their academic objectives. In addition, the implementation of data-driven teaching offers a significant contribution to educational research and analysis. Through meticulous collection and scrutiny of information relating to instructional techniques, curriculum efficiency, as well as academic performance indicators among students; educators are presented with evidence-supported grounds for making sound deductions aimed at enhancing both instructional strategies and fostering optimal student engagement.

In conclusion, the utilization of data-driven pedagogy with technological tools presents an array of methods to enhance student engagement and motivation. Through the effective deployment of techniques such as personalized learning, differentiated instruction, and data visualization analysis among others; teachers can establish a dynamic and compelling educational atmosphere that enables students' success.

8.10 Using Data Analytics for Monitoring and Improving Student Progress

In the contemporary era of technology, data analytics holds significant relevance for educators to monitor and enhance student progress. By leveraging the wealth of information available, teachers can effectively gain meaningful insights into their students' learning patterns including identifying strengths as well as areas that require improvement. This subchapter aims to investigate how data analytics empowers monitoring of student performance while exemplifying its potential impact in modernizing education practices.

In recent years, data-driven teaching approaches in the field of Science, Technology, Engineering and Mathematics (STEM) have garnered considerable interest. Through leveraging analytical tools to parse through student performance metrics for patterns, educators can modify their instructional strategies accordingly. By way of illustration: in circumstances where certain students persistently demonstrate difficulty understanding specific mathematical concepts or topics - adjustments may be made towards the pedagogical methods employed with a view toward addressing identified knowledge gaps.

The domain of personalized education stands as another sphere wherein data analysis tools can contribute notably. By scrutinizing individual student records, instructors may recognize peculiar requirements for their students and develop tailored lesson plans to cater to these needs. This approach guarantees specific guidance for each pupil, ultimately enhancing academic outcomes in a significant manner.

Utilizing data analytics for assessment and feedback is vital in achieving effective education. Teachers can track student progress in an up-to-date manner, detect areas that require improvement, and offer prompt guidance to enhance the students' learning trajectory. This approach not only assists learners in remaining on course but also encourages them to assume responsibility for their educational journey.

The utilization of data visualization tools in the academic setting has observed an upward trend. Through presenting information and statistics visually, educators can effectively communicate intricate concepts to learners in a comprehensible and captivating manner. Visual representations of data aid students' identification of patterns, linkage between ideas as well as facilitating their comprehension level on the subject matter at hand.

Utilizing data-driven methodologies for differentiated instruction presents an especially advantageous approach for students with varying learning requirements. Thorough analysis of student performance statistics enables teachers to pinpoint and address areas in which supplementary assistance is necessary, thus customizing their course delivery methods as deemed fit. This method results in a comprehensive support system that guarantees every individual receives the required level of attention needed to maximize their educational potential.

Data-driven teaching techniques can provide substantial advantages for special education students. Through the examination of progress and individual requirements, instructors can construct customized intervention plans that effectively address unique learning needs. Such methods facilitate an inclusive instructional environment while guaranteeing requisite support is provided equitably to all students to foster academic success.

Furthermore, the utilization of data analytics holds significant importance in enhancing students' engagement and motivation. A meticulous analysis of the statistics concerning student involvement assists instructors to identify efficacious strategies that can effectively capture their interest, subsequently augmenting their enthusiasm towards learning. This approach not only contributes to cultivating a congenial atmosphere for education but also prompts pupils to participate actively in shaping their educational journey.

The observation and enhancement of student progress represent fundamental constituents of proficient pedagogy. Through the implementation of data analytics, educators can acquire pertinent perspectives on learner achievements, pinpoint deficiency zones and leverage evidence-based judgments. This methodological approach endows teachers with competence to offer focused teaching strategies, curate bespoke education schemes thereby transforming training paradigms that culminate in better edification for all students.

8.11 Transforming Education with Learning Analytics in the Digital Age

Technology has revolutionized the education sector, providing teachers with a vast array of digital tools that can enhance their teaching practices and improve student learning outcomes. Among these tools, learning analytics holds immense potential to empower teachers with valuable insights into student performance, engagement, and learning patterns.

8.11.1 What is Learning Analytics?

Learning analytics is a process that involves collecting, analyzing, and reporting data on learners and their contexts to optimize learning. With the aid of digital tools and platforms, teachers can collect a wealth of data on various aspects of student learning, such as assessment performance, online discussion participation, and time spent on different learning activities.

8.11.2 How Can Learning Analytics Improve Teaching Practices?

By analyzing this data, teachers can uncover patterns and trends that provide valuable insights into student learning behaviors, enabling them to make informed decisions to optimize their teaching strategies. Learning analytics can help identify struggling students who may require additional support or intervention, highlight areas of the curriculum where students are excelling, and personalize instruction by tailoring content and activities to individual student needs.

In addition, learning analytics can support formative assessment practices by continuously monitoring student progress and performance, providing timely feedback, and making immediate adjustments to instructional strategies. This iterative feedback loop fosters a culture of continuous improvement, ensuring that students are always on track and that their learning needs are being met.

8.11.3 Ethical Considerations

It is crucial to approach learning analytics with caution and consider ethical considerations such as data privacy and security. Teachers must ensure that student data is collected and used in compliance with relevant regulations and guidelines.

Learning analytics is a powerful tool that has the potential to transform education and create a more effective and engaging learning experience for all students in the digital age. By leveraging the data collected through digital tools and platforms, teachers can gain valuable insights into student learning patterns, personalize instruction, and provide timely feedback. With the right approach, learning analytics can significantly enhance teaching practices and improve student outcomes.

8.11.4 Enhancing Student Learning Outcomes with Assessment Software

In today's digital age, educators have access to an array of tools that can help them improve their teaching methods and students' learning outcomes. Assessment software is one such tool that has become increasingly popular among modern teachers. This subchapter examines the advantages and applications of assessment software in monitoring student progress, enabling informed instruction, and ultimately advancing overall student achievement.

Assessment software offers teachers a comprehensive and efficient method of tracking student progress. The manual grading of papers and the decoding of handwritten responses are things of the past. With assessment software, teachers can effortlessly create and administer tests, gather and analyze student data, and generate detailed reports on individual and class performance. This enables teachers to quickly identify areas of strength and weakness, tailor their instruction accordingly, and provide prompt feedback to students.

The beauty of assessment software lies in its ability to provide real-time data. Teachers can quickly obtain and comprehend student performance data, allowing them to make informed instructional decisions. By analyzing the data, teachers can recognize patterns, trends, and gaps in understanding. This information empowers teachers to modify their teaching strategies, reteach certain concepts, or modify their lesson plans to target specific areas where students may be struggling.

Moreover, assessment software encourages personalized learning experiences. Teachers can differentiate their instruction to meet the diverse needs of their students by tracking individual student progress and identifying students who may require additional support or enrichment opportunities. This ensures that no student is left behind or held back by the pace of the entire class. Assessment software also fosters greater accountability and transparency. With comprehensive reports and data, teachers can effortlessly communicate student progress to parents, administrators, and even students themselves. Parents can access their child's performance data, monitor progress, and actively participate in their child's education. Administrators can monitor overall class performance, identify areas of concern, and provide targeted professional development for teachers if necessary. Students can see their progress and development, fostering a sense of ownership and motivation to improve.

In conclusion, assessment software is a valuable tool for modern educators. It simplifies the assessment process, provides real-time data, facilitates personalized instruction, and promotes accountability. By embracing assessment software, teachers can effectively track student progress, make data-driven instructional decisions, and ultimately create a more engaging and successful learning environment for their students.

8.11.5 Enhancing Instructional Practices with Data in Modern Education

In today's educational landscape, data is a valuable resource for teachers to improve their instructional practices. This section will explore how data can be used to make informed decisions in the classroom, with a focus on digital tools that aid in this process.

The primary benefit of using data to inform instructional decision-making is the ability to personalize and differentiate instruction for each student. By collecting and analyzing data, teachers can gain valuable insights into their students' strengths, weaknesses, and learning preferences. This allows educators to tailor their lessons and activities to meet the specific needs of individual students, ensuring that every learner is engaged and making progress. Digital tools have revolutionized the way data is collected and analyzed in the classroom. Online assessments, learning management systems, and educational apps make it easier for teachers to gather data on student performance and progress. This data can be visualized and interpreted using data analysis tools, providing teachers with a clear picture of each student's academic journey.

Data can also be used to identify trends and patterns at the classroom or school level. By examining data on a larger scale, teachers can identify areas of strength and areas in need of improvement. This information can guide instructional decision-making at a broader level, leading to more effective teaching practices and better outcomes for all students. It is important to note that using data to inform instructional decision-making requires a thoughtful and ethical approach. Teachers must ensure that student privacy and confidentiality are protected when collecting and analyzing data. Additionally, data should be used as a tool to support and enhance teaching practices, rather than as a sole determinant of success or failure.

In conclusion, the use of data to inform instructional decision-making is a powerful tool for modern teachers. By leveraging digital tools and analyzing data, teachers can personalize instruction, identify trends, and communicate progress effectively. However, it is crucial to approach data analysis ethically and responsibly, ensuring that student privacy is protected, and data is used in conjunction with professional expertise. By embracing data-driven decision-making, teachers can create dynamic and engaging learning experiences that meet the needs of every student.

8.12 Empowering Educators: The Significance of Data Literacy in Modern Teaching

In today's digital age, data has become more accessible than ever before, and its effective utilization can greatly enhance teaching practices and student learning outcomes. Teachers must embrace and understand the power of data to adapt to the evolving landscape of modern education. This subchapter aims to promote data literacy among teachers, providing them with the necessary knowledge and skills to harness the full potential of digital tools in their classrooms.

8.12.1 What is Data Literacy?

Data literacy refers to the ability to interpret and analyze data effectively, making informed decisions based on evidence. It involves understanding data sources, collecting and organizing data, interpreting patterns and trends, and making data-driven decisions to enhance teaching and learning experiences.

8.12.2 The Importance of Data Literacy in Modern Teaching

This subchapter emphasizes the significance of data literacy, exploring the role of data in informing instructional strategies, identifying student needs, and monitoring progress. By promoting data literacy among teachers, we empower them to leverage digital tools to transform their instructional methods and optimize student success.

8.12.3 Digital Tools for Data Collection and Analysis

We delve into various digital tools that facilitate data collection and analysis, offering practical guidance on how to utilize them effectively. We explore tools such as learning management systems, online assessment platforms, and data visualization software, highlighting their features and benefits. Teachers will gain hands-on experience in utilizing these tools to collect, analyze, and interpret data through step-by-step instructions and real-life examples.

8.12.4 Ethical Considerations Surrounding Data Usage

This subchapter emphasizes the ethical considerations surrounding data usage, ensuring that teachers understand their responsibilities in handling student data appropriately and protecting privacy. It also addresses potential challenges and limitations of data-driven instruction, offering insights on how to mitigate these challenges effectively.

In conclusion, this subchapter equips teachers with the necessary knowledge and skills to become data literate, enabling them to harness the full potential of digital tools in their classrooms. By promoting data literacy, teachers can develop a mindset that values evidence-based decision-making and continuous improvement, leading to improved student learning outcomes and preparing them to navigate the ever-evolving digital landscape.

8.12.5 Prioritizing Privacy and Security in Educational Data during the Digital Age

The rise of technology in education has brought with it a wealth of digital tools that can enhance classroom instruction. However, it is imperative to address privacy and security concerns to safeguard sensitive information such as students' personal details, grades, and learning preferences.

As educators, we bear the responsibility of protecting our students' personal information. When selecting digital tools, it's crucial to ensure that they have robust security measures in place to prevent data breaches. Furthermore, reviewing the platform's terms of service and privacy policies is essential to ensure that student data is not being misused.

To protect students' data, teachers can also implement best practices in the classroom. This includes practicing strong password protection, regularly updating software and applications, and limiting access to student data to authorized personnel. By educating students and their parents about the privacy and security implications of using digital tools in the classroom, we can empower them to make informed decisions.

Involving students and parents in discussions about data privacy can help to ensure that they understand the risks and benefits of using digital tools. Educating students on safe online practices, such as avoiding sharing personal information online and being wary of suspicious links or emails, is also essential.

In summary, as technology continues to integrate into education, we must prioritize privacy and security concerns to protect student data. By adopting secure digital tools, implementing best practices in the classroom, and educating students and parents about data privacy, we can ensure that educational data is protected and used responsibly.

8.12.6 Upholding Privacy and Security in Educational Data in the Digital Age

With the increasing use of digital tools in education, students' personal information, such as their names, addresses, grades, and learning preferences, are at risk. It is critical to address privacy and security concerns to safeguard their data.

As educators, we must prioritize the protection of our students' personal information. When selecting digital tools, it's important to ensure that they have robust security measures in place to prevent data breaches. It's also essential to review the platform's terms of service and privacy policies to ensure that student data is not being used inappropriately.

In addition to choosing secure digital tools, teachers can also implement best practices in the classroom to protect students' data. This includes using strong passwords, regularly updating software and applications, and limiting access to student data to authorized personnel. Educating students and their parents about the privacy and security implications of using digital tools in the classroom is also critical.

By involving students and parents in discussions about data privacy, we can empower them to make informed decisions about the use of digital tools. This includes teaching students safe online practices, such as avoiding sharing personal information online and being wary of suspicious links or emails.

In conclusion, as we continue to integrate technology into education, it's vital to prioritize privacy and security concerns to protect student data. By adopting secure digital tools, implementing best practices in the classroom, and educating students and parents about data privacy, we can ensure that educational data is protected and used responsibly.

Upholding privacy and security in educational data is essential for building trust in digital learning environments. Educational institutions, technology providers, and regulatory bodies must uphold the highest standards of data privacy and security in the digital age.

8.13 Implementing Data-Driven Interventions for Struggling Students

Within the field of education, adopting a universal approach seldom produces ideal outcomes. Owing to students' distinctiveness, it is imperative that their needs are dealt with on an individual basis to guarantee success. This principle holds especially true for pupils experiencing academic challenges. Fortunately, data-based interventions furnish teachers with invaluable resources for identifying and effectively supporting such learners.

In recent times, there has been a notable rise in the adoption of data-based teaching methodologies for STEM subjects. Through an analysis of students' performance metrics, educators can pinpoint areas where difficulties may arise and thus customize their instructional approach consequently. Specifically speaking about algebraic equations as an example - if assessment suggests that certain pupils struggle repetitively with this topic area, targeted interventions like supplementary practice exercises or direct one-on-one tutoring can be implemented by the teacher to tackle such robust challenges aptly within these learners.

The incorporation of digital tools has significantly transformed data-driven teaching by facilitating personalized learning experiences. Through the utilization of cutting-edge data analysis software, educators can gather meticulous details regarding individual students' academic patterns, aptitudes, and limitations. This knowledge enables them to construct customized educational strategies that are designed to precisely meet each student's distinctive requirements. For instance, a pupil grappling with comprehending course materials through conventional methods but visually adept may benefit from interactive multimedia resources while another learner who favors auditory techniques might prefer recorded lectures or podcasts as an integral part of their study regimen.

Utilizing data-driven assessment and feedback is an integral part of monitoring student progress and implementing timely interventions. By consistently gathering and scrutinizing evaluation data, educators can accurately identify areas in which learners are encountering difficulties, consequently modifying their instructional methods to better facilitate learning outcomes. This method ensures that students experiencing academic challenges receive prompt feedback accompanied by customized strategies aimed at addressing particular hurdles thereby ensuring equitable educational opportunities for all pupils.

The utilization of data visualization tools presents educators with an efficient means to render intricate sets of information more comprehensible and accessible for students. Deploying digital platforms for data representation in pedagogical settings can facilitate the presentation of sophisticated concepts through visually stimulating formats, thereby enabling academically challenged learners to assimilate essential themes effectively. Illustratively, graphical depictions like bar graphs or pie charts hold significant potential in enhancing a student's comprehension relating to datasets and patterns beyond conventional text-based strategies.

The application of data-driven methodologies for personalized instruction is particularly advantageous to academically challenged students. Through thorough analysis and assessment of individual student needs, educators are empowered to tailor their pedagogical approach in a manner that effectively addresses each pupil's respective impediments while providing appropriate supplemental guidance when required. For example, if it becomes evident that one or more learners require added practice within discrete skills sets, the teacher has the ability to modify lesson plans by introducing supplementary activities as well as creating additional learning resources with which they can reinforce fundamental concepts.

Data-driven teaching methodologies are particularly advantageous for special education learners. By acquiring and scrutinizing data on pupils' personalized educational blueprints, educators can pinpoint zones where supplementary support may be required. In the instance of a special needs learner battling with reading comprehension, designated interventions can be employed by teachers such as providing auxiliary materials or presenting small group instruction to tackle this precise obstacle.

Captivating and inspiring pupils who are struggling can be a challenging undertaking. Nonetheless, evidence-based methodologies provide significant insights into learner engagement and motivation. Through scrutinizing records of student attendance, involvement, and achievements; educators can recognize patterns or trends that could signify their disengagement or shortage of drive. Equipped with this knowledge base, instructors may create schemes to rekindle the interest of individuals faltering in learning such as featuring project-oriented teaching techniques or fusing practical examples into pedagogy materials.

The surveillance and enhancement of student advancement constitute a crucial element in data-informed instruction. Through the utilization of data analytics, educators are equipped to monitor long-term progress among students, pinpoint areas that require further development, and intervene effectively as needed. Such forward-thinking measures pave the way for disadvantaged learners to access essential assistance with their studies thereby leveling academic playing fields relative to their peers while increasing overall achievement rates alike.

Ultimately, data-oriented teaching methodologies are indispensable in the realm of educational research and analysis. Through the gathering and examination of student performance metrics alongside instructional techniques, scholars can gain valuable perspectives on divergent interventions' efficacy in tandem with informed judgments to enhance pedagogical practices. This empirically based approach guarantees that students facing challenges inch learning benefit from evidence-supported methods yielding noteworthy outcomes.

To conclude, the utilization of data-driven interventions for students who are experiencing difficulties is a significant asset in the arsenal of educators. Through leveraging analysis tools capable of processing data to identify personalized learning techniques and differentiated instruction strategies that cater to individual student requirements, along with visualization resources allowing teachers complete insight into their class's overall performance instructors can effectively recognize and support struggling pupils. These approaches founded on empirical evidence not only foster stronger pupil engagement and motivation but also permit objective monitoring by tutors as they strive toward improving their progress ultimately culminating in better academic outcomes across all members within a given classroom setting.

8.14 Tracking and Analyzing Student Progress with Data Analytics Tools

In the current digital era, teachers possess a wealth of data that possesses immense potential to transform education and elevate student learning. Data analytics represents an influential resource at their disposal which empowers them to monitor and assess student advancement in real-time. Through this technique of leveraging data-driven pedagogy, educators can customize instruction methods for individuals, offer pertinent evaluations specific to each learner's needs while simultaneously improving overall educational outcomes.

In contemporary times, data-informed pedagogical techniques for subjects encompassed under STEM have garnered substantial favor. Teachers can leverage analytical tools to detect the domains where pupils face challenges and alter their dispensation correspondingly. Such an approach facilitates targeted identification of areas wherein math learners struggle by diligent employment of data analytics; subsequently enabling instructors in furnishing personalized support or supplementary teaching tactics as demanded.

The employment of data analysis tools holds great potential for effective implementation in the practice of personalized learning. By gathering and scrutinizing information on individual student academic progress, instructors can adeptly customize instruction to cater to each pupil's distinctive predispositions and methodological preferences. Consequently, this approach may lead to heightened involvement, incentive, ultimately culminating in enhanced scholarly accomplishment.

The integration of data-driven assessment and feedback are fundamental aspects of successful teaching. Through the utilization of data analytics tools, educators can swiftly evaluate students' academic progress with precision and efficiency to pinpoint areas where they excel or require improvement quickly. This enables teachers to provide prompt corrective measures that assist pupils in making necessary adjustments towards enhancing their comprehension.

In addition to its widespread applications in various fields, data visualization tools also offer undeniable advantages within the educational setting. Through conveying information via visually captivating and readily comprehensible formats, educators can leverage these technologies towards facilitating students' comprehension of intricate ideas and patterns. Thusly applied, a greater capacity for learning engagement is fostered alongside improved rates of knowledge retention among learners.

The implementation of differentiated instruction is a crucial practice in catering to the varying needs among students. Employing data-driven techniques can aid educators in identifying learners who necessitate supplementary support or stimulating material and subsequently adapting instructional methodologies suitably. By customizing lesson plans according to individual learning predispositions, instructors can ensure all pupils make significant headway while fulfilling their maximum potential.

In the realm of education, students in special needs programs necessitate distinct pedagogical strategies and aid. The application of data-oriented teaching techniques enables educators to pinpoint precise areas presenting difficulties for such individuals thereby providing tailored interventions. By consistently monitoring student achievement levels over time, teachers can make prudent choices concerning personalized instruction avenues as well as support services rendered particularly per child's unique requirements.

The utilization of data-driven methodologies can be employed to enhance student engagement and motivation. Through careful analysis of behavior, attendance, and participation patterns among students, educators may identify recurrent trends while devising effective strategies for heightened class involvement and overall motivation levels. Such efforts are paramount in fostering a conducive atmosphere that promotes positive learning experiences with the potential to benefit all pupils involved.

The proper supervision and enhancement of student progress represent a fundamental pillar in achieving successful teaching outcomes. The implementation of data analytics tools provides educators with the ability to continually monitor individual academic performances, analyze trends over time, and formulate informed decisions aimed at optimizing instructional practices. Through consistent analysis of students' information patterns, teachers can accurately identify areas requiring attention or improvement while adapting their strategies effectively towards fulfilling learner objectives.

Data-driven teaching not only provides tangible advantages for educators and learners but can also significantly contribute to educational research and analysis. By collecting comprehensive data sets on an extensive scale, experts in the field as well as policymakers can extract valuable insights into productive instructional techniques that facilitate academic progress among students from diverse backgrounds. Moreover, such meticulous investigation would help locate critical gaps in current methods of education delivery allowing stakeholders to make informed decisions grounded in reliable evidence-base approaches aimed at improving student outcomes across a wider spectrum.

To summarize, the utilization of analytical tools for data can significantly transform education by affording instructors a wealth of valuable insights into student progress and learning. By applying data-driven instructional methods, educators can optimize personalized teaching practices through targeted feedback mechanisms which ultimately improve overall academic outcomes among students. This transformative ability extends beyond monitoring achievement levels or reinforcing individualized subject matter, analytics tools also bear considerable potential to enhance program efficacy via bolstered engagement from learners while promoting equal opportunity for success across all subsets within educational institutions.

8.15 Data-Driven Teaching for Educational Research and Analysis

Within the context of our contemporary digital landscape, data-driven methods have catalyzed a transformative shift in education. Through these sophisticated and impactful tools, educators are endowed with powerful techniques which serve to fortify their pedagogical practices and promote meaningful progress across student outcomes. This particular section provides an examination into how data-driven approaches can be employed within educational research endeavors, facilitating teachers' acquisition of invaluable insights as well as informed decision-making processes that ultimately cultivate positive transformations within their classrooms.

Empirical evidence affirms that pedagogical techniques centered around data analysis have yielded exceptional results in science, technology, engineering and mathematics (STEM) disciplines. By harnessing digital tools and methodologies for scrutinizing student information; teachers are able to pinpoint which subject areas where students may be encountering difficulties thus directing apt interventions towards rectifying these shortcomings effectively. Consequently, this personalized approach guarantees each pupil is accorded the requisite support enabling them to thrive academically- a circumstance that invariably leads to enhanced educational accomplishments.

The utilization of data-driven assessment and feedback is pivotal in the domain of education. Through exploitation of digital tools, educators can amass immediate and accurate information on student performance to dispense timely and specialized feedback. The provision of such guidance not only helps learners identify personal strengths as well as areas that require improvement, but also allows instructors to tailor their pedagogical approach according to individual needs. This methodological process ensures a comprehensive coverage whereby every learner stands accounted for with equal opportunity towards reaching maximum potential sans any experience or feeling overlooked by virtue thereof being consigned into an ambiguous category characterized by mere numerical attribution indicative solely at its surface level evaluation exclusively considering conventional metrics while disregarding core learning requirements necessary pertaining there innovation led holistic educational ecosystem incumbent upon inclusive paradigms encompassing all strata equivalently begetter ignited transformed enlightener equating true edification awesomeness.

Data visualization tools present a potent method of conveying complicated information in an articulate and compelling approach. By integrating digital data visualization techniques into the classroom, educators may successfully convey pivotal ideas, making learning more attainable and pleasing for students. Additionally, visual depictions of statistics can help learners cultivate critical thinking capabilities as well as competencies relating to analyzing information - instrumental skills required for achievement within today's 21st-century professional environment.

Data-driven techniques have proven to be highly effective in the implementation of differentiated instruction. Through analysis of student data, teachers can identify specific learning needs and personalize their instructional approach accordingly. By adopting this methodology, students receive education at a level appropriate for them, thereby maximizing their potential for academic growth while maintaining an inclusive classroom atmosphere conducive for positive development.

The adoption of data-driven teaching techniques is paramount in facilitating effective education for special needs students. Through careful analysis of individual student progress, educators can tailor interventions and accommodations specifically suited to their distinct requirements. This approach fosters a culture of inclusivity towards all learners and guarantees that each has equitable prospects for attainment regardless of ability level.

Moreover, utilizing data-driven methodologies can markedly enhance student involvement and incentive. Employing data analytics to track students' advancement and detect areas of captivation permits educators to create learning encounters that are pertinent and captivating. This individualized approach endows learners with a sense of responsibility for their education while cultivating autonomous motivation from within themselves.

To conclude, the utilization of data-driven teaching techniques presents significant possibilities for educational research and analysis. Through the application of digital tools and proficient data analysis methods, instructors can acquire valuable insights into student learning that inform their instructional practices while driving positive change within classrooms. Whether focused on personalized instruction, enhanced assessment and feedback or augmented student engagement levels; employing a data-driven approach has immense transformative potential in education space – enabling teachers to become even more effective as educators.

8.16 Analyzing Data for Educational Policy and Decision-Making

Amidst the dynamic landscape of education, it is imperative for educators to exercise informed judgment based on empirical evidence. Data-informed pedagogy serves as a potent mechanism that has the potential to revolutionize conventional paradigms and digital advancements play an indispensable role in enabling this paradigm shift.

The utilization of digital tools in data-driven teaching presents a promising prospect for the advancement of STEM subjects. This approach offers considerable benefits to educators by equipping them with valuable insights into student performance and learning patterns, thereby enabling them to efficiently identify areas where students may be struggling and adjust their instruction correspondingly. Additionally, data analysis techniques can facilitate customized educational experiences geared towards individual learners while accounting for their distinctive aptitudes and limitations.

In contemporary education, data-driven assessment and feedback play fundamental roles in enhancing instructional effectiveness. Educational practitioners can leverage digital tools to collect and scrutinize student performance metrics which provide the basis for furnishing pertinent critiques promptly. The personalized nature of this evaluation process accords learners valuable insights into their level of progress as well as opportunities requiring optimization- a scenario that culminates in holistic learning outcomes improvement.

Data visualization tools offer teachers an efficacious means of presenting intricate information in a visually captivating manner. By integrating these instruments into their instruction, educators have the ability to facilitate students' comprehension of complex datasets and enhance their analytical abilities. Further, data-informed strategies may be employed to customize pedagogy according to individual student requirements for optimal learning outcomes.

Students who require special education services necessitate personalized instruction that caters to their distinct learning requirements. Data-driven pedagogical practices empower educators with the capability to scrutinize data pertaining solely to these individuals and establish customized tactics which stimulate academic progress. Additionally, utilizing this approach can heighten student involvement and incentivization by delivering instantaneous feedback alongside monitoring of advancement in real-time.

The role of data analytics in monitoring and enhancing student progress is critical. Educators can leverage digital tools to monitor the performance trajectory of students, enabling them to identify any areas that may require supplemental assistance. By adopting a data-driven approach, educators can intervene at an early stage providing targeted interventions that ultimately drive academic success among students.

In conclusion, the application of data-driven teaching methodology not only advances individual classroom performance but also contributes to educational research and analysis through its ability to assess larger sets of data. By scrutinizing a broader spectrum of information, experts can access valuable insights into prevailing styles in education while molding evidence-based approaches that promote growth-oriented policies and practices within the sector.

In conclusion, conducting data analytics for the purpose of educational policy and decision-making is an imperative practice among educators in today's digital age. Employing techniques such as data-driven teaching methods along with advanced technological tools aids teachers in tailoring learning experiences to individual needs, delivering focused feedback, and customizing instruction delivery while ensuring enhanced student engagement and motivation levels. Furthermore, analyzing academic progress through efficient monitoring methodologies facilitated by comprehensive data analysis contributes positively towards progressive edification research endeavors. Wholeheartedly adopting a process-of-empirical-comprehension approach coupled with embracing cutting-edge technological innovations has significant potential to reform contemporary education paradigms which would enable informed decisions by all stakeholders that positively impact the overall success rates of students 'academic outcomes.

8.17 Ethical Considerations in Data-Driven Educational Research and Analysis

Considering the era of vast amounts of data, educators now have access to substantial information that has immense potential for transforming teaching and learning. Nevertheless, with this significant capability comes a correspondingly great responsibility. As teachers adopt data-focused approaches to their pedagogy through analytical means, it becomes vital to consider the ethical considerations inherent in collecting, analyzing, and employing student-related statistics.

An essential ethical consideration in the education sector is safeguarding student data privacy and security. It is incumbent upon educators to take measures that guarantee collected information remains confidential, protect against unauthorized access, and observe strict regulatory provisions on data protection. Furthermore, teachers should obtain explicit consent from both students and their respective parents or guardians before collecting personally identifiable details used exclusively for educational purposes.

Another crucial factor to consider is the transparency and candor of data-driven methodologies. Educators should be transparent about the kinds of information being gathered, its intended purpose, and those authorized personnel who shall have access to it. Such a practice helps create an atmosphere of trust among students, parents/guardians as well as members of the broader society. In addition, instructors ought also to demonstrate openness towards feedback from stakeholders while fostering collaborative efforts amongst them in decision-making processes regarding anything related to data collection or analysis endeavors.

Furthermore, educators must consider the potential partialities and preconceptions that may emanate from data-oriented methodologies. Software tools for analyzing information and algorithms are prone to biases since they frequently rely on inputs created by humans who might inadvertently involve their personal predilections in the system's makeup. It is incumbent upon instructors to undertake a scrupulous analysis of both their data sets as well as any corresponding algorithms employed therein so as not to propagate discriminatory practices or entrench extant inequalities.

Additionally, educators ought to be cognizant of the inadvertent outcomes that may arise from data-based pedagogical approaches. Despite its capacity to offer valuable discernment, data examination must not override teachers' proficiency and intuition. Teachers should harness the power of data as an instrument for guiding their instruction while retaining a thorough recognition of each student's individualized necessities and situations.

Finally, educators must engage in continuous professional development to remain informed on the newest ethical standards and most effective practices regarding data-driven educational research and analysis. They should also play an active role in discussions and investigations related to the ethical consequences of utilizing data for instructional purposes by exchanging their experiences with peers within this domain while learning from others' insights.

By considering the ethical considerations involved in data-driven educational research and analysis, educators can effectively utilize data while concurrently upholding principles of privacy, transparency, fairness, and efficacy within their teaching practices. Consequently, resulting in advancements towards improved student outcomes as well as an education system that exemplifies equality and inclusivity.

CHAPTER 9

Empowering Student Creativity with Digital Tools

In today's ever-evolving educational landscape, instilling creativity in students has become a critical aspect of preparing them for success in the 21st century. This chapter elaborates on the integration of digital tools to unleash the creative potential of students across various educational settings.

9.1 The Importance of Creativity in Education

The concept of creativity is widely debated in human culture regarding innovation and potential resources. It encompasses the origin, excavation, and development of original ideas, or novel solutions to prior obstacles. These inventive conquests can manifest themselves as tangible products such as smartphones; organizations like Google Inc.; services and computer software programs (e.g., Windows Operating system); social-economic plans; artistic mastery evident through sculptures, visual drawings fashion designs, or animations. Moreover, Creativity also pertains to an individual's capability for imaginative contemplation coupled with the art of questioning skills when presented with new tasks. The developed technologies witnessed globally serve as commendable evidence showcasing mankind's creative capacity since everything around us including household items are all attributed works from intellectual brilliance despite its occasional nonchalant approach by some people who fail to realize that it still demands skillset together combined knowledge about technology leading up towards better results achieved overtime.

Every person possesses the powerful skill of creativity, yet learners excel in this area as it enhances their future career accomplishments and motivates them from the beginning. Early on, imaginative thinking is necessary to discover new methods for improving technical skills leading to a prosperous future. Children absorb abilities, concepts, and experiences from those around them during development, manifesting changes both apparent or personal based upon these interactions. Once ignited, creativity becomes an enjoyable experience that urges learners towards innovative solutions ultimately resulting in increased achievement levels and success down the line.

Moreover, cognitive characteristics play a crucial role in creative work within specific contexts. Problem-solving skills and the acquisition of relevant knowledge are essential factors that contribute significantly to this process. The ability to apply pre-existing knowledge effectively in diverse environments fosters growth and development. Numerous educators and scholars have emphasized creativity as an engine for modern education and career success among learners due to its potential for driving innovation. Additionally, governments worldwide have invested heavily in creating resources that promote fresh ideas and innovations while opening new markets with increased job opportunities. For instance, countries such as Japan, China, Germany UK & US continue improving their scientific manufacturing industries by enhancing creative learning systems and equipping students with the necessary skills to foster breakthroughs. This paper emphasizes the vital significance of integrating creativity into various levels of education despite limitations so that set goals can be achieved more efficiently through our current educational system today.

To examine the significance of creativity in education, it is necessary to respond to these inquiries.

Education that fosters creativity is essential for a learner's cognitive development to meet the demands of today's complex job market and innovation-oriented societies. The cultivation of creative skills depends on external factors such as social conditions, technical knowledge acquisition, skill-building exercises, and long-term commitment toward future aspirations; not just individual ability or talent alone. In addition to physical constructions like infrastructure facilities, products, etc., it also includes developing new solutions through inventive thinking that address societal needs or challenges. Furthermore, cultivating creativity also involves social transformations such as organizational structures for economic entities/businesses, traditions specific to certain geographies/geographical cultures/paradigm shifts (where enforced rules decide how these units function). Innovation plays an integral role within this process - thus contributing positively both at a personal level by improving quality of life and nationally/economically with growth following in its wake.

9.2 Active Learning and Creativity

Active learning and creativity are closely linked, as an active learner needs to use their creative thinking skills to select the best program, game, film, or song from various options. Governments and non-profit organizations have recognized the importance of creativity in higher education institutions for effective problem-solving in future job markets. This approach aims at maximizing human potential with minimal waste between training and performance levels. Creativity encourages learners to actively engage in all aspects of their education thus avoiding passiveness which hinders progress, leading them towards purposeful lives by unlocking untapped potentials necessary for development. Methods that foster more participatory processes vary but share a common objective: leveraging on humanity's potentiality through innovation and ideas aimed at shaping modern civilization's growth while also providing efficient solutions catering directly toward individual success within any given market sector context. However, some developing nations prioritize uplifting society collectively regarding happiness alongside improving living standards along these lines propelling similar communications around its inception aim/focusing mainly on addressing societal concerns related/unrelated work engagement demands/needs beyond just earning income/profits.

One compelling discovery shows that interactive teaching is essential for cultivating creative thinking in students and preparing them for their future careers. Unlike traditional frontal lectures, active learning engages learners through attractive elements that encourage greater participation, such as detailed examples tailored to attentive students. Nonetheless, creativity remains the key driver behind student productivity and realizing their full potential. However, these teachings don't usually involve students actively participating in the learning process; instead, "active teaching" requires inspired pupils who are well-versed in their work to lead by example. According to research, self-regulation is linked to both long-term academic success and short-term creativity achievement in students. The immediate advantages of self-regulation for promoting creative development are particularly noticeable as it can guide students towards innovative thinking and idea generation. Creative individuals who possess effective planning skills have a better ability to manage their learning experience within the prescribed timeframe while also acquiring sufficient knowledge.

The findings of the research indicate that academic success in the future is highly associated with active learning accomplishment. This correlation hinges on a learner's innovation and accountability towards their actions, alongside an imaginative setting promoting more advantageous outcomes within the classroom. Students characterized by superior performance and self-control ability are observed as well.

9.2.1 The Importance of Teaching Creativity to Students

The survey data from nineteen students provides insight into the challenges and solutions for active learning among students. It is evident that there are diverse learning patterns and needs within student populations, which this study reflects accurately. The findings highlight a need for more detailed profiling of larger cohorts to better understand their requirements. Interestingly, most of the surveyed students gravitate towards stimulating, inspiring and challenging environments despite individual differences in preferences (except two who were neutral). Small class sizes paired with active teaching methods enable teachers/supervisors to have one-on-one discussions with each student thus eliminating fear or shyness they may otherwise face when surrounded by peers during group sessions, allowing them freedom explore all possibilities without feeling embarrassed before others watching on as spectators!

Some students crave deeper, faster, broader and more intensive experiences. Others express a desire to halt rapid achievement and become standardized in terms of both experience and accomplishment. This creates tension between the need for intense involvement with rigorous learning opportunities within limited time constraints. Rojstaczer suggests that inadequate investments have left most learners feeling as though they lack important out-of-classroom experiences necessary for personal growth. More than half of graduating students require increased standardization and improved teaching methods which cater to their individual needs while also challenging them aggressively at every turn - thereby providing a flow across creative training programs where self-motivation is encouraged through active engagement rather than passive memorization. By incorporating creativity into active learning strategies, developmental changes can be achieved rapidly; allowing individuals access to different skills otherwise neglected by traditional modes of instruction. A diverse pool of engaged learners who embrace new challenges has proven highly impactful on effective academic outcomes when facilitated correctly with educators initiated creatively-driven curricula approaches foster collaboration over competition methods among peers thus minimizing exclusionary behavior tendencies from classroom culture seamlessly transforming the overall learner's dynamics imprint towards unity-solving mindset adoption enhancing societal cohesiveness prospectively aligned around inclusive value systems embracing diversity prospected universality avant-garde enlightenment fostering intellectual evolution way beyond mere accreditation appended paperwork nomenclature-symbolism generation attributions bounty accruing essentially practicality exploring approachability dimensions thereof authenticated productivity translating positively via symbolism-laden rungs respectively escalating accredited measurements termed dual-practicality-enhanced attaining lifelong endowment validations cascading globally accessible breakthroughs culminating individuation heights lifting humanity essence futurological visionaries-bodied embodiments prospered therein symbolizing potential outputs morpho genetically apt evidential basis underpinned proverbial axiom 'actions speak louder words'.

The students' learning motivation profile and performance exhibit noticeable alterations depending on various experiences, influenced by factors like diversification, learning to lead a good life, career choices influence, and setting future rhythms. Active teaching is crucial in providing learners with the necessary tools for developing an appropriate level of motivation and inspiration.

Fostering creativity in teaching has a positive impact on students' engagement and enjoyment of school. By involving learners through open discussion that incorporates creative ideas into lesson plans, educators can CONVEY INFORMATION BETTER. This approach also encourages innovation and allows teachers to tap into their students' hidden talents, which boosts confidence during the learning process. Conversely, traditional methods often lead to student boredom and decreased concentration levels - detrimental factors that can result in unproductive behavior among learners. Integrating active discussions helps cultivate dedicated pupils who remain committed throughout classroom activities while preparing for future success by making efficient use of resources and time management skills.

Promoting creative education is key in helping teachers inspire students' creativity and encourage lifelong learning. This approach fosters independent thinking, responsibility, problem-solving skills for social and everyday issues, collaboration with others, and a focus on fulfilling human needs rather than traditional subjects through available technology. Additionally, promoting student-centered learning allows learners to draw from diverse perspectives leading them towards better careers upon graduation while positively contributing to society's well-being. Although critics believe that creativity does not equate democracy; the collaborative technological resources online as well as small instructional groups allow educators opportunities for employing such activities crucial when developing creative-learning abilities among their students who will learn more efficient techniques which strengthen active analytical processes over just passively acquiring textbooks knowledge without true understanding & critical-thinking ability enhancements. By encouraging innovative practices within educational institutions worldwide via individualized approaches beyond compulsory coursework offerings- ultimately benefiting communities at large since it helps facilitate an organized classroom where everyone can understand what they are being taught using LCD screens/projectors plus enhancing communication involving all parties involved achieving optimal integrations across-generalizing bodies of constructive knowledge faster/easier.

9.3 Restrictions on Creative Expression in the Field of Education

The development of learners' creativity and ability to express themselves freely is crucial for holistic growth and critical thinking in the ever-evolving realm of education. Yet, educators grapple with a convoluted web of regulations that define the limits on creative expression within educational contexts. Such constraints are influenced by an array of factors - cultural traditions or legal mandates included- which pose both obstacles and avenues for fostering innovation and self-expression among students.

Cultural and Societal norms: The impact of cultural and societal norms on educational contexts is substantial. Acceptable or appropriate conduct can be influenced by these aspects, with some cultures labeling specific topics or expressions as taboo or controversial thereby prompting self-censorship amongst pupils while institutions restrict creativity. In this regard, educators must demonstrate a competent understanding of each culture's sensitivities to safeguard the promotion of open dialogue whilst encouraging critical thinking to balance out respect for values tied up within that society against creative exploration requirements for students' betterment.

Legal Regulations: The parameters of creative expression in schools are shaped by both legal regulations and educational policies. These guidelines, such as curriculum standards, administrative directives, and laws that promote student safety can limit educators' discretion when selecting teaching materials or broaching certain subjects. The issue also involves reconciling freedom-of-speech legislation with education practice, which sparks arguments over whether constitutional rights may be upheld while still permitting schools to regulate students' means of self-expression.

Parental and Community Expectations: The expectations of parents and the community can impact school policies regarding creative expression, potentially limiting certain forms due to controversial topics or divergent perspectives. In response, educators must work alongside stakeholders in an open and understanding way while advocating for the value of creative exploration in education.

Technological Challenges: The infusion of technology into education poses fresh obstacles for imaginative expression. Although electronic media presents chances for inventive learning adventures, it also gives rise to apprehensions regarding cyber safety, online harassment and conforming to acceptable usage guidelines. Teachers must steer these challenges by cultivating digital know-how as well as accountable conduct online while utilizing technological means to promote creativity and cooperation among pupils.

Restrictions on budget: The scarcity of resources, either inadequate funding for art-related activities or unavailability of required materials and equipment, can limit educators' potential to promote creative expression in the classroom. Nevertheless, teachers can harness their creativity and adaptability skills to create interesting educational opportunities that stimulate inventiveness while encouraging individuality among students.

Despite numerous obstacles and limitations, educators hold significant influence in cultivating creativity and unrestrained expression within educational contexts. By maneuvering boundaries sensibly through advocacy and inventive techniques, they can foster an all-encompassing learning atmosphere that endows students to investigate, challenge norms, form a vision meaningfully; thus, preparing them for success amid dynamic global changes ahead.

9.4 Encouraging Digital Storytelling and Multimedia Projects

In today's technological age, educators must incorporate digital tools into their teaching practices. Utilizing digital storytelling and multimedia projects provides students with dynamic educational opportunities that encourage creativity, critical thinking, and communication skills. In this subchapter, we will introduce educators to digital storytelling and provide practical strategies to promote its implementation in the classroom.

9.5 What is Digital Storytelling?

Digital storytelling involves the use of digital tools such as videos, images, audio, and interactive elements to create and share stories. This method allows students to express themselves in a variety of media formats, solidify their understanding and retention of information, and breathe new life into traditional teaching methods.

9.5.1 How to Encourage Digital Storytelling?

To encourage educators to engage their students with digital storytelling and multimedia projects, we will begin by providing an overview of popular digital tools such as video-editing software, presentation tools, and interactive platforms. Additionally, we will explore websites and online resources that provide pre-made templates, images, and sound effects to enhance digital projects.

9.5.2 Developing Project-Based Assignments

We will guide educators in the development of project-based assignments that incorporate digital storytelling. By providing clear objectives and guidelines, educators can empower students to take ownership of their learning and unleash their creativity. We will showcase different project ideas, such as creating digital portfolios, producing mini-documentaries, or designing interactive presentations.

9.5.2.1 Assessment Strategies

To assess both the content and technical aspects of students' projects, educators will learn to evaluate the quality of their work. By providing constructive feedback and encouraging collaboration, students can improve their creativity, research, and presentation skills.

9.5.3 Benefits of Digital Storytelling

Lastly, we will highlight the benefits of digital storytelling and multimedia projects in developing 21st-century skills. By engaging in these projects, students can develop digital literacy, critical thinking, collaboration, and communication skills, which are essential for success in the modern world.

In conclusion, this subchapter provides educators with the necessary knowledge and strategies to encourage digital storytelling in their classrooms. By integrating digital tools into their teaching practices, educators can enhance the learning experience for their students and prepare them for the digital world ahead.

9.6 Fostering Collaboration and Communication with Online Tools

Today's teachers play a broader role than traditional educators. They must embrace digital tools to enhance student engagement, foster collaboration, and facilitate effective communication in the classroom. The subchapter titled "Fostering Collaboration and Communication with Online Tools" introduces teachers to various online platforms and applications that can revolutionize their teaching methods and create a more interactive learning environment.

Online tools enable collaboration among students, which is one of their key benefits. Google Classroom, Edmodo, and Microsoft Teams are some of the platforms that create a virtual space where students can work together on projects, share resources, and provide feedback to one another. These tools promote teamwork and allow for seamless communication between students and teachers, creating an open and inclusive learning environment.

Furthermore, online tools offer interactive features that engage students in the learning process. Kahoot, Quizlet, and Nearpod are some of the platforms that allow teachers to create interactive quizzes, flashcards, and presentations respectively, making learning more fun and interactive. Teachers can cater to different learning styles and capture students' attention in a way that traditional methods may not achieve.

Online tools also facilitate effective communication between teachers and students, which is crucial in a digital society. Remind and ClassDojo, for instance, provide a secure and convenient way for teachers to communicate important announcements, share resources, and provide timely feedback to students. These tools enhance the overall learning experience by eliminating barriers and ensuring seamless communication.

To keep up with the demands of the modern world and provide their students with the skills they need to succeed, teachers must familiarize themselves with online tools and explore their potential in the classroom. This subchapter serves as an introduction to the vast array of digital tools available, providing teachers with the necessary foundation to incorporate these tools into their teaching practices.

In conclusion, "Fostering Collaboration and Communication with Online Tools" emphasizes the importance of using digital tools to enhance teaching methods. By embracing these tools, teachers can promote collaboration, engagement, and effective communication in their classrooms. As the education landscape continues to evolve, teachers must adapt and leverage technology to create a dynamic and inclusive learning environment.

9.7 Cultivating Critical Thinking Skills through Digital Projects

In today's digital era, teachers must incorporate technology into their classrooms to enhance student engagement and foster critical thinking skills. The vast amount of information available online makes it imperative for educators to equip their students with the necessary skills to navigate and analyze the content critically.

This subchapter from "From Chalkboard to Keyboard: An Introduction to Digital Tools for Teachers" aims to guide teachers on how to use digital projects to promote critical thinking skills in their students. By integrating digital tools into their teaching strategies, teachers can create an interactive and dynamic learning environment that fosters higher-order thinking.

Project-based learning is one effective way to promote critical thinking. Digital projects allow students to explore real-world problems, collaborate with peers, and think critically to find solutions. By engaging in these projects, students develop essential skills such as problem-solving, analysis, evaluation, and creativity. Teachers can guide students to think critically about the information they find, analyze its credibility, and synthesize it to create meaningful outcomes.

This subchapter explores various digital tools and platforms that can be used to promote critical thinking through projects. Teachers will learn how to guide students to use online research and data analysis, multimedia presentations, and virtual simulations to develop their critical thinking skills. Practical examples and case studies illustrate successful implementation in different subject areas.

Assessing critical thinking skills in digital projects is also crucial. Teachers can design rubrics and evaluation criteria that focus on critical thinking skills, ensuring students' learning outcomes align with the project objectives. By providing feedback and guiding students in reflection, teachers can further enhance their critical thinking abilities.

In conclusion, this subchapter provides teachers with the knowledge and tools necessary to promote critical thinking skills through digital projects. Integrating technology into the classroom and guiding students in utilizing digital tools effectively prepares them to navigate the digital world confidently and think critically about the information they encounter. Through project-based learning, students develop essential skills that will serve them well in their academic and professional lives.

9.8 Enhancing Critical Thinking Skills through Digital Projects: Tools to Consider

To promote critical thinking skills in students, it's important to leverage a variety of tools that encourage analysis, creativity, and problem-solving. Here are some tools in different categories that can help achieve this goal:

- Mind Mapping: MindMeister, Coggle, MindMup
- Collaborative Writing: Google Docs, Zoho Writer, Dropbox Paper
- Digital Storytelling: Adobe Spark, Book Creator, StoryMap JS

- Game-Based Learning: Kahoot!, Quizlet, Minecraft Education Edition

By utilizing these tools, students can strengthen their critical thinking skills while engaging in a fun and interactive learning experience (See Table 9.1). Integrating these tools into educational activities can create a rich, interactive learning environment that fosters critical thinking skills. Teachers can leverage these digital projects to engage students and promote learning.

Table 9.1 Tool for Enhancing Critical Thinking Skills.

Activity	Tool	Platform	Features
Collaboration and Communication Tools	Google Workspace: • Encourages collaborative document editing, real-time feedback, and communication.	Microsoft 365: • Provides tools like Teams and OneNote for collaborative projects and discussions.	Slack: • Facilitates team communication and collaboration on projects.
Mind Mapping Tools	MindMeister: • Allows for collaborative mind mapping, brainstorming, and organizing ideas.	XMind: • Enables the creation of mind maps for visualizing and structuring thoughts.	Coggle: • A collaborative mind-mapping tool that promotes visual thinking.
Presentation Tools	Prezi: • Offers a dynamic, non-linear presentation style to encourage creative thinking.	Canva: • Allows students to create visually appealing presentations, posters, and infographics.	Emaze: • Offers visually engaging presentation templates.
Project-Based Learning Platforms	Edmodo: • Supports project-based learning through collaboration, discussion, and resource sharing.	Project Pals: • Facilitates the creation, organization, and sharing of digital projects.	Trello: • A project management tool that helps students plan and track progress.
Coding and Programming Tools	Scratch: • Introduces coding concepts through a visual, block-based interface.	Code.org: • Provides a variety of coding activities for students of all ages.	Thunkable: • Enables the creation of mobile apps with a drag-and-drop interface.

Table 9.1 ***Contd...***

Activity	Tool	Platform	Features
Digital Storytelling Tools	Storybird: • Allows students to create and share digital stories collaboratively.	Adobe Spark: • Facilitates the creation of multimedia stories, web pages, and videos	Book Creator: • Enables the development of interactive digital books
Simulation and Virtual Labs	PhET Interactive Simulations: • Offers interactive math and science simulations.	Labster: • Provides virtual labs for science subjects, promoting experimentation and critical analysis.	Google Earth: • Allows exploration and analysis of geographical data.
Online Debate Platforms	Debate.org: • Facilitates online debates on various topics, encouraging critical argumentation.	Kialo: • Provides a platform for structured, thoughtful debates on complex issues	
Critical Thinking Games	Minecraft Education Edition: • Encourages creativity, problem-solving, and collaboration.	Kahoot!: • Offers interactive quizzes and games to stimulate critical thinking.	Mystery Skype: • Fosters critical thinking through global connections and problem-solving.
Virtual Reality (VR) Tools	Google Expeditions: • Takes students on virtual field trips to enhance experiential learning.	CoSpacesEdu: • Allows students to create and explore virtual environments.	Merge Cube: • Offers augmented reality experiences for hands-on learning.
Assessment and Reflection Tools	Flipgrid: • Encourages video responses for reflection and discussion.	Padlet: • Facilitates collaborative brainstorming and reflection.	Socrative: • Provides real-time assessments to gauge understanding.

9.9 Promoting Global Connections with Virtual Exchange Programs

In today's interconnected world, fostering global connections and cultural understanding is more important than ever. As educators, we have a unique opportunity to help our students develop a global mindset and prepare them for the challenges and opportunities of the modern world. One powerful tool that can assist us in achieving this goal is virtual exchange programs.

Virtual exchange programs utilize digital tools to connect students from different countries and cultures, allowing them to collaborate, communicate, and learn together. These programs offer a range of benefits for both educators and students, making them an invaluable addition to the modern teacher's toolkit.

First and foremost, virtual exchange programs provide a platform for students to engage in meaningful cross-cultural interactions. Through video conferencing, online discussions, and collaborative projects, students can gain firsthand knowledge and understanding of different cultures, traditions, and perspectives. This exposure helps break down stereotypes and promotes empathy, tolerance, and respect among students from diverse backgrounds.

Furthermore, virtual exchange programs enhance students' digital literacy and global competence. By participating in online collaborations, students develop crucial 21st-century skills such as communication, collaboration, critical thinking, and problem-solving. They also learn to navigate digital tools and platforms effectively, preparing them for a future where technology is an integral part of their personal and professional lives.

For educators, virtual exchange programs offer an opportunity to expand their teaching repertoire and connect with colleagues from around the world. By collaborating with teachers from different countries, teachers can exchange ideas, share resources, and gain new perspectives on pedagogy. This professional development aspect not only enhances their teaching practices but also enriches their students' learning experiences.

To implement virtual exchange programs successfully, teachers need to familiarize themselves with a range of digital tools and platforms. These tools can facilitate communication, collaboration, and project management, ensuring seamless interactions between students and educators from different countries. Some popular platforms for virtual exchange programs include eTwinning, iEARN, and PenPal Schools, among others.

In conclusion, virtual exchange programs are an excellent way to promote global connections and cultural understanding among students. By leveraging digital tools, teachers can provide their students with unique learning experiences that prepare them for a globally interconnected world. So, let's embrace these virtual exchange programs and empower our students to become global citizens of the future.

9.10 Supporting Student Digital Portfolios for Reflection and Growth

In the digital age, educators must incorporate technology into their teaching to provide engaging and effective learning experiences for students. Digital portfolios are a prime example of a powerful digital tool that can benefit both students and teachers.

Unlike traditional paper-based portfolios, digital portfolios offer a multimedia-rich platform for students to showcase their best work. They can include documents, images, videos, and audio recordings, enabling students to demonstrate their creativity and digital literacy skills.

Another significant advantage of digital portfolios is that they facilitate self-reflection, promoting metacognition and student ownership of learning. Students can curate and update their portfolios regularly, assess their progress, identify areas for improvement, and set goals for future learning.

To maximize the effectiveness of digital portfolios, teachers need to provide clear guidelines for portfolio creation and evaluation. Ongoing feedback and guidance are also crucial to help students refine their portfolios and develop their reflective skills.

Digital portfolios can serve as useful assessment tools, enabling teachers to gain valuable insights into their students' strengths, weaknesses, and learning styles. This information can inform instructional decisions and facilitate personalized learning experiences tailored to individual student needs.

However, educators must also consider issues related to privacy and digital citizenship. Students should be educated on how to protect their personal information and respect the intellectual property rights of others. Teachers can also teach students how to critically evaluate online sources and use technology responsibly.

In conclusion, digital portfolios offer a powerful tool for supporting student reflection and growth. By providing a platform for students to showcase their work, engage in self-reflection, and receive feedback from teachers, digital portfolios foster both academic and personal development. As educators, we must embrace digital tools like portfolios to create meaningful learning experiences and prepare students for success in the digital age.

CHAPTER 10

E-Learning Platforms for Technical Skills Development

E-learning platforms have revolutionized the teaching and learning experience among students and provide supplementary resources to instructors. Such platforms provide a large amount of information and knowledge, access to certain sources that might not be easily accessible otherwise, and time to manage according to students' ease.

E-learning platforms grant an easy approach for students, making accessibility easier. New ways of learning do not require students to be there in person, unlike the older methods. Through the higher level of flexibility provided, it can be said that education has no boundaries- it is open to all.

Electronic learning is the way to go for multiple technical domains such as programming, augmented reality, virtual design and so on. This way the teacher can provide a fruitful learning exposure to their students and make up with new ways to teach and elucidate the older teaching methods.

E-learning platforms provide a pathway for learning many different skills effectively. These include digital marketing, web development, data analytics etc. The classroom gives us the right amount of knowledge needed to be good at rapidly changing fields.

Another significant advantage of e-learning platforms is the availability of virtual laboratories and simulations for science and engineering education. These virtual tools allow students to conduct experiments and simulations in a safe and controlled environment, without the need for expensive equipment or physical lab space. This not only saves costs but also enhances the learning experience by providing hands-on practice and real-world applications.

In conclusion, e-learning platforms are crucial in shaping the future of technical education. By providing accessibility, flexibility, and a wide range of resources for teachers and scholars, these platforms have revolutionized the way we learn. In an ever-changing world of technology, it is essential to embrace e-learning platforms to enhance teaching methods and ensure students' success.

10.1 Popular E-Learning Platforms for Technical Skills Development

In today's digital age, the demand for technical skills is higher than ever before. As a teacher or scholar in the field of technical education, it is crucial to stay up to date with the latest tools and platforms that can help enhance the learning experience for your students. In this subchapter, we will explore the most popular e-learning platforms for technical skills development that cater to a wide range of niches within the realm of digital tools and technical education.

One of the leading platforms in online coding courses and tutorials is Code academy. With a user-friendly interface and interactive lessons, Code academy offers courses in various programming languages such as Python, Java, and HTML/CSS. Students can practice coding in a real-time coding environment and receive immediate feedback, making it an ideal platform for beginners and experienced coders alike.

For those interested in digital design and graphic arts education, Adobe Creative Cloud is a must-have tool. This platform provides access to a wide range of industry-standard software such as Photoshop, Illustrator, and InDesign. With comprehensive tutorials and project-based learning, students can develop their skills in graphic design, web design, and digital art.

Virtual reality (VR) and augmented reality (AR) are rapidly gaining popularity in education. Platforms like Unity and Unreal Engine offer comprehensive courses and tools for educators interested in incorporating VR and AR into their technical education curriculum. These platforms provide resources for creating immersive experiences and simulations that enhance learning in fields such as engineering, architecture, and healthcare.

When it comes to e-learning platforms for technical skills development, Udemy and Coursera are two giants in the industry. Both platforms offer a wide range of courses and programs in digital marketing, data science, web development, and more. Featuring courses from renowned universities and industry experts, these platforms provide students with the opportunity to gain practical skills and certifications that are highly valued in the job market.

Online project management and collaboration tools are essential for technical education. Platforms like Trello and Asana allow educators and students to manage and collaborate on projects seamlessly. These tools provide features such as task assignment, progress tracking, and file sharing, making them invaluable resources for teaching project-based courses and fostering teamwork.

Lastly, virtual laboratories and simulations are transforming science and engineering education. Platforms like Labster and PhET Interactive Simulations offer virtual labs and interactive simulations that enable students to conduct experiments and explore complex scientific concepts in a safe and controlled environment. These platforms provide a hands-on learning experience that enhances understanding and retention of technical knowledge.

In conclusion, the world of e-learning platforms for technical skills development is vast and diverse. By incorporating these popular platforms into your teaching strategies, you can provide your students with the necessary tools and resources to succeed in today's digital world. Whether it's coding, digital design, virtual reality, or project management, there is a platform out there that caters to your specific niche within technical education.

10.2 The Advantages of E-Learning in EDUCATION

E-learning has become a crucial aspect of education in our digital age, extending to technical education. In this subchapter, we will explore the benefits of e-learning in technical education, highlighting its positive impact on both teachers and scholars in various niches, including digital tools, online coding courses, virtual reality, and augmented reality education tools, and more.

One significant advantage of e-learning in technical education is its flexibility and accessibility. Teachers can create and deliver engaging and interactive lessons, allowing students to access the content anytime and anywhere. This flexibility accommodates different learning styles and preferences, enabling scholars to learn at their own pace. Additionally, e-learning eliminates geographical barriers, making technical education accessible to a wider audience.

Moreover, e-learning provides a wealth of digital tools and resources that enhance technical education. For instance, online coding courses and tutorials allow scholars to acquire programming skills efficiently, while e-learning platforms that offer advanced software and tools benefit digital design and graphic arts education. Virtual reality and augmented reality education tools create immersive learning experiences for technical subjects, enhancing understanding and retention.

E-learning platforms also provide personalized learning experiences. Teachers can track scholars' progress, tailor content accordingly, and identify areas of improvement. This individualized approach ensures that each scholar receives the necessary support and challenges, ultimately enhancing their technical skills and knowledge.

E-learning bridges the gap between theory and practice through virtual laboratories and simulations. Scholars can conduct experiments and simulations in a safe and controlled environment, enhancing understanding and preparing them for real-world technical challenges.

Lastly, e-learning offers opportunities for collaboration and networking. Online project management and collaboration tools facilitate group work and teamwork skills, crucial in technical professions. Scholars can connect with industry professionals through e-learning platforms, gaining valuable insights and networking opportunities.

In conclusion, the integration of digital tools, online courses, and collaborative platforms revolutionizes the way technical subjects are taught and learned. The benefits of e-learning in technical education are vast and diverse, from flexibility and accessibility to personalized learning experiences and practical simulations. Teachers and scholars in various niches can benefit from these advantages, ultimately enhancing technical education in the modern era.

CHAPTER 11

Digital Marketing and Analytics Training Programs

In the constantly evolving digital landscape, educators need to keep up with the latest tools and techniques to enhance technical education. One area that has gained significant traction is digital marketing and analytics. This subchapter provides an overview of how these areas can revolutionize education, catering specifically to teachers, scholars, and individuals interested in digital tools and technical education.

11.1 The Importance of Digital Tools in Technical Education

As the world becomes increasingly digital, educators must equip students with the necessary skills to navigate this digital terrain. Online coding courses, digital design, and graphic arts education, virtual reality and augmented reality education tools, and e-learning platforms for technical skills development are just a few of the digital tools that can enhance the learning experience.

11.2 The Role of Digital Marketing and Analytics in Education

Digital marketing and analytics offer educators the opportunity to reach a wider audience and measure the impact of their efforts. By leveraging digital marketing strategies, teachers can promote their courses, connect with potential students, and create a strong online presence. Analytics tools enable educators to gather data on student engagement, performance, and learning patterns, allowing for more personalized instruction and targeted interventions.

11.3 The Power of Data Science and Analytics in Education

Data science and analytics courses and tools play a pivotal role in empowering educators to make informed decisions. By analyzing data collected from various sources, such as online platforms and virtual classrooms, teachers can gain deep insights into student progress and effectively tailor their teaching approaches. This data-driven approach enables educators to identify areas where students may be struggling and devise targeted interventions to support their learning.

11.4 Collaboration and Project Management Tools in Technical Education

Online project management and collaboration tools facilitate seamless communication and teamwork in technical education. These tools enable students to collaborate remotely, share resources, and work together on complex projects. Web development and programming boot camps provide students with intensive training and hands-on experience, equipping them with the skills needed to thrive in the digital age.

11.5 Virtual Laboratories and Simulations in Technical Education

Virtual laboratories and simulations offer a safe and cost-effective alternative to traditional science and engineering education. With these tools, students can conduct experiments, analyze data, and explore complex concepts in a virtual environment. This immersive experience enhances learning outcomes and prepares students for real-world challenges.

In conclusion, digital marketing and analytics have the potential to transform education by providing educators with the tools and insights needed to enhance technical education. By embracing digital tools, teachers can engage students, reach a wider audience, and create a more personalized learning experience. With the rapid advancements in technology, educators must adapt and leverage these digital tools to prepare students for success in a digital world.

11.6 Incorporating Digital Marketing and Analytics in Technical Education

In this technology-driven era, it is crucial that technical education incorporates teachings on digital marketing and analytics. The integration of these subjects will equip students with skills to keep up with the growing trend of online businesses, giving them a competitive edge in the job market. Digital marketing involves promoting products or services through social media and email platforms while data analysis yields vital insights for effective decision making.

There are several benefits for students when technical education includes these tools. By gaining knowledge in digital areas like analytics and SEO optimization, they can obtain a competitive advantage that modern employers seek. Additionally, incorporating these tools allows the acquisition of essential skills such as social media proficiency and data analysis useful across various industries.

Institutions have multiple options of boosting the integration of courses that cater to contemporary industry demands. The first approach involves arranging workshops focusing exclusively on topics pertaining to practical applications. Alternatively, professionals from distinct disciplines could invite educators at events or talks for divulging insights and guidance on how specialized work processes can be harmonized suitably for optimal outcomes. It is crucially important to prioritize individual career sustainability while considering these methods always.

In summary, offering customized courses that equip students with analytical abilities and improve their aptitude in contemporary marketing principles will better prepare them for graduation. Given the varied demands of markets requiring distinct skill sets from individuals over time, embracing this approach guarantees a seamless pathway towards career development without unnecessary obstacles. Incorporating digital marketing and analytics into technical education can enrich students' skill sets and equip them for the ever-changing demands of the digital age. Check out this comprehensive guide to learn how to seamlessly integrate these concepts into technical education.

1. **Foundational Concepts:**
   - **Introduction to Digital Marketing:** Provide an overview of digital marketing principles, including SEO, content marketing, social media marketing, email marketing, and paid advertising.
   - **Understanding Analytics:** Introduce the basics of analytics, focusing on key metrics and the importance of data-driven decision-making.
2. **Practical Workshops:**
   - **Hands-on Exercises:** Conduct workshops where students can apply digital marketing concepts in real-world scenarios, such as creating social media content, designing ad campaigns, and optimizing website content for search engines.
   - **Tool Proficiency:** Familiarize students with digital marketing tools such as Google Analytics, SEMrush, and social media management platforms.

3. **Integrated Projects:**
   - **Capstone Projects:** Assign comprehensive projects that require students to develop and execute a digital marketing strategy for a fictitious or real business.
   - **Cross-Disciplinary Collaboration:** Encourage collaboration between students from technical and non-technical disciplines to simulate real-world working environments.
4. **Guest Lectures and Industry Insights:**
   - **Invite Industry Experts:** Bring in professionals from the digital marketing and analytics fields to share their experiences, industry insights, and emerging trends.
   - **Panel Discussions:** Conduct panel discussions with experts covering various aspects of digital marketing, analytics, and their intersection with technology.
5. **Certifications and Training Programs:**
   - **Google Analytics Certification:** Encourage students to pursue certifications like Google Analytics Individual Qualification (GAIQ) to demonstrate proficiency in analytics.
   - **HubSpot Academy:** Leverage resources like HubSpot Academy for free certifications in inbound marketing, content marketing, and social media strategy.
6. **Web Analytics Integration:**
   - **Google Analytics Workshops:** Conduct workshops on setting up Google Analytics, tracking website performance, and extracting actionable insights.
   - **Conversion Rate Optimization (CRO):** Teach students the principles of CRO and how analytics can be used to optimize user journeys on websites.
7. **Social Media Marketing:**
   - **Social Media Campaigns:** Guide students in planning and executing social media campaigns, considering target audiences, content creation, and performance tracking.
   - **Social Media Analytics:** Explore analytics tools within social media platforms and third-party tools to measure the impact of social media efforts.

8. Content Marketing Integration:

- **Content Creation Workshops:** Conduct workshops on creating engaging and relevant content for websites, blogs, and social media.
- **Content Performance Analysis:** Teach students how to analyze the performance of content through metrics such as engagement, shares, and conversions.

9. Email Marketing Practices:

- **Email Campaign Management:** Provide insights into crafting effective email campaigns, including segmentation, personalization, and A/B testing.
- **Email Analytics:** Introduce tools for measuring the success of email campaigns through metrics like open rates, click-through rates, and conversions.

10. Data Visualization Techniques:

- **Introduction to Data Visualization:** Teach students how to visually represent marketing data using tools like Tableau, Google Data Studio, or Microsoft Power BI.
- **Creating Dashboards:** Guide students in creating dashboards that provide a holistic view of marketing performance.

11. Ethical Considerations and Privacy:

- **Data Ethics Discussions:** Engage students in discussions about the ethical use of data in digital marketing.
- **Privacy Compliance:** Ensure students are aware of privacy regulations (e.g., GDPR, CCPA) and their implications for digital marketing practices.

12. Continuous Learning and Industry Updates:

- **Encourage Lifelong Learning:** Emphasize the importance of staying updated on industry trends and advancements in digital marketing and analytics.
- **Online Communities:** Recommend participation in online communities and forums to foster continuous learning and networking.

11.7 Digital Tools for Digital Marketing and Analytics Training

When it comes to educating students in digital marketing and analytics, having access to the right combination of tools is critical. These tools enable students to gain hands-on experience and valuable insights into real-world situations. Look at this list of digital tools that are beneficial for digital marketing and analytics training.

By leveraging a combination of digital tools, educators can create a comprehensive and hands-on learning experience for students pursuing digital marketing and analytics training. The integration of these tools into coursework enables students to develop practical skills and be well-prepared for the dynamic and data-driven field of digital marketing (See Table 11.1, Table 11.2).

Table 11.1 Digital Marketing Tools.

Tools	Purpose:	Usage:
Google Analytics	Comprehensive web analytics tool for tracking and analyzing website traffic.	Students can learn to set up Google Analytics, analyze user behavior, and generate reports.
SEMrush	SEO and competitive research tool.	Students can conduct keyword research, analyze competitor websites, and track the performance of SEO strategies.
HubSpot Marketing Hub	All-in-one inbound marketing platform.	Students can use HubSpot for content creation, social media management, and email marketing.
Hootsuite	Social media management and scheduling tool.	Students can learn to manage multiple social media accounts, schedule posts, and track social media performance.
Mailchimp	Email marketing and automation platform.	Students can design and execute email campaigns, analyze email performance, and understand audience engagement.
Google Ads	Online advertising platform by Google.	Students can set up and manage ad campaigns, analyze and performance, and understand the bidding process.
Canva	Graphic design tool for creating visual content.	Students can design social media posts, infographics, and other visual content for digital marketing campaigns.
Buffer	Social media management and scheduling tool.	Students can schedule posts, analyze social media performance, and engage with audiences.

Table 11.2 Analytics Tools.

Tools	Purpose	Usage
Tableau	Data visualization and business intelligence tool.	Students can create interactive dashboards and visualizations to analyze marketing data.
Google Data Studio	Free data visualization tool by Google.	Students can create customizable reports and dashboards using data from various sources.
Hotjar	User behavior analytics and feedback tool.	Students can understand how users interact with websites through heatmaps, session recordings, and surveys.
Crazy Egg	Website optimization and user tracking tool.	Students can analyze user behavior on websites using heatmaps, scroll maps, and A/B testing.
Mixpanel	Analytics platform for tracking user interactions.	Students can gain insights into user engagement and retention by analyzing events and user behavior.
Kissmetrics	Customer engagement and analytics platform.	Students can track customer journeys and understand how different marketing channels contribute to conversions.
Moz	SEO and link analysis tool.	Students can perform website audits, track keyword rankings, and analyze backlink profiles.
Trello	Project management tool using boards, lists, and cards.	Students can plan and organize digital marketing campaigns collaboratively.
Slack	Team collaboration and communication platform.	Students can communicate in real-time, share updates, and collaborate on projects.

CHAPTER 12

Data Science and Analytics: Courses and Tools

Data science and analytics have become powerful tools utilized in many industries, including education. The increasing availability of data and digital tools has made educators recognize its potential to improve teaching and learning experiences. This section aims to provide an overview of how the integration of data science and analytics can benefit teachers across different educational niches.

Technical education is increasingly relying on digital technology, making it inseparable from computer-based courses that involve programming or coding language studies. By analyzing student performance during online tutorials, educators can identify areas where students struggle most while adapting their instructional strategies accordingly with targeted interventions.

Graphic arts instruction similarly benefits from demonstration techniques like those used for technical groups by tailoring class lessons based on individual progress analysis according to preference towards certain approaches offered alongside VR simulation software accessible separately via a feature-rich e-learning platform system all readily available at your fingertips regardless if you are using desktops as part-and-parcel hardware components essential pieces such taught material development process setups designed catered specifically around curriculum devised solely promoting work outcome improvements over timeframes outlined upfront within each program guidance plan we offer nationally accredited digitally scoped examination frameworks suited perfectly just right for every type candidate seeking\u00a0their next academic degree.

For Technical Skills Development E-Learning Platforms revolutionized training methods through personalized feedback options giving insights into knowledge gaps never realized! It ensures skills mastery with marketing campaigns optimized post-performance review resulting overall improved scores marked against industry-standard exams expected produce consistent results more accurate conclusions.

To acquire necessary skill sets includes procuring appropriate collaborated toolsets boasting modern-day adaptability namely implemented upon evidence-oriented decision-making practices; supported primarily by nowhere else centralizing pool resources team dynamics projects monitoring capabilities enabling future subversive success opportunities analyzed utilizing reliable statistical research meta-data collected throughout amongst similar institutions integrated datasets highlighting self-driven productivity efforts without outside assistance far too casual hence integrating Alexis default web browser updated weekly recommended mandatory use inclusion perfect only detection systems correlation indicative observations conclusion endless possibilities detailed within easy access portfolios career oriented type of temperament.

Lastly, Data Science and Analytics courses have gained popularity for their focus on evidence-based decision-making techniques applied towards refining teaching practices. By providing educators with the latest skills in data collection, analysis, interpretation they can ensure improved student performance and engagement across all niches including virtual labs simulations involving engineering science subject matter inevitably leading guides students toward attaining higher levels conceptual understanding resulting more nuanced knowledge acquisition over time!

Data science and analytics have become integral parts of various industries in the modern world. Therefore, it is crucial for teachers and scholars to equip themselves with the necessary knowledge and skills in this field. Fortunately, a wide range of digital tools are available that greatly enhance data science education.

Online coding courses and tutorials are key tools for teaching programming languages such as Python or R which are essential for data analysis. These resources offer interactive lessons containing real-life examples enabling learners to grasp complex concepts easily.

Digital design graphics play a significant role too since visualizing information is an essential skill taught through visualization software like Tableau or Power BI creating interactive dashboards transforming raw datasets into compelling visuals making them easier to analyze by students.

Virtual reality (VR) & augmented reality (AR) provide immersive learning experiences simulating real-world scenarios allowing interaction with virtual representations aiding understanding of complex ideas while e-learning platforms cover many topics including machine learning ensuring a comprehensive flexible experience incorporating hands-on projects personalization quizzes options etcetera catering for different needs/tastes/preferences…

Marketing/analytics training programs also exist helping develop market research/data-driven decision-making competencies via access/update feedback about latest trends using diverse digital instruments hone specialized abilities preparing better future careers overall technical ed…

Project management/collaboration utilities include Trello/Asana make task-sharing efficient/effective facilitating effective collaboration among educators/students adding value next-generation developers' curriculums/ beyond benefiting career paths applaudable job sector worth pursuing long-term-wise opportunities ...

Web development /programming bootcamps represent valuable assets offering practical/hands-on sessions building strong foundations manipulation techniques inclusive foundation prerequisites help attain competence covering related areas script writing language builds critical thinking problem-solving capacities subject matter confidence …

Lastly, virtual laboratories/simulations go hand-in-hand w/science/ engineering educations promoting "conduct experiments," analyzing info, /exploring complexities scientific fields given simulate experimentation environments safe secure risk-free experiential practices prior real-life testing implementations.

To conclude, digital tools revolutionize data science/analytic education. Combining online coding courses/design graphics software/e-learning platforms/marketing analytics training programs/project management/ collaboration utilities/web development programming bootcamps/virtual laboratories/simulations opens many possibilities of creating interactive &engaging lessons that promote critical thinking problem-solving skills in the next generation developers' curriculums beyond benefiting career paths and the job sector's future opportunities.

CHAPTER 13

Online Project Management and Collaboration Tools for Technical Education

The technical education sector has undergone a significant transformation in the rapidly advancing digital age. Digital tools and technology have revolutionized teaching methods, enabling educators to impart knowledge more effectively while students acquire valuable skills. Project management and collaboration have emerged as critical components of this shift. This chapter highlights how these two elements enhance technical education by catering to both teachers' needs, scholars', various niches within the field.

Digital learning environments that simulate real-world scenarios are now achievable thanks to technological developments. At the forefront is project management which allows hands-on practical experiences for students with methodologies such as Scrum or Agile fostering problem-solving abilities, teamwork, reflective ownership of ideas for individuals preparing them adequately before they enter industry demands.

Collaboration plays an essential role in facilitating complex discussions among peers from all corners regardless if online coding platforms transcend geographical barriers locally enhancing creativity across diverse backgrounds exponentially at no cost adding invaluable multilateral insights into solutions cooperation being vital-design graphics arts educational spaces benefit just like science laboratories too where virtual reality (VR)and augmented reality(AR) chase new horizons on interactive immersive training experiences digitization affords us. VR& non-virtual AR labs continue offering secure experimental exploration avenues complemented nicely using integration advantages afforded once combined projects incorporate effective online suitably placed skill-based assignments data analytics courses utilizing project coordination. Collective brainstorming harnessed through collaborative efforts pushing motivational levels forward accelerating progress generating positive results. Promoting greater accountability channels important group dynamics strengthening career development possibilities.

In conclusion, powerful agents supporting informative educational functionalities incorporating proper e-learning channel choices assisting creating media-rich content reaching target audiences promoting cross-functional collective insight regarding decision-making processes reaping untold benefits. Linked communal minds epitomize creative zenith flow inducing self-motivation embracing interdisciplinary work division initiatives granting exceptional growth trajectories mentioned above offers limitless potential qualifying graduates possessing well-rounded competencies. Being conscious heeding carefully selected inputs necessary adapting successfully benefited ahead thus participants leveraging innovative technologies providing truly transformative quality technical education indeed.

13.1 Popular Online Tools for Project Management and Collaboration

In today's digital age, project management and collaboration have become crucial skills for teachers and scholars in various fields of technical education. Luckily, there is a wide range of online tools available that can simplify and enhance these processes. Whether you are managing a coding course, designing graphics, teaching virtual reality, or analyzing data, these tools can streamline your workflow and improve productivity. Here are some popular online tools for project management and collaboration that are highly recommended for individuals in the digital tools and technical education niche:

1. **Trello:** Trello is a popular project management tool that uses boards, lists, and cards to help you organize and prioritize tasks. It allows you to collaborate with team members, assign tasks, set due dates, and track progress. With its intuitive interface and customizable features, Trello is an ideal tool for managing projects in technical education.

2. **Slack:** Slack is a communication and collaboration platform that enables real-time messaging, file sharing, and project discussions. It offers channels for different topics, direct messaging, and integration with other tools like Google Drive and Trello. Whether you are coordinating a coding bootcamp or collaborating on a graphic design project, Slack can help you stay connected and streamline communication.

3. **Google Drive:** Google Drive is a cloud-based file storage and sharing platform that allows you to create, store, and collaborate on documents, spreadsheets, presentations, and more. With its real-time editing and commenting features, Google Drive is an essential tool for teachers and scholars in digital design, data science, and virtual reality education.

4. **Asana:** Asana is a versatile project management tool that allows you to create and manage tasks, assign responsibilities, set deadlines, and track progress. It offers visualizations like Gantt charts and Kanban boards, making it ideal for managing complex projects in technical education.
5. **GitHub:** GitHub is a web-based platform for version control and collaboration in software development. It allows multiple developers to work on the same project, track changes, and merge their code seamlessly. GitHub is widely used in web development and programming bootcamps to facilitate collaboration and code sharing.

These are just a few examples of the many online tools available for project management and collaboration in technical education. Whether you are teaching coding, digital design, data science, or virtual reality, integrating these tools into your workflow can enhance efficiency and productivity. By leveraging the power of technology, teachers and scholars can create engaging and interactive learning experiences for their students, ultimately preparing them for success in the modern digital world.

13.2 Advantages of Online Project Management and Collaboration in Technical Education

The modern world requires technical education to incorporate online project management and collaboration tools for effective learning. These digital platforms present immense benefits both for teachers and learners, changing the traditional approach to teaching technical skills. This section examines these perks in-depth.

One significant advantage of utilizing online project management tools is that it allows streamlined communication between students and educators while improving teamwork among them irrespective of their locations through virtual engagement mediums on such a unified platform as this presents real-time feedback options resulting in meeting deadlines without hassle by tracking progress till completion enhancing problem-solving expertise crucially needed across various specialties within technology-based professions.

Online Project Management solutions also provide an opportunity where one can build essential computer literacy valued highly concerning employability portfolios due to training based on task allocation techniques encompassing methodologies relevant towards properly understanding projects from inception until delivery stage thus making graduates capable of completing tasks efficiently enough opening doors not merely locally but globally too.

Moreover, deploying Online Project Management Tools provides delightful incentives like centralized access points inhibiting misplaced records reducing physical storage requirements simultaneously allowing accessibility unlimited times anywhere anytime if internet-enabled empowering individualized schedules catering diverse needs demand dynamics forming suitable pacing delivering exquisite outcomes.

Finally, adopting Digital Platforms enhances collaborative efforts flawlessly with other innovative educational deployments providing mechanisms ranging specific examples spanning AR/VR avenues transforming different coursework types into comprehensive yet immersive undertakings when integrated finely.

In summary, there exist several advantages accessible via implementing digital means aimed at engaging optimum potentialities functioning seamlessly amongst learners tackling STEM-related fields effectively equipping future professionals' aptitude handling technological challenges proficiently pursuing career paths confidently.

CHAPTER 14

Web Development and Programming Bootcamps

In the era of digital technology, there is an ever-increasing demand for web developers and programmers. To meet this need, individuals require skills in maintaining websites and applications that keep pace with advancing technologies. The purpose of this subchapter is to present teachers and scholars with an overview of web development and programming bootcamps as a popular method for acquiring these essential abilities.

Web development and programming bootcamps are short-term training programs designed to provide participants intense instruction on coding basics like HTML, CSS, JavaScript etc., website construction techniques which includes interactive user interfaces creation along with application developing techniques. They enable immersive hands-on learning while imparting computer education at high speeds- learners quickly gain practical insights into new knowledge areas thanks to their format. Endowing practitioners or students who have learnt rudimentary aspects supporting them acquire necessary competencies regarding succeeding within the industry tends be mastered during such sessions.

For educators seeking ways through which they can revamp their curricula towards building just some technical skill sets; attending tech camps becomes quite helpful since attendees receive information from qualified professionals conversant about current project requirements realities. One big merit associated relates towards networking opportunities prospect s availed among fellow-bench-markers partaking live events but virtually –which later culminate relevance once key decisions settings become enacted afterwards.

The flexible online courses option available across numerous PHP Boot Minnesota (as many customarily get referred); means almost everybody regardless location may hone themselves via becoming skilled personnel relating undertaking apps/website needs real-time work locally/domestically. Regardless level i.e. beginner, intermediate / advanced stage - having access toward gateways enabling transition going pro-level remains one game changing chance whenever we speak matters pertinent traditional educational classes scheduling constraints wherever they exist, in contrast beyond remote entertainment distance-wise.

In conclusion, web development and programming bootcamps offer numerous benefits to teachers and scholars in the field of digital tools and technical education. From accelerated learning to practical experience and networking opportunities, these bootcamps provide a valuable resource for staying current in the fast-paced world of web development and programming. By attending a bootcamp, teachers and scholars can enhance their technical skills and provide their students with the best possible education.

14.1 Digital Tools for Web Development and Programming Education

Teaching web development and programming requires a set of digital tools that facilitate hands-on learning, collaboration, and project management. Here is a list of digital tools across various categories that can enhance web development and programming education:

Integrated Development Environments (IDEs):

- **Visual Studio Code:**
    - **Purpose:** A lightweight and powerful code editor with support for various programming languages.
    - **Usage:** Ideal for web development projects, offering features like syntax highlighting, debugging, and extensions.
- **Sublime Text:**
    - **Purpose:** A versatile text editor with a sleek interface and extensibility.
    - **Usage:** Supports syntax highlighting, multiple selections, and a wide range of plugins for web development.
- **Atom:**
    - **Purpose:** A hackable text editor built on web technologies.
    - **Usage:** Offers a user-friendly interface, customizable themes, and a rich package ecosystem for web development.

Version Control:

- **Git and GitHub:**
    - **Purpose:** Version control system and hosting platform for Git repositories.

- **Usage:** Teaches collaborative coding, version tracking, and project management through repositories.

Web Development Frameworks:

- **Bootstrap**:
  - **Purpose:** A front-end framework for building responsive and visually appealing websites.
  - **Usage:** Simplifies the development of responsive and mobile-first web projects.
- **React**:
  - **Purpose:** A JavaScript library for building user interfaces.
  - **Usage:** Ideal for teaching component-based development and creating interactive UIs.
- **Django**:
  - **Purpose:** A high-level Python web framework for rapid development.
  - **Usage:** Introduces concepts of MVC architecture and backend development using Python.

Code Collaboration:

- **Code Pen:**
  - **Purpose:** An online community for testing and showcasing user-created HTML, CSS, and JavaScript code snippets.
  - **Usage:** Enables collaborative coding and sharing of projects in an interactive environment.
- **JSF idle**:
  - **Purpose:** An online IDE for web development with a focus on JavaScript.
  - **Usage:** Great for experimenting with and sharing JavaScript, HTML, and CSS code snippets.

Learning Platforms:

- **Code academy**:
  - **Purpose:** An interactive learning platform offering coding courses in various programming languages.
  - **Usage:** Provides hands-on exercises and projects for beginners.

- **Free Code Camp:**
  - **Purpose:** A nonprofit platform offering free coding lessons and projects.
  - **Usage:** Focuses on full-stack development and includes practical coding challenges.

Project Management:

- **Trello:**
  - **Purpose:** A project management tool using boards, lists, and cards.
  - **Usage:** Helps organize and track coding projects collaboratively.
- **Asana**:
  - **Purpose:** A project management and collaboration tool.
  - **Usage:** Useful for managing coding projects with task assignments, timelines, and communication features.

Cloud Services:

- **Heroku**:
  - **Purpose:** A cloud platform that enables developers to deploy, manage, and scale applications.
  - **Usage:** Simplifies the process of deploying web applications for educational purposes.
- **Netlify**:
  - **Purpose:** A cloud platform for continuous deployment that simplifies web hosting.
  - **Usage:** Supports the deployment of static websites and serverless functions.

Code Review:

- **GitHub Actions:**
  - **Purpose:** Automate workflows and perform various tasks directly on GitHub repositories.
  - **Usage:** Integrate automated testing and code quality checks into the development workflow.

- **Code Climate:**
    - **Purpose:** A tool for automated code review to improve code quality.
    - **Usage:** Analyzes code and provides insights into potential issues and improvements.

Documentation:

- **Swagger/OpenAPI:**
    - **Purpose:** A framework for API documentation and testing.
    - **Usage:** Teaches API design principles and documentation for web development projects.
- **JSDoc**:
    - **Purpose:** A tool for adding inline documentation to JavaScript code.
    - **Usage:** Encourages the practice of documenting code for better collaboration and understanding.

These tools cover a range of aspects in web development and programming education, from coding and version control to collaboration and project management. Depending on the curriculum and specific goals, educators can integrate these tools to create a comprehensive and hands-on learning experience for students.

CHAPTER 15

Virtual Laboratories and Simulations for Science and Engineering Education

As technology continues to advance at an unprecedented rate, educators must adapt to these changes and utilize digital tools to enhance technical education. One such tool that has gained significant popularity in recent years is virtual laboratories and simulations. These digital resources have revolutionized the way students learn and apply technical skills, making them an essential component of modern technical education.

Benefits of Virtual Laboratories and Simulations:

- Enable hands-on learning experiences without the constraints of physical equipment or materials.
- Encourage critical thinking and problem-solving skills through the ability to manipulate variables and receive immediate feedback.
- Offer a level of interactivity and customization that traditional labs cannot match.
- Highly cost-effective compared to setting up and maintaining physical labs, making them accessible to a broader range of educational institutions and students.
- Easily integrated into online learning platforms, allowing for seamless remote education and expanding access to technical skills development.
- Proven valuable in science and engineering education, allowing students to conduct experiments, design prototypes, and analyze data in a virtual setting.
- Foster teamwork and communication skills that are essential in technical fields.

In conclusion, incorporating virtual laboratories and simulations in technical education provides students with unique opportunities to learn, explore, and apply technical skills in a safe and interactive environment. Teachers and scholars in the field of technical education must embrace these digital tools and leverage their potential to enhance the learning experiences of our students. By doing so, we can equip the next generation of technical professionals with the skills and knowledge they need to thrive in an increasingly digital world.

15.1 Digital Tools for Virtual Laboratories and Simulations

Virtual laboratories and simulations are valuable tools for providing hands-on learning experiences in various scientific and technical disciplines. Here are digital tools/ Platforms that can be utilized for virtual laboratories and simulations in education (See Table 15.1). Simulations are ideal for exploring intricate systems or phenomena that may not be possible otherwise due to restrictions on observation or manipulation opportunities available offline.

Digital tools for virtual laboratories offer a significant benefit of accessibility, allowing students to access these resources from anywhere and at any time when they have an internet connection. This flexibility promotes self-directed learning and empowers learners to take responsibility for their education. Additionally, virtual labs often incorporate interactive tutorials and quizzes that reinforce fundamental concepts while assessing comprehension level in real-time. Such personalized feedback helps boost student engagement during the learning process by targeting areas requiring remediation through highly customized sessions catering explicitly towards everyone's strengths or weaknesses.

Digital platforms also enable simulation scenarios that might be dangerous or expensive to implement in physical labs, thereby protecting student safety while saving costs linked to procuring materials or maintaining equipment. Digital platforms also enable simulation scenarios that might reduce chemicals usage in Chemistry lab or Environmental Lab, thereby protecting green earth and switching to Green Chemistry.

Table 15.1 Digital tools / Platforms for Virtual Labs and Simulations.

Tool/Platform	Purpose	Feature
Labster	Offers a wide range of virtual labs in biology, chemistry, physics, and more.	Interactive simulations, 3D animations, and assessments.
PhET Interactive Simulations	Provides free interactive math and science simulations.	Covers physics, chemistry, biology, earth science, and math topics.
ChemCollective	Offers virtual labs and scenario-based learning for chemistry.	Simulations cover topics like stoichiometry, thermodynamics, and acid-base chemistry.

Table 15.1 ***Contd...***

Tool/Platform	Purpose	Feature
Labster VR	Virtual reality (VR) labs for a more immersive experience.	VR simulations in biology, chemistry, and physics.
ExploreLearning Gizmos	Interactive math and science simulations.	Covers topics from elementary to high school level.
MERLOT	A collection of online resources, including virtual labs.	Covers various disciplines, searchable by subject.
Labster Direct Integration with Learning Management Systems	Integrates Labster directly into LMS platforms for seamless access.	Easy access to virtual labs within the LMS environment.
Labster Lab Safety Simulator	Teaches lab safety through a simulated environment.	Immersive scenarios for learning safety protocols.
Anatomy and Physiology Revealed (APR)	Virtual dissection and exploration of anatomy.	Detailed 3D models and interactive modules for studying anatomy and physiology.
LabXchange	An online platform with virtual labs and learning pathways	Curated content covering various biology-related topics
Zygote Body	Interactive 3D human anatomy visualization.	Allows exploration of the human body in detail.
McGraw-Hill Virtual Labs	A collection of virtual labs covering various science disciplines.	Interactive simulations for biology, chemistry, and physics.
Explore Learning Gizmos	Interactive math and science simulations.	Covers topics from elementary to high school level.
Explore Learning Gizmos	Interactive math and science simulations.	Covers topics from elementary to high school level.
WW Norton's Virtual Labs	Virtual labs for biology, chemistry, and environmental science.	Engaging simulations for a range of scientific concepts.
BioMan Biology	Educational games and virtual labs for biology.	Interactive simulations for learning biological concepts.
ChemCollective	Offers virtual labs and scenario-based learning for chemistry.	Simulations cover topics like stoichiometry, thermodynamics, and acid-base chemistry.
NeuroLab	Virtual lab for neuroscience education.	Interactive simulations and experiments related to neuroscience.

These tools provide a diverse range of virtual labs and simulations, allowing educators to enhance the learning experience and provide practical, hands-on training in scientific and technical disciplines.

Chapter 16

Professional Development for Tech-Savvy Teachers

In today's digital age, it is important for teachers to acquire and continuously develop their technology skills to keep up with the ever-changing digital landscape. Professional development for tech-savvy teachers is essential to ensure that they are equipped with the necessary skills to integrate technology effectively in the classroom.

One way to achieve this is through attending workshops and conferences, where teachers can learn about the latest technology trends and best practices for implementing them in the classroom. These events provide an opportunity for educators to network and share ideas with other like-minded professionals.

Another way to develop technology skills is by taking online courses or webinars. There are numerous online platforms that offer courses specifically designed for teachers, covering topics such as classroom management, digital literacy, and coding. These courses are often self-paced, allowing teachers to work on their own schedules.

Lastly, it is important for schools to provide ongoing support and resources to their teachers. This can include access to technology coaches or mentors who can provide guidance and support, as well as access to digital tools and resources to use in the classroom.

By investing in professional development for tech-savvy teachers, schools can ensure that their educators are equipped with the skills and knowledge necessary to prepare students for success in the digital age.

16.1 Strategies and Resources for the Professional Development of Tech-savvy Teachers

Tech-savvy teachers' professional development is a non-stop expedition that calls for taking charge, teaming up with colleagues and being open to lifelong education. Merging various strategies and tools amplifies teachers' digital knowledge, enables them to smoothly incorporate technology in their teaching methodology, hence empowering learners to excel in the era of digitization.

Technology integration in education is vital for student engagement, fostering collaboration and equipping them with the skills required to succeed in a technologically driven society. To fully harness classroom technology's potential, educators must continually enhance their digital literacy proficiency through continued professional growth. Professional development for tech-savvy teachers is essential to keep educators updated on the latest trends, tools, and methodologies in technology integration. Here are some strategies for the professional development of tech-savvy teachers. (See Table 16.1).

1. **Needs Assessment and Goal Setting**
   Before starting professional development, teachers should evaluate their current skills, areas for growth, and technology-related learning objectives. This can be done through surveys, self-assessment, or discussions with colleagues. Setting SMART goals based on these needs guides their professional development journey effectively.

2. **Collaborative Learning Communities**
   Joining collaborative learning communities allows teachers to share knowledge, exchange ideas, and learn from peers' experiences. Participation in professional learning communities, online forums, or social media groups focused on technology integration offers peer support, collaborative projects, and resource sharing.

3. **Workshops and Training Sessions**
   Attending workshops, training, and conferences on educational technology helps educators stay updated on trends, tools, and teaching strategies. Hands-on experiences in workshops provide practical skills that can be directly applied in the classroom.

4. **Online Courses and Webinars**
   Online courses and webinars offer flexible professional development options for busy teachers. Platforms like Coursera, edX, and Khan Academy provide courses on digital literacy, blended learning, coding, and multimedia creation. Webinars by educational technology organizations feature expert speakers and innovative tools.

5. **Coaching and Mentoring**
   Personalized coaching and mentoring support teachers in integrating technology effectively. Experienced coaches provide guidance, address challenges, offer feedback on lesson plans, and model effective teaching strategies.

6. **Online Resources and Learning Platforms**
   Accessing online resources and platforms empowers teachers to explore new ideas and technologies. Websites like Edutopia and Commonsense Education offer articles and teaching guides. Platforms such as Google for Education and Microsoft Educator Community provide tutorials and certifications.
7. **Action Research and Reflective Practice**
   Engaging in action research and reflective practice helps teachers assess technology integration's impact on student learning outcomes. This process fosters continuous improvement and innovation in teaching practices.

Professional development for tech-savvy teachers is an ongoing journey that requires proactive learning, collaboration, and openness to lifelong learning. Here are some tools/platforms for the professional development of tech-savvy teachers. (See Table 16.1).

Table 16.1 Tools/Platforms for the professional development of tech-savvy teachers.

Activity	Tools/Platforms
Online Courses and Certifications	**1. Coursera** Offers courses and specializations on various educational technology topics. **2. edX** Provides online courses and certifications from universities and institutions. **3. Google for Education Training Center** Offers free online courses and certifications for educators using Google tools. **4. Microsoft Educator Center** Provides training courses and certifications for educators using Microsoft products.
Webinars and Virtual Conferences	**5. Ed Surge** Hosts webinars and virtual events covering edtech trends and tools. **6. ISTE (International Society for Technology in Education)** Organizes conferences, webinars, and workshops on educational technology. **7. SimpleK12** Offers on-demand webinars and virtual summits for educators.
Educational Technology Blogs	**8. EdTech Magazine** Provides articles and insights on the latest educational technology trends. **9. Edutopia - Technology Integration** Focuses on best practices and strategies for integrating technology in education.

Table 16.1 ***Contd...***

Activity	Tools/Platforms
Professional Learning Communities (PLCs)	**10. Twitter Chats** Participate in education-related Twitter chats to connect with other tech-savvy educators. **11. LinkedIn Groups** Join LinkedIn groups focused on educational technology discussions and resources.
Collaborative Learning Platforms	**12. Google Educator Groups:** Join local or online Google Educator Groups for collaborative learning. **13. Microsoft Teams for Education:** Utilize Microsoft Teams for collaborative discussions and resource sharing.
Maker Spaces and Tech Labs	**14. Create a Maker Space** Establish a Maker Space in the school for hands-on tech projects. **15. Tech Labs and Workshops** Organize tech workshops and labs for teachers to experiment and learn.
Coaching and Mentoring	**16. Peer Coaching** Encourage peer coaching where tech-savvy teachers support colleagues. **17. Mentorship Programs** Establish mentorship programs for new teachers interested in technology integration.
Attend Tech Conferences	**18. FETC (Future of Education Technology Conference):** Attend conferences like FETC for in-depth exposure to educational technology. **19. TCEA (Texas Computer Education Association):** Participate in TCEA conferences for professional development opportunities.
Online Communities	**20. EdTech Reddit** Engage in discussions on the EdTech subreddit to connect with educators. **21. Tech & Learning Community** Join the Tech & Learning online community for sharing ideas and resources.
Stay Informed Through Newsletters	**22. EdSurge News** Subscribe to EdSurge newsletters for updates on edtech news and trends. **23. ISTE Community Update:** Subscribe to ISTE newsletters for information on educational technology.
Continuous Self-Learning	**24. Podcasts** Listen to educational technology podcasts for insights and interviews. **25. Read Books on Educational Technology** Explore books by edtech experts to deepen your understanding.

Professional development for tech-savvy teachers is an ongoing process that involves staying informed, collaborating with peers, and actively participating in the broader educational technology community. By leveraging various resources and strategies, educators can enhance their skills and contribute to the effective integration of technology in the classroom.

16.2 Attending Technology Conferences and Workshops

In today's rapidly evolving digital age, it is crucial for teachers to stay up to date with the latest advancements in technology and how they can be effectively integrated into the classroom. One of the best ways to achieve this is by attending technology conferences and workshops specifically designed for educators. These events not only provide valuable insights into the latest digital tools but also offer opportunities for networking and professional development.

Technology conferences and workshops offer teachers a unique platform to explore and learn about new digital tools that can enhance their teaching practices. These events bring together experts, industry leaders, and like-minded professionals who share a common goal - to revolutionize education through technology. By attending these conferences, teachers can discover innovative tools and strategies that can transform their classrooms into engaging and interactive learning environments.

Moreover, these conferences and workshops facilitate hands-on learning experiences, allowing teachers to gain practical knowledge and skills that they can immediately implement in their classrooms. Through interactive workshops, educators can explore different digital tools, learn how to integrate them into their lesson plans, and discover creative ways to engage students in their learning journey. The hands-on approach provides valuable experiential learning opportunities, ensuring that teachers are equipped with the necessary skills to navigate the digital landscape confidently.

Networking is another significant advantage of attending technology conferences and workshops. Teachers can connect with industry experts, fellow educators, and edtech companies, fostering professional relationships that can lead to collaborations and shared resources. Networking at these events opens doors to new opportunities and provides a platform for teachers to exchange ideas, experiences, and best practices.

Furthermore, technology conferences and workshops offer teachers a chance to engage in professional development. Many of these events offer workshops and sessions that provide insights into effective teaching strategies, the latest educational research, and emerging trends in digital learning. By participating in these sessions, teachers can expand their knowledge, enhance their teaching skills, and stay ahead of the curve in terms of educational technology.

In conclusion, attending technology conferences and workshops is crucial for teachers seeking an introduction to digital tools for the modern classroom. These events provide valuable opportunities to explore the latest digital tools, gain practical knowledge and skills, network with industry professionals, and engage in professional development. By actively participating in these conferences, teachers can enhance their teaching practices, create engaging learning environments, and ultimately prepare students for success in the digital age.

16.3 Engaging in Continuous Learning with Online Courses

In the fast-paced digital world today, it is crucial for educators to stay up-to-speed with the latest technological advancements and educational tools. Online courses provide an exceptional opportunity for teachers to continuously enhance their skills, broaden their knowledge, and create a more engaging learning environment for students.

The flexibility of online courses offers significant advantages to teachers as they can learn at their own pace from home. With interactive modules, video tutorials and discussion forums connecting them with experts globally; such resources enable instructors worldwide access valuable insights into various digital tools making teaching practice easier.

Online courses also empower lifelong learners who become role models in displaying commitment towards professional growth by staying current on technology education trends, fostering excitement among students while inspiring self-driven discovery leading towards sustained academic progress beyond classrooms. Utilizing techniques learned from taking these continuous online classes allows school settings managers or leaders excellent opportunities train newly hired faculty members mentorship programs providing plenty tailored development chances promising sharing-environment beneficial collectively ultimately enabling organization success built upon past workforce successes!

16.4 Collaborating with Colleagues for Peer-to-Peer Support

In today's dynamic educational landscape, it is crucial for educators to remain updated with the latest digital tools and technologies that can enhance their teaching methodologies. In this regard, continual learning and development are of utmost importance. Collaborating with peers proves to be a successful technique towards achieving such goals. This discourse aims to shed light on why collaborating with colleagues holds significant value when utilizing modern teacher-centric digital tools.

By collaborating, teachers cultivate a sense of community and gain the ability to share their knowledge in practical ways. Working together enables them to uncover fresh ideas, tackle issues with creative approaches that effectively integrate digital tools into classroom instructions. This allows for tapping into diverse perspectives on teaching methodologies from various experts which enhances everyone's pedagogical techniques.

The initial crucial step in establishing collaborative peer-to-peer support among colleagues involves forming supportive networks within schools or districts. This can be accomplished by reaching out to educators who share an interest in utilizing a range of technological resources. Once such like-minded individuals have been identified, they are invited to join professional learning communities or dedicated online groups focused on these topics.

These forums offer convenient spaces for people to connect and freely ask relevant questions while sharing insightful materials and extensions. Active involvement from various school partners fosters close collaboration, making them readily available as go-to resource persons offering mutual assistance based on partnership efforts.

Successful collaborations are characterized by receptivity and open-mindedness, which aim to achieve optimal support outcomes. When partners exchange feedback or suggestions during constructive dialogues facilitated through reach-outs, it can lead to surpassing our boundaries and comfort zones while further enhancing creativity and talent expression in future sessions. This approach helps teams focus on project-related drive endeavors both now and into the future.

Collaborating through co-teaching and co-planning presents several advantages for fostering collaborative engagement. The inclusion of expert input adds significant value, enabling peers to gain hands-on experience while observing work ethics in action. This, in turn, yields enjoyable moments when implementing exposure-relevant strategy sets that facilitate the transferability of acquired aptitudes over time.

Moreover, such collaboration promotes greater efficiency and productivity as each party applies mutually shared learnings productively across their individual classrooms. Reinforced positively via informal conversations during lunch hours or breaks from work environments following fruitful classroom interactions earlier established culminates into deeper insightful revelations born of interdependence between colleagues committed toward professional growth within their field.

When modern teachers collaborate with their peers for mutual support, they can master diverse digital tools crucial to their profession. Engaging constructively and actively seeking opportunities to work together allows colleagues goals' regarding requests structures in the learning experience and enhances innovation towards proactive career advancement. By working collaboratively, trainers interact more effectively while embracing deep insights that lead to enhanced growth among co-collaborators. This drives transformative evolution, enriches overall classroom experiences advanced by technological exploitation benefits which are actionable at all levels of education without reservations-driving professional transformational potentials collectively harnessed through fostering block-oriented relationships yielding long-lasting partnerships unparalleled diversity/ranges enriched interpersonal relations amplifying targeting options/resultants from resources already available/implemented when power is embraced mutually dependent correlation facilitating uplift on evolutionary paths made smoother whenever collaborating relentlessly driven focused units realize collective team spirit exemplified during joint ventures ensuring positive sustainable educational translations means progressive results obtained prodigious/huge.

16.5 Embracing Lifelong Learning as a Tech-Fluent Educator

As the digital world rapidly evolves, it is imperative for educators to become proficient in technology. Educators have a responsibility to prepare students for their future by embracing lifelong learning and continually updating skills using new digital tools.

This subchapter focuses on introducing teachers to lifelong learning, its significance in becoming tech-fluent educators, benefits of incorporating updated teaching practices with advanced technological advancements including online collaboration platforms as well as educational apps amongst others.

Lifelong education involves acquiring knowledge and upgrading one's skill set throughout life. Staying up to date through adopting growth mindset strategies that allow exploration into different innovative classroom management techniques can enhance student engagement while promoting efficiency at instruction delivery time leading ultimately towards fostering creativity alongside critical thinking development among learners respective.

To upgrade technological expertise continuously requires active participation within professional networks' resources like workshops or conferences focused solely on advancing our abilities such us attending webinars related explicitly around specific areas targeting improvement needed when trying faultlessly delivering lesson content efficiently without hindering individual performance-wise respectively - this way supporting collective attainment goals simultaneously contributing positively during every child's journey increasingly facing ever-increasing demands arising from international competitiveness stakes relative today's challenging workspace environments globally speaking consequently affecting any country worldwide striving-for international excellence achievements now obtainable thanks mainly but not exclusively due primarily via utilizing enabling technologies always available-on-demand anytime anywhere!

We should also encourage collaboration between colleagues working together exchanging ideas sharing best practice experiences collectively discovering innovations pushing integration further enhancing pupils' output performances regardless grade placement possibilities exist onwards-upwards accelerated progressions reflective long-term target projections shapes societies social welfare integrating fully embracing official policies delegating mandated requirements fulfilling contemporary demographics so valued opening pathways corresponding changing tendencies shifting thought patterns inevitable progressing transformational necessity referring excelling equitably lecturing imposing bias viewpoints unsuitable equality justice intentions meaning-lasting impact generations present-future rendering solidly eternalizing sensitivity considering cultural acceptance respect conceptual norms entailing crucial survival humanity never overlooking positively taking advantage transformative opportunities offered elevating standard living standards immeasurably.

In conclusion, enhancing skills through lifelong learning as tech-fluent educators central to success in the digital age; let us embrace this journey together and optimize opportunities with new tools transforming education by crafting engaging personalized life-long knowledge enabling creativity critical thinking throughout learners' developing exposure levels vastly effectively within mark achieving spearheading desired objectives at present onward shaping history positively being remembered forever collectively.

16.6 Strategies to Support Lifelong Learning for Teachers in Digital Education

Ensuring lifelong learning for teachers in digital education is crucial to keep them abreast of the latest trends, tools, and methodologies in the rapidly evolving field of education technology. Here are strategies to promote lifelong learning among teachers in the digital education landscape (See Table 16.2)

Table 16.2 Strategies to promote lifelong learning among teachers in the digital education landscape.

Strategies	Features
Establish a Culture of Continuous Learning:	• Foster a school culture that values continuous professional development. • Recognize and celebrate teachers' efforts in their professional growth
Provide Access to Ongoing Professional Development	• Offer a variety of professional development opportunities, including workshops, webinars, and conferences. • Utilize online platforms for convenient access to self-paced courses and resources. • Support teachers in pursuing advanced degrees or certifications related to digital education.
Implement a Mentorship Program	• Pair experienced educators with newer teachers to facilitate knowledge transfer. • Create mentorship programs specifically focused on digital education. • Encourage collaborative problem-solving and idea sharing.
Encourage Collaboration and Communities of Practice	• Foster a sense of community among teachers by creating collaborative spaces. • Use platforms like social media, forums, and online groups to facilitate communication.
Incorporate Peer Learning	• Promote peer learning and collaboration within school teams. • Encourage teachers to share best practices and lessons learned from their experiences. • Organize regular peer observation and feedback sessions.
Offer Incentives and Recognition	• Provide incentives such as stipends, extra time off, or recognition for completing professional development milestones. • Recognize and celebrate teachers who demonstrate excellence in digital education.

Table 16.2 ***Contd...***

Strategies	Features
Support Self-Directed Learning	• Empower teachers to pursue topics of interest through self-directed learning. • Provide resources and access to online courses that align with individual interests and professional goals.
Stay Informed About Emerging Technologies	• Establish a mechanism for sharing information about emerging technologies. • Encourage teachers to explore and experiment with new tools and platforms. • Foster a culture of curiosity and exploration.
Create a Digital Learning Hub	• Establish a centralized digital hub where teachers can access resources, tutorials, and updates. • Use the hub to curate information on digital tools, pedagogies, and best practices. • Ensure that the hub is user-friendly and regularly updated.
Promote Reflective Practice	• Encourage teachers to regularly reflect on their teaching practices. • Incorporate reflective components into professional development activities. • Provide opportunities for educators to share insights gained from reflection.
Address Barriers to Learning	• Identify and address any barriers that may hinder teachers' access to professional development opportunities. • Provide support for time management, technology access, and other logistical challenges.
Collaborate with External Experts	• Bring in external experts for workshops, webinars, or training sessions. • Facilitate partnerships with educational technology companies and organizations. • Offer opportunities for teachers to attend conferences and events.
Feedback and Evaluation	• Establish a feedback loop for professional development programs. • Regularly evaluate the effectiveness of professional development initiatives. • Use feedback to tailor future programs to teachers' needs and preferences.

By implementing these strategies, educational institutions can create an environment where teachers feel supported, motivated, and empowered to engage in lifelong learning, particularly in the realm of digital education.

CHAPTER 17

Overcoming Challenges and Ensuring Equity

Overcoming challenges and ensuring equity can be a difficult task, but it is necessary for creating a just and inclusive society. One of the biggest challenges is identifying the root causes of inequality and addressing them in a systematic way. This requires a deep understanding of the historical and social context that has led to disparities in access to resources, opportunities, and power.

One way to overcome these challenges is to promote education and awareness. This can be done through public campaigns, training programs, and community outreach. By educating people about the nature of inequality and its impact on individuals and communities, we can empower them to act and promote change.

Another important strategy is to engage in policy reform. This might involve advocating for new legislation or changes to existing laws and regulations that promote greater equity. It might also involve working to ensure that institutions and organizations are held accountable for their actions and policies.

Ultimately, creating a more equitable society requires a commitment to collaboration and cooperation across all sectors of society. This means working together to identify and address the root causes of inequality, and to develop and implement effective solutions that promote justice and inclusion for all.

To establish fairness across societies requires cross-sectoral collaboration with all involved parties taking part actively establishing solutions geared around rooting out requirements promoting equal opportunity stressing justice complied coupled alongside inclusion for all persons irrespective of variances within groups seeing each other's differences as resemblances celebrating diversity when uniting together seeking harmony over discordance contributing positively making cooperatively-driven visions adversarial-free reality someday. Here are strategies to overcome common challenges and promote equity in digital teaching (See Table 17.1)

Table 17.1 Strategies to overcome common challenges and promote equity in digital teaching.

Digital teaching	Challenge	Strategies
Access to Technology	Not all students have equal access to devices and the internet.	• Provide school-issued devices for students. • Implement a device loan program. • Partner with community organizations to secure devices. • Utilize offline resources for students with limited internet access. • Consider low-bandwidth teaching methods.
Digital Literacy	Students may have varying levels of digital literacy skills.	• Offer digital literacy workshops for students. • Provide resources and tutorials for using online tools. • Encourage peer support and collaboration. • Integrate digital literacy into the curriculum.
Engagement and Participation	Maintaining student engagement in a digital environment can be challenging.	• Use interactive and multimedia content. • Incorporate gamification elements. • Foster a sense of community through online discussions. • Provide varied and interesting assignments. • Encourage student collaboration on projects.
Differentiated Instruction	Adapting teaching methods to meet the diverse needs of students can be challenging.	• Provide options for content delivery (videos, text, audio). • Use adaptive learning platforms. • Implement a flipped classroom model. • Offer choice in assignments and assessments. • Provide additional support for struggling students.
Assessment and Feedback	Assessing student understanding and providing timely feedback can be complex.	• Use a variety of assessment methods (quizzes, projects, discussions). • Leverage digital assessment tools. • Provide clear assessment criteria. • Offer timely and constructive feedback.

Table 17.1 ***Contd…***

Digital teaching	Challenge	Strategies
Teacher Professional Development	Teachers may need training to effectively use digital tools and platforms.	• Provide ongoing professional development opportunities. • Offer workshops on effective online teaching strategies. • Foster a culture of collaboration and knowledge sharing among teachers. • Utilize mentorship programs for peer support.
Accessibility and Inclusivity	Ensuring that digital materials are accessible to all students.	• Use accessible design principles for online content. • Provide alternative formats for materials. • Caption videos and use alt text for images. • Be mindful of diverse learning needs.
Home Environment	The home environment may not be conducive to learning for all students.	• Encourage open communication with parents/guardians. • Provide resources for creating a productive learning space at home. • Consider flexible assignment deadlines.
Language and Cultural Diversity	Students may come from diverse linguistic and cultural backgrounds.	• Provide multilingual resources. • Encourage cultural inclusivity in the curriculum. • Use translation tools for communication.
Digital Divide Awareness	Some students and families may not be aware of the digital divide issues.	• Communicate openly about access challenges. • Advocate for policies addressing the digital divide. • Collaborate with community organizations to raise awareness. • Share success stories of overcoming digital access challenges.

Promoting equity in digital teaching requires a proactive and inclusive approach that considers the diverse needs and circumstances of students. By addressing these challenges with strategic planning and ongoing support, educators can create a more equitable learning experience for all students.

17.1 Addressing Access and Connectivity Issues

Access to technology and connectivity is essential in today's education system. As educators, it's important to address any issues that students may face with regards to access and connectivity so they can benefit from digital tools. This section will explore different strategies for promoting inclusivity within the classroom by tackling these challenges.

To start addressing access barriers, teachers must first understand what problems their students might have such as limited internet connection or affordability concerns regarding hardware devices like laptops or tablets. Once identified resource acquisition then next moves towards solving them often involves collaboration between administrators, parents of children attending schools offering facilities where necessary equipment could be utilized alongside building collaborations among community organizations too.

One effective solution would be a lending program established inside the school wherein underprivileged kids got given an opportunity-whereby lenders extend gadgets (like Laptops & Tablets) without paying back fees later-they get free use during study time only; this way all pupils participate well digitally regardless of personal means preventing possible discrimination when completing said homework/assignments/tasks together amongst classmates through sharing device(s).

Further aspects worthy focusing on include extending/introducing more alternative options outside traditional broadband e.g. adopting hotspot mobile Wi-Fi units etc..., seeking discount plans if service providers are open negotiating rates allowing sponsorship packages obtainable at lower costs particularly designated networks communities nearby residents lacking steady net presence due location constraints (remote areas/periphery). Also factoring in designing learning modules centered around non-online resources establishes inclusive best practices complimenting modern era teaching utilizing educational apps accessed offline interactive eBooks digitized libraries potentially unlocked via Free/Open-Source software (FOSS), giving everyone equal opportunities financially speaking while introducing diverse approaches taken into consideration being able join sessions platforms proving less costly thereby boosting cooperation/livelihoods providing upward mobility goals shared achieving greater prosperity wellbeing For example bills required covering data usage frequently getting reviewed cheaper alternatives discussed acceptable substitutes made available upon request translating reduced pressure expenditure ensuring balance preserved encouraging innovative projects blossom idea exchange fostered enhancing knowledge depth diversity within education strengthening society as a whole through technical adoption done justly according to each respective schools' financial capabilities.

17.2 Supporting Digital Literacy for All Students

In the current digital era, it is essential for educators to equip themselves with skills and knowledge that support their students' digital literacy. Traditional teaching methods are no longer sufficient as technology advances rapidly. Instead, teachers must embrace digital tools in classrooms for better learning experiences.

This section aims to provide comprehensive education on why digital literacy matters and practical strategies of supporting all learners digitally through effective communication online or resource evaluation while navigating the internet successfully.

Firstly, this subchapter opens about how enabling access to various service providers like Google caps (Gmail) brings a lot of benefits; these include accessing vast resources efficiently contextualizing what they learn by working together effectively with others within an inclusive system building critical thinking skills preparing them adequately before possible future careers involving technological proficiency.

To achieve success in deploying successful strategies idealize towards developing everyone's technical proficiencies from integrating such programs into school curricula at varying levels catered differently depending upon need until achieving one common goal- well-educated children who can become responsible users over time similar global trends alike amongst many countries worldwide-we have got you covered.

Additionally, and not limited: A significant acknowledged issue challenges bridging divisions created by unequal distribution according accessibility since everybody cannot afford gadgets during non-school hours where there exist disparities between different student groups due mainly based influence policies put national boards regarding whose responsibility providing accessible devices rest finally lying so digits life-rooting lays evenly across entire classroom full potential realizing equality opportunity irrespective budgeting circumstance among challengers lay domain agents trough blessings propel society forward-minded than divided backward ones limiting futuristic possibilities.

Overall when applying scientific creative consideration thought implementing equitable justice needs foremost present fundamentally driving behind every decision taken even further monitoring continuous developments waves changing times always staying vigilant fostering conceptual development ideas advancements shaping alloy mixture particularized practices individualizes affects diverse thrilling vibrant flow student lives reaching dreamed horizon beyond endless sky-scraping ceiling proved previously uncrossable simply determining destiny.

17.3 Promoting Inclusive Practices in the Digital Classroom

In today's era of technology, classrooms have incorporated digital tools and platforms, which has revolutionized teaching by allowing teachers to create engaging learning experiences for students. However, it is crucial to ensure that these technological advancements are accessible to all students irrespective of their background or abilities.

To achieve inclusivity in the digital classroom environment, ensuring accessibility should be a priority through incorporating closed captions for videos, alternative text for images and using screen readers. Moreover, universal design principles need implementation when designing materials so they can be used equally across all student's preferences & needs.

Equity and access issues also multiply as not every student may hold equal internet connectivity or electronic devices – this creates hindrance within education delivery at increasing paces as more educational settings move online amid global health conditions such as COVID-19 pandemic.

Promoting inclusive practices is reliant upon understanding the needs of each individual learner. Our commitment lies here whereby investing into unconventional diversified-future-ready methods, strategic steps taken build unison culture celebrating positive diversity amongst blended generations, becoming goal focused on enlightening enriched insight distinguished future leaders building paths cross cultural lines - an ideal representative mindset fitting our increasingly connected world advancing thought processes toward brighter tomorrows closing gaps we overlooked previously.

17.4 Strategies to Promote Inclusivity in the Digital Classroom

To create an environment where all students feel valued, respected, and engaged in their learning, it is essential to promote inclusive practices in the digital classroom. Here are some strategies to foster inclusivity (See Table 17.2).

Table 17.2 Strategies to foster inclusivity.

Strategies	Description
Accessible Digital Content	• Ensure that all digital materials are accessible to students with diverse needs. • Use platforms that support screen readers, captions, and alt text for images. • Provide content in multiple formats to accommodate various learning preferences.
Universal Design for Learning (UDL):	• Embrace the principles of Universal Design for Learning to create flexible and customizable learning experiences. • Offer multiple means of representation, engagement, and expression. • Provide varied options for students to access and demonstrate their understanding.
Diverse Learning Resources:	• Incorporate diverse perspectives and voices in learning materials. • Use multimedia, such as videos, podcasts, and articles, that reflect a variety of cultural backgrounds and experiences. • Offer content in multiple languages when appropriate.
Differentiated Instruction:	• Tailor instruction to meet the individual needs of students. • Provide options for content delivery, assessment formats, and learning pathways. • Use adaptive learning technologies to personalize the learning experience.
Collaborative Learning Opportunities:	• Encourage collaborative projects and group activities. • Foster a sense of community through online discussions and forums. • Use breakout rooms for small-group discussions during virtual classes.
Scaffolded Support:	• Provide scaffolded support for complex tasks. • Break down assignments into smaller, manageable steps. • Offer additional resources and guidance for students who may need extra support.
Clear Communication	• Use clear and concise language in all communications. • Provide instructions in multiple formats (written, verbal, video). • Establish open channels for students to ask questions and seek clarification.

Table 17.2 ***Contd…***

Strategies	Description
Technology for Inclusion	• Utilize assistive technology tools to support students with diverse learning needs. • Ensure that digital platforms are compatible with accessibility features. • Explore features like closed captioning, speech-to-text, and text-to-speech.
Regular Check-ins and Feedback	• Conduct regular check-ins with students to gauge their well-being and understanding. • Provide constructive feedback that focuses on growth and improvement. • Offer multiple channels for feedback, such as written comments, audio, or video.
Culturally Responsive Teaching	• Incorporate culturally responsive teaching practices. • Acknowledge and celebrate cultural diversity in the classroom. • Be mindful of cultural nuances and sensitivities in discussions and assignments.
Professional Development on Inclusive Practices	• Provide ongoing professional development for teachers on inclusive practices. • Offer training on accessibility features, diverse teaching strategies, and culturally responsive teaching. • Create a supportive community for educators to share best practices.
Flexible Assessment Options	• Offer flexible assessment options that accommodate diverse learning styles. • Allow students to choose from a range of assessment formats (e.g., written, oral, project-based). • Consider alternative methods of assessment beyond traditional exams.
Promote a Positive Classroom Culture	• Foster a culture of respect, empathy, and understanding. • Address instances of bias or discrimination promptly. • Establish clear expectations for inclusive behavior.
Student Voice and Choice	• Empower students by giving them a voice in their learning. • Provide opportunities for students to express their preferences and interests. • Allow for choice in topics, projects, or assignments.
Family and Community Engagement	• Collaborate with families and the community to support student learning. • Keep families informed and involved in their child's education. • Seek input from families on inclusive practices.

By implementing these strategies, educators can create a learning environment that respects and values the diversity of all students. It is important to remember that promoting inclusivity in the digital classroom requires intentional planning and ongoing commitment.

17.5 Fostering Inclusivity in the Digital Classroom: Tools for Diverse Learning Needs

Promoting inclusivity in the digital classroom is essential. It involves utilizing tools that support diverse learning needs and create an environment where all students feel valued and engaged. Here are some tools that can help you achieve that goal:

- Closed captioning and transcripts for videos.
- Screen readers and text-to-speech software.
- Online whiteboards and collaboration tools
- Virtual breakout rooms for group activities
- Digital polls and quizzes to check for understanding.
- Accessible and customizable learning management systems

By incorporating these tools into your digital classroom, you can ensure that all students have equal opportunities to learn and succeed. Implementing these tools (See Table 17.3) in the digital classroom can contribute to creating a more inclusive learning environment that meets the diverse needs of students. Regularly assessing the effectiveness of these tools and seeking feedback from students can help refine their use for optimal inclusivity. Tools for diverse learning needs refer to various resources, strategies, and techniques designed to support individuals with different abilities and learning styles. These tools aim to create an inclusive educational environment where every student can thrive and reach their full potential. They may include assistive technologies, adaptive materials, specialized software, visual aids, modified instructional approaches, and personalized learning plans. By implementing these tools, educators can provide tailored instruction that addresses the unique requirements of each learner, promoting equal opportunities for academic success.

Table 17.3 Tools for Diverse Learning Needs.

Tools	Features
Microsoft Learning Tools	• Immersive Reader: Supports reading comprehension with features like text-to-speech and customizable text spacing. • Dictation: Allows students to dictate content, promoting accessibility for diverse learning styles.
Google Classroom	• Integration with Google Translate for multilingual support. • Collaboration tools for group projects and inclusive learning activities.
Otter.ai	• Real-time transcription and closed captioning for virtual classes. • Supports students with hearing impairments and language differences.
Flipgrid	• Video discussion platform that gives every student a voice. • Encourages diverse forms of expression and communication.
Padlet	• Collaborative digital boards for sharing ideas and resources. • Inclusive space for visual learners to express themselves.
Bookshare	• Accessible eBook library for students with print disabilities. • Provides a wide range of books in accessible formats.
EquatIO	• Mathematical expression editor for creating accessible math content. • Supports diverse learners, including those with dyscalculia.
Read&Write by Texthelp	• Text-to-speech, speech-to-text, and other literacy support tools. • Designed to assist students with reading and writing difficulties.
Symbaloo EDU	• Visual bookmarking tool for organizing and sharing resources. • User-friendly interface for easy navigation, suitable for diverse learners.
Quillionz	• AI-powered question generation tool. • Supports diverse learning styles and assessment preferences.
Seesaw:	• Digital portfolio platform that accommodates various types of student work. • Encourages reflection and self-expression.
Kahoot	• Game-based learning platform that engages students with quizzes and challenges. • Inclusive for different learning styles and preferences.
Cricksoft Clicker 7	• Word prediction, speech feedback, and other literacy support features. • Designed to assist students with writing difficulties.

Table 17.3 ***Contd…***

Tools	Features
Learning Ally	• Audiobook library for students with print disabilities. • Provides a wide range of educational content in audio format.
Vocaroo	• Online voice recording tool. • Encourages verbal expression and accommodates different learning styles.
StoryJumper	• Digital platform for creating and sharing interactive storybooks. • Supports diverse learning preferences and encourages creativity.
Edpuzzle	• Interactive video lessons with built-in assessments. • Accommodates various learning styles through visual and auditory components.
Trello	• Project management tool for collaborative planning and organization. • Inclusive for visual learners and those who benefit from structured organization.
Edutopia - Culturally Responsive Teaching Resources	• Online resources and articles on culturally responsive teaching. • Provides insights and strategies for creating an inclusive classroom.
Aida Calculus Tutor	• AI-driven math tutor that adapts to individual learning styles. • Supports diverse learning needs in mathematics.
Minecraft: Education Edition	• Virtual learning environment that promotes creativity and collaboration. • Inclusive for students with different interests and learning styles.
Assistive Technology Extensions (Chrome)	• Extensions like "Read Aloud" and "Speechnotes" for Chrome can enhance accessibility. • Support students with reading and writing difficulties.
Accessibyte Online	• Suite of online tools for students with visual and learning impairments. • Includes games and educational activities.
Buncee	• Visual creation tool for interactive presentations and projects. • Supports diverse ways of expressing ideas.
Screen Reader Software (e.g., JAWS, NVDA)	• Assistive technology for students with visual impairments. • Enables access to digital content through auditory feedback.

17.6 Cultivating Responsible Digital Citizenship

In today's digital age, where technology is becoming increasingly integrated into our lives, it is crucial for teachers to equip themselves with the knowledge and skills to navigate the digital world responsibly. As educators, we have a responsibility to guide our students in becoming responsible digital citizens, ensuring that they use digital tools effectively and ethically. This subchapter aims to introduce cultivating responsible digital citizenship and empower teachers with the necessary tools to guide their students in this digital journey.

The subchapter begins by defining what it means to be a responsible digital citizen. It emphasizes the importance of understanding the rights and responsibilities that come with using digital tools, such as respecting others' privacy, practicing online safety, and being mindful of the impact of one's digital footprint. It also highlights the significance of promoting a positive online culture where inclusivity, empathy, and digital ethics are upheld.

Next, the subchapter explores strategies for fostering responsible digital citizenship in the classroom. It provides practical tips for incorporating digital citizenship education into the curriculum, such as integrating lessons on digital etiquette, cyberbullying, and online privacy. It also suggests engaging students in discussions and activities that encourage critical thinking and ethical decision-making when using digital tools.

Furthermore, the subchapter delves into the role of teachers as digital role models. It emphasizes the need for teachers to demonstrate responsible digital behavior and model ethical digital practices. By doing so, teachers can inspire their students to emulate these behaviors and develop a sense of digital responsibility.

Additionally, the subchapter addresses the importance of parental involvement in cultivating responsible digital citizenship. It provides guidance on how teachers can collaborate with parents to create a cohesive approach to digital citizenship education, ensuring that students receive consistent messages both at home and in school.

Finally, the subchapter concludes with a discussion on the benefits of cultivating responsible digital citizenship. It highlights how responsible digital citizens are better equipped to navigate the digital world, engage in meaningful online interactions, and contribute positively to the digital community.

Overall, this subchapter serves as an essential guide for teachers in their journey towards creating responsible digital citizens. By incorporating these principles into their teaching practices, teachers can empower their students to become responsible, ethical, and informed digital citizens in the modern world.

17.7 Strategies for Fostering Responsible Digital Citizenship in Digital Education

In the world of digital education, cultivating responsible digital citizenship is critical. It enables students to navigate the online landscape securely, ethically, and responsibly. Here are some effective strategies for promoting responsible digital citizenship in digital education (See Table 17.4). Cultivating responsible digital citizenship involves a comprehensive and continuous approach that integrates digital literacy, ethical behavior, and critical thinking skills. Educators can help students become ethical, responsible, and empowered digital citizens by incorporating these strategies into digital education.

To encourage responsible digital citizenship in digital education, a range of tools can be used to teach, monitor, and reinforce positive online behaviors. Here are some effective tools that can be employed to promote responsible digital citizenship (See Table 17.5)

To make the most of digital tools in education, it is crucial to integrate them into a comprehensive digital citizenship curriculum. This should include active student engagement and the involvement of parents and guardians in the learning process. To ensure that students adopt responsible online behavior, ongoing discussions and reflections should be part of the overall digital education strategy.

Table 17.4 Effective strategies for promoting responsible digital citizenship in digital education.

Strategies	Activity
Digital literacy education	**1. Curriculum Integration:** a. Embed digital literacy lessons into the curriculum at various grade levels. b. Cover topics such as online safety, information literacy, and responsible social media use. **2. Critical Thinking Skills:** a. Teach students to critically evaluate online information. b. Provide exercises that develop critical thinking skills when consuming digital content.
Cybersecurity awareness	**3. Basic Cybersecurity Education:** a. Educate students about the importance of strong passwords and secure online practices. b. Highlight the risks of sharing personal information online. **4. Awareness of Cyber Threats:** a. Teach students to recognize common cybersecurity threats, such as phishing. b. Provide guidance on how to report suspicious activities.

Table 17.4 ***Contd...***

Strategies	Activity
Online safety and privacy	**5. Privacy Settings and Permissions:** a. Instruct students on adjusting privacy settings on various platforms. b. Emphasize the importance of understanding and managing permissions. **6. Personal Boundaries:** a. Teach students about setting and respecting personal boundaries in online interactions. b. Discuss the potential consequences of sharing inappropriate content.
Digital etiquette	**7. Online Communication Skills:** a. Teach students about effective and respectful online communication. b. Address the potential impact of tone and language in digital communication. **8. Netiquette Guidelines:** a. Establish guidelines for online etiquette in virtual classrooms and discussions. b. Encourage positive and inclusive communication.
Copyright and fair use	**9. Understanding Copyright Laws:** **Educate students on copyright laws and intellectual property.** **10. Creative Commons and Open Educational Resources (OER):** Introduce Creative Commons licenses and OER as alternatives to copyrighted materials.
Digital footprint awareness	**11. Permanent Nature of Digital Content:** a. Emphasize the permanence of digital footprints. b. Discuss the potential impact of online actions on future opportunities. **12. Managing Digital Identities:** a. Teach students how to curate and manage their digital identities. b. Highlight the importance of showcasing positive achievements online.
Media literacy	**13. Identifying Bias and Misinformation:** a. Train students to recognize bias and misinformation in digital content. b. Provide tools for fact-checking and verifying information. **14. Understanding Media Influence:** a. Discuss the influence of media on opinions and perspectives. b. Analyze how media shapes societal norms and values.
Ethical online behavior	**15. Respecting Others' Digital Spaces:** a. Teach students to respect others' online spaces and contributions. b. Discuss the implications of cyberbullying and online harassment.

Table 17.4 *Contd…*

	16. Promoting Positive Digital Citizenship: a. Encourage students to be positive contributors to online communities. b. Highlight the power of kindness and empathy in online interactions.
Digital citizenship pledges and agreements	**17. Student Commitment:** a. Engage students in creating digital citizenship pledges or agreements. b. Have discussions about the responsibilities associated with being a digital citizen. **18. Parental Involvement:** a. Share digital citizenship principles with parents and caregivers. b. Encourage a collaborative effort between schools and families.

Table 17.5 Effective tools that can be employed to promote responsible digital citizenship

Tools	Features
Common Sense Education	• Curriculum resources for teaching digital citizenship. • Interactive lessons on topics such as privacy, cyberbullying, and media literacy.
Google's Be Internet Awesome	• Online game-based learning to teach digital safety and citizenship. • Lesson plans for educators covering topics like privacy and online etiquette. • Resources for parents and guardians.
Nearpod	• Interactive lessons on digital citizenship topics. • Real-time assessments and quizzes to gauge understanding. • Collaboration features for student engagement.
Common Lit	• Reading passages with questions that promote digital literacy. • Lessons on media literacy, information literacy, and responsible online behavior.
Pear Deck	• Interactive presentations for teaching digital citizenship. • Engaging activities and discussions within presentations. • Real-time feedback and insights.
Edpuzzle	• Video lessons on digital citizenship topics with embedded quizzes. • Allows teachers to track students' progress and understanding. • Engages students with interactive video content.

Table 17.5 ***Contd...***

Tools	Features
Digital Passport by Common Sense Education	• Game-based platform for teaching elementary students' digital citizenship skills. • Modules covering topics like cyberbullying, privacy, and online communication. • Teacher resources and tracking tools.
Newsela	• Articles with quizzes that promote media literacy and critical thinking. • Content covering current events and relevant digital citizenship issues. • Differentiated reading levels.
iKeepSafe	• Curriculum and resources for teaching digital citizenship. • Lessons on topics such as online safety, privacy, and cyberbullying. • Interactive games and videos.
Kahoot	• Gamified quizzes and challenges on digital citizenship. • Customizable quizzes for different grade levels. • Interactive and competitive learning environment.
Quizizz	• Interactive quizzes on digital citizenship topics. • Real-time feedback and analytics.
BrainPOP	• Animated videos and quizzes on digital citizenship. • Engaging characters and scenarios to teach important concepts.
Flipgrid	• Video discussion platform for student collaboration. • Teachers can pose questions related to digital citizenship. • Encourages thoughtful and respectful communication.
Storyboard That	• Create digital stories and comics to illustrate digital citizenship scenarios. • Encourages creative expression and critical thinking. • Suitable for various age groups.
Netsmartz Workshop	• Resources and interactive tools for teaching internet safety. • Educational videos, games, and presentations. • Lesson plans for educators.
Classcraft	• Gamified platform that promotes positive online behaviors. • Encourages collaboration and teamwork. • Allows teachers to track students' behavior and achievements.

Table 17.5 *Contd…*

Tools	Features
Social Express	• Interactive lessons and games on social and emotional learning. • Addresses social skills, empathy, and responsible online behavior. • Suitable for younger students.
Privacy Playground: The First Adventure of the Three Little CyberPigs	• Interactive game for teaching online privacy. • Engages students in a story-based scenario to learn about privacy issues. • Designed for upper elementary and middle school students.
Family Link by Google	• Parental control app to manage children's online activities. • Allows parents to set digital ground rules and monitor screen time. • Encourages responsible device use.
Seesaw	• Digital portfolio platform that fosters positive online behavior. • Encourages student reflection and collaboration. • Provides a secure environment for sharing work.

17.8 Advocating for Equitable Technology Integration in Education

Technology presents incredible opportunities to enhance teaching methods and personalize student experiences by making them more interactive and engaging; however, there are issues surrounding equitable access to these tools for all students regardless of their background or abilities.

By ensuring equal access for everyone - no matter what their socioeconomic status might be- digital resources can help bridge this gap between those who have internet at home versus others without immediate accessibility from home computers/smartphones/tablets etc., eliminating any disadvantage caused by lack thereof electronic devices/tools required in creating inclusive opportunity within academic settings such classrooms.

Only when on board with supporting responsible usage through classroom initiatives could full potential impact truly come into play!! Advocacy efforts take teamwork – working together collaboratively toward achieving goals helps ensure success not only benefiting teacher associations among colleagues but ultimately benefitting learners holistically enabling transitions necessary for basic skill sets while still embracing advanced virtual curricula innovations! The applications speak volumes about diversified approaches bringing improvements effectively across various subjects compounds dividends invaluable WebDriver Wait responsive listening skills & logic application essential encouraging landscape shifts accordingly adapting amidst changing progressions revolutionizing generations' edification completing gaps left behind traditional one-way directions. Advocating for equitable technology integration in education is crucial to ensure that all students have access to the benefits of digital tools and resources.

Over the past few years, technology has completely transformed how we live, work and communicate. This change is felt in every aspect of our daily lives, including education. As educators today it's increasingly important that we recognize technological integration as a vital part of improving learning outcomes.

17.9 Promoting Equal Technology Integration in Education: Strategies and Key Points

Making sure that all students have access to digital tools and resources is critical for their success. Advocating for fair technology integration in education is vital. Here are strategies and key points to consider when advocating for equitable technology integration:

1. Highlight the Educational Opportunities:

- Emphasize how technology can enhance learning experiences for all students.
- Showcase examples of successful technology integration that resulted in improved engagement, collaboration, and achievement.

2. Address the Digital Divide:

- Advocate for initiatives that bridge the digital divide by ensuring access to devices and internet connectivity for all students.
- Propose programs or partnerships that provide technology resources to underserved communities.

3. Advocate for Professional Development:

- Highlight the importance of ongoing professional development for teachers to effectively integrate technology.
- Support initiatives that provide training for educators to use technology tools in ways that benefit diverse learners.

4. Promote Inclusive Design:

- Stress the importance of adopting inclusive design principles when developing or selecting educational technology tools.
- Encourage the use of tools that cater to diverse learning needs, including those of students with disabilities.

5. Advocate for Open Educational Resources (OER):

- Promote the use of OER to reduce costs and ensure equitable access to educational content.
- Encourage educators to create and share resources that can benefit students across different socioeconomic backgrounds.

6. Highlight the Impact on Underserved Communities:

- Share data and stories that illustrate the positive impact of technology on education in underserved communities.
- Advocate for targeted initiatives that address the unique needs of students in disadvantaged areas.

7. Engage with Stakeholders:

- Collaborate with parents, community leaders, and advocacy groups to build a coalition for equitable technology integration.
- Involve all stakeholders in discussions and decisions related to technology initiatives.

8. Advocate for Culturally Responsive Technology:

- Stress the importance of culturally responsive technology that reflects the diverse backgrounds of students.
- Encourage the development and use of educational technology that respects and includes various cultural perspectives.

9. Policy Advocacy:

- Advocate for policies that support equitable technology integration in schools.
- Engage with policymakers to ensure that funding and resources are allocated to address technology disparities.

10. Collaborate with Industry Partners:

- Partner with technology companies to develop initiatives that support equitable access to their products.

- Encourage tech companies to invest in educational programs that benefit underserved communities.

11. Highlight the Future Workforce Implications:

- Emphasize the importance of preparing students for the technology-driven workforce.
- Illustrate how equitable access to technology in education contributes to closing the skills gap.

12. Advocate for Flexible Learning Models:

- Support flexible learning models that allow students to access educational content both in and outside the traditional classroom setting.
- Promote blended learning approaches that combine online and in-person instruction.

13. Data-Driven Advocacy:

- Use data to demonstrate disparities in technology access and its impact on student outcomes.
- Advocate for data-driven decision-making in allocating resources and implementing technology initiatives.

14. Engage in Public Awareness Campaigns:

- Launch public awareness campaigns to educate the community about the importance of equitable technology integration.
- Share success stories and testimonials from students, teachers, and parents.

15. Monitor and Evaluate Equity Initiatives:

- Advocate for ongoing monitoring and evaluation of equity initiatives in technology integration.
- Use data to assess the effectiveness of programs and make adjustments as needed.

16. Advocate for Student Voice:

- Include students in discussions about technology integration, seeking their input on tools and resources.
- Empower students to advocate for equitable access to technology.

17. Collaborate with Education Advocacy Organizations:

- Partner with education advocacy organizations that prioritize equity in education.
- Leverage collective efforts to influence policy changes and resource allocation.

18. Emphasize Universal Design for Learning (UDL):

- Advocate for the adoption of UDL principles that cater to diverse learning styles and abilities.
- Highlight how UDL promotes inclusive and equitable education.

19. Advocate for Accessible Technology:

- Stress the importance of adopting and creating educational technology that is accessible to students with disabilities.
- Encourage the use of tools that support accessibility features.

20. Share Research and Best Practices:

- Stay informed about research on equitable technology integration.
- Share best practices with educators, administrators, and policymakers.

Ensuring that technology is inclusive and benefits all students, regardless of their backgrounds or circumstances, requires a multifaceted approach. Education stakeholders must collaborate, advocate for policy changes, engage with local communities, and address disparities. By championing these efforts, we can guarantee that technology is used equitably in education.

CHAPTER 18

A Roadmap for Implementing and Operating Digital Tools

The adoption of digital tools in education has increased significantly, and their effective implementation is crucial for its success. However, using these tools can be challenging; thus, having a road map would aid the process.

To begin with, it's essential to identify set goals/objectives for digital learning while considering learners' needs before selecting suitable tech applications that align appropriately towards achieving those objectives. Moreover, taking into consideration cost implication, cost accessibility, & practicality comes in handy. To ensure effectiveness, a sound knowledge of handling usage must be acquired.

Secondly, tutors &learners need enough training/coaching on functionalities offered by selected digital tools. This will maximize utility value when incorporated within applicable coursework. Support options include workshops, tutorials as well as remote assistance provisioned via appropriate online resources/solutions.

Thirdly, to benefit from chosen tool deployment maximum utilization benefits, it should be fully integrated currently. As this expose tutor pupil alike. Companywide evaluation helps access product efficiency, giving room to necessary adjustment.

As noted above, a strategic plan/roadmap covering aspects such as objective/goal setting, lens-based selection guidelines, effective capacity building, on-going assessment dividend maximization. At end-users' level, digital educational system would impact them positively if adopted optimally incorporating intelligent usage whichever required technology platforms/ products utilized.

18.1 Overview of the Roadmap for Implementing and Operating Digital Tools

Developing a Plan for Implementing and Operating Digital Tools in Digital Education Using digital tools in digital education requires a well-planned approach that entails effective execution and consistent assessment. Follow this roadmap to guide your process:

1. Needs Assessment:

- Identify educational goals and objectives that digital tools can help achieve.
- Assess the current technological infrastructure and identify any gaps.
- Gather input from teachers, students, and administrators to understand their needs and preferences.

2. Define Objectives and Outcomes:

- Clearly define the objectives and expected outcomes of integrating digital tools.
- Align these objectives with educational standards and institutional goals.
- Set measurable targets to gauge the success of the implementation.

3. Budgeting and Resource Allocation:

- Estimate the costs associated with acquiring, implementing, and maintaining digital tools.
- Allocate budgetary resources for hardware, software, training, and ongoing support.
- Explore grant opportunities or partnerships that may help fund the initiative.

4. Technology Selection:

- Research and choose digital tools that align with educational objectives.
- Consider the scalability, interoperability, and compatibility of the selected tools.
- Ensure that the tools meet accessibility and usability standards.

5. Infrastructure Development:

- Upgrade or expand the technological infrastructure to support the chosen tools.
- Ensure sufficient bandwidth, reliable connectivity, and secure data storage.
- Implement necessary hardware and software configurations.

6. Professional Development:

- Provide comprehensive training for educators on how to effectively use the selected digital tools.
- Offer ongoing professional development opportunities to keep educators updated on best practices.
- Include training sessions on pedagogical strategies for integrating technology into the curriculum.

7. Create Implementation Teams:

- Form implementation teams comprising administrators, teachers, IT staff, and support personnel.
- Assign roles and responsibilities to ensure a coordinated and collaborative effort.
- Establish a communication plan to keep all stakeholders informed.

8. Pilot Testing:

- Conduct a pilot program with a small group of teachers and students.
- Collect feedback on the usability, effectiveness, and impact of the digital tools.
- Use pilot testing to identify and address any issues before full-scale implementation.

9. Scale-Up Implementation:

- Based on the feedback and success of the pilot, scale up the implementation to the entire institution.
- Communicate changes, expectations, and support mechanisms to all stakeholders.
- Monitor the implementation closely and address any challenges promptly.

10. Monitoring and Evaluation:

- Establish a system for ongoing monitoring and evaluation of the digital tools.
- Use data and feedback to assess the impact on student outcomes and overall effectiveness.
- Regularly review and update the implementation plan based on evaluation results.

11. Support Mechanisms:

- Implement a robust support system for educators and students.
- Provide helpdesk services, online resources, and troubleshooting guides.
- Foster a community of practice where educators can share insights and support each other.

12. Feedback and Iteration:

- Continuously seek feedback from teachers, students, and administrators.
- Use feedback to make iterative improvements to the implementation.
- Encourage a culture of innovation and adaptability.

13. Data Privacy and Security:

- Implement strong data privacy and security measures to protect sensitive information.
- Ensure compliance with relevant data protection regulations.
- Educate all stakeholders on data privacy best practices.

14. Parent and Community Engagement:

- Keep parents and the community informed about the implementation of digital tools.
- Provide resources and information to help parents support their children's use of technology.
- Seek input and feedback from the community.

15. Assessment and Accountability:

- Develop assessment mechanisms to measure student progress and achievement.
- Establish accountability measures to ensure that the implementation aligns with educational goals.
- Regularly review and adjust assessment strategies based on data and feedback.

16. Continuous Improvement:

- Foster a culture of continuous improvement and innovation.
- Encourage educators to share success stories and best practices.

- Stay informed about emerging technologies and pedagogical approaches.

17. Sustainability Planning:

- Develop a long-term sustainability plan for the digital tools initiative.
- Consider the scalability of the program and its long-term impact.
- Plan for future upgrades, replacements, and evolving educational needs.

18. Documentation and Knowledge Transfer:

- Maintain comprehensive documentation on the implementation process.
- Facilitate knowledge transfer by documenting best practices and lessons learned.
- Create a repository of resources for ongoing reference.

19. Celebrating Success and Recognition:

- Acknowledge and celebrate successes and milestones achieved through digital tools.
- Recognize the efforts of educators, students, and support staff.
- Share success stories internally and externally.

20. Community of Practice and Collaboration:

- Foster a community of practice where educators can collaborate and share insights.
- Encourage interdisciplinary collaboration and cross-functional teams.
- Promote a collaborative culture that values teamwork and shared learning.

Navigating the Complexities of Digital Implementation in Educational Institutions By adhering to this roadmap, educational institutions can successfully implement and operate digital tools to maximize their impact on student learning outcomes and support equal access to technology-enhanced education.

CHAPTER 19

Conclusion and Future of Digital Tools in Technical Education

Technical education has been revolutionized by digital tools, providing teachers and scholars with various opportunities to enhance teaching methods and create a more engaging learning experience for students. This subchapter explores the significance of such tools in technical education, catering to different niches like data science, e-learning platforms, virtual reality simulation labs along with online coding courses.

Digital resources ensure access to tutorials on programming languages that help learners develop essential skills regardless of their location or pace. Tools also allow graphic arts & design enthusiasts manipulate digital media effectively fostering creativity amongst them. Virtual Reality (VR), Augmented Reality (AR) programs have become quite sought-after as they offer immersive interactive experiences making it easy to comprehend complicated engineering& scientific concepts through VR simulations.

E-Learning Platforms further provide choice-based course options while acclimatizing pupils with practical technology know-how. Data Science, AI modules coupled alongside Analytics training present aspirants' ample opportunity towards acquiring appropriate competences required for today's world.

Project Management software, & Collaboration apps support teamwork enhancing communication adeptness. Technical Boot camps enable intensive crash-courses necessary for thriving digitally guided curriculum. It's not surprising therefore that embracing technologies is imperative among educators preparing individuals accordingly- staying par-to-date is tantamount should one prepare young minds - ready for the techno-fueled times ahead.

19.1 Emerging Trends and Future Developments in Digital Tools for Digital Education

Digital tools have revolutionized technical education and have become an essential part of the learning process. As technology advances, new tools are being developed to enhance the way technical education is delivered. In this document, we will explore the emerging trends and future developments in digital tools for technical education.

One of the most significant emerging trends in digital tools for technical education is the use of virtual and augmented reality. These technologies provide an immersive learning experience, allowing students to interact with digital objects and environments in a way that was previously impossible. For example, students can explore complex machinery or systems in detail, gaining a deeper understanding of how they work. This trend is expected to continue, with more schools and institutions investing in virtual and augmented reality technology.

Another trend in digital tools for technical education is the increased use of mobile devices. With the growing popularity of smartphones and tablets, educators are finding new ways to deliver content directly to students' devices. This provides students with the flexibility to learn at their own pace and on their own schedule. Mobile devices also offer a variety of apps and tools that can be used to enhance learning and collaboration.

Finally, the future of digital tools for technical education is likely to include more personalized and adaptive learning experiences. With the help of artificial intelligence and machine learning, educational platforms will be able to tailor content and assessments to each student's individual needs and abilities. This will allow students to learn more efficiently and effectively and will help educators to identify areas where students may need additional support.

In conclusion, digital tools have already transformed technical education, and the emerging trends and future developments discussed in this document are likely to continue this transformation. As technology continues to advance, educators and students alike will benefit from new and innovative ways of learning and collaborating.

19.2 Advancements in Technology Transforming Technical Education

The field of technical education has undergone a dramatic transformation in recent years, due to the rapid advancement of technology. As teachers and scholars operating within this ever-changing landscape, it is essential to stay up-to-date on emerging trends and future developments related to digital tools. These technologies have the potential to enhance technical skills training for students seeking success in today's modern world. This article will explore some of the exciting new advances that are improving education opportunities within various niches.

19.3 Online Coding Courses and Tutorials

One notable trend gaining traction involves online coding courses and tutorials which enable learners an interactive educational experience while acquiring valuable knowledge about programming at their own pace. This enhanced learning experience could offer greater employability potential as these courses are increasingly incorporated into tech ed contexts, and technological industries currently experiencing labor shortages.

19.4 Technical Design Curriculums

Technical design curriculums such as graphic arts can now utilize powerful software that is more accessible than ever before. Numerous e-tools are hosted presently online, allowing classrooms across borders – access typically made available only internally via office spaces with costly licensing fees attached. This new digital frontier provides creative pursuits beyond prior limitations set by traditional classroom setups previously limited geographically or economically.

19.5 VR and AR in Education

Virtual reality (VR) and augmented reality (AR) have not been left behind with growing popularity amongst educators seeking advanced coursework delivery methods. These simulations range in subject areas from science laboratory modules to created digitally providing tours of already constructed architectural environments or visualizing complex engineering concepts come true using simulated platforms bespoke-designed entirely tailor-made immersive experiences drawing deeply upon its capacity revolutionize how teaching occurs altogether compared more conventional approaches taken until recently most popularly still relied heavily textbook printouts.

19.6 E-Learning Platforms

E-learning platforms have generated increased popularity for developing technical skills amongst students and professionals alike while seeking to improve proficiency relating analytics, digital marketing or web development. Teachers within these fields can further explore ideas uniquely suited towards supplementing traditional classroom teaching tactics.

19.7 Looking Ahead

Looking ahead, educators will need to keep current with trends continuing revolutionizing how we think about pedagogy in general employment at all levels, including other aspects like project management collaboration featuring prominently on the horizon. Alongside cutting-edge advancements concerning VR/AR adoption that presently play significant roles addressing areas needing improved student performance or require custom-made microlearning – processes adapted contextual experiences using targeted knowledge sharing leading personalized understanding among users, coupled with rapidly evolving AI technologies enmeshed connectedness through smart devices. Individuals are increasingly dependent on computers, network popular demand pushing technological solutions making waves across every facet of our lives.

In conclusion, digital tools are now an intrinsic part of modern-day society bringing immense benefits even to tech ed challenges facing us today. Expect solution providers typically forthcoming as they strive to cater to learning better ever-evolving needs next decade future students, researchers, and policymakers remain ready to tackle complexities together informed decisions aimed at resolving issues related quickly and effectively. The way forward involves institutions situated positioning themselves to meet arising demands rather than becoming bypassed by unforeseen changes in local/global landscapes enabled rapid global computer networking systems underlying principles involved correspond transforming formats updated progressively time various respective stakeholders allowing efficient resource sharing promoting balanced equal education opportunity globally integrating innovative e-tools seeking intelligently emphasized being applied design synergies cut beneficiation curve not left behind chance innovation occurs fostering collaborative efforts since exchanging information freely open access nature stuck outdated models stifling creativity nonetheless leaving young learners wanting more long-term engagements sidestepping counterproductivity measures unprecedentedly optimized transformative impacts generation intending to see potential given rise indeed implementations realizable constructing policies innovating educate inspire quite unlike anything witnessed before scale paradigm shift promises to achieve commodified affordances without previous developmental setbacks associated bloated expenditures reducing reliance upon physical infrastructures placing increased focus widening skills improvement equipping earliest age groups toward employment purses advancing critical thinking aptitudes towards addressing modernity's most daunting challenges.

19.8 Recommendations for Utilizing Digital Tools in Technical Education

As technology continues to evolve, it's essential for technical education to keep pace with these changes. Digital tools can offer numerous benefits, such as enhancing engagement, providing practical experiences, and promoting collaboration. Here are some recommendations for teachers and scholars seeking to incorporate digital tools into technical education:

1. Explore e-learning platforms: E-learning platforms offer a flexible, interactive learning environment. Teachers and scholars should consider using these platforms to provide students with comprehensive courses, tutorials, and certifications in areas such as coding, digital design, data science, and more.
2. Use virtual reality and augmented reality: Virtual reality (VR) and augmented reality (AR) tools provide immersive experiences that enable students to visualize complex concepts and explore real-world scenarios. Incorporating VR and AR into lessons can boost understanding and engagement in technical subjects.
3. Incorporate digital marketing and analytics tools: Digital marketing and analytics are increasingly crucial in various industries. Teachers and scholars should incorporate training programs that offer hands-on experience with digital marketing tools and data analytics platforms to equip students with relevant skills.
4. Foster collaboration with online project management tools: Technical education often requires teamwork and collaboration. Online project management and collaboration tools can facilitate group work, enabling students to collaborate effectively, track progress, and manage tasks.
5. Offer web development and programming bootcamps: Bootcamps focusing on practical coding skills can help meet the growing demand for web developers and programmers. Teachers and scholars should consider organizing such programs to equip students with the necessary skills and a solid foundation in web development and programming.
6. Integrate virtual laboratories and simulations: Virtual laboratories and simulations provide students with hands-on experience and enhance their understanding of theoretical concepts in a safe, controlled environment. Teachers and scholars should consider incorporating these tools into science and engineering education.

By implementing these recommendations, teachers and scholars can effectively utilize digital tools to enhance technical education. It's crucial to continuously explore new technologies and adapt teaching methods to keep pace with the ever-changing digital landscape. Ultimately, the successful integration of digital tools into technical education will empower students with the skills and knowledge they need to thrive in the modern world.

Conclusion

Teaching in the Digital Age: A Guide to Modernizing Higher Education (From Chalkboard to Keyboard: An Introduction to Digital Tools for Teachers)

This book examines how digital equipment can empower educators today, highlighting a essential edition of coaching methods that meet college students' virtual talent. Incorporating those assets into lesson plans fosters an interactive getting to know surroundings selling creativity, critical wondering, and collaboration.

This book advocates for instructors developing their own abilities with generation thru understanding basic notions like online privateness safety even as being added on diverse educational apps and whiteboards created specifically helping student training content material shipping.

Relying totally upon simply technological aid isn't enough - it falls under the instructor's responsibility strategically harness this system as supportive factors improving individualized learner instruction beyond traditional programming obstacles permitting exploratory environments where all voices are endorsed same participation fostering creative community-generated problem-solving exchanges amongst equally contributing friends at every step.

Potential drawbacks contain risks such as safety invasion or accountable conduct transmission needing regular interest with the aid of teachers illustrating moral use patterns, creating conscientious virtuous "virtual residents".

Teaching in the Digital Age: A Guide to Modernizing Higher Education (From Chalkboard to Keyboard: An Introduction to Digital Tools for Teachers)

This book delves into the ways wherein virtual tools can empower educators within the contemporary age, highlighting the need for instructors to embrace technology and adapt their teaching methods to healthy the desires of modern day digital-savvy college students. By incorporating virtual equipment into their lesson plans, instructors can create a fascinating and interactive mastering environment that promotes creativity, essential wondering, and collaboration.

Throughout this adventure, the book emphasizes the significance of virtual literacy and the need for instructors to become proficient in using digital tools. An array of digital tools are explored, which includes academic apps and interactive whiteboards, and the way they can be utilized to enhance scholar mastering.

The book also acknowledges the capacity challenges and issues that accompany digital gear in the lecture room, inclusive of privacy, security, and virtual citizenship. Teachers need to guide their college students to turn out to be accountable virtual residents who understand the ethical and accountable use of technology.

To conclude, the digital age affords both possibilities and challenges for instructors. By integrating virtual equipment into their teaching practices, educators can deliver more personalized, engaging, and effective practice. However, this adventure requires continuous mastering, adaptation, and collaboration among teachers. With this technique, the destiny of education can be transformed through generations.

www.ingramcontent.com/pod-product-compliance
Ingram Content Group UK Ltd.
Pitfield, Milton Keynes, MK11 3LW, UK
UKHW021322190726
13845UKWH00003B/16